"John Wesley was clearly an explosive force in hi… but, like most charismatic leaders of hi… of most people's consciousness. What's … organising church life have either grown … an overgrowth of custom and distortion. … on the challenge of releasing the raw energ… boggling and heart-warming ideas, which g… unique place in the gallery of great Christian thinkers and …ers of the past. I've been trying to do this for decades and I know how difficult a task it is. So, in all honesty, I picked up Stephen Poxon's book with some hesitation. But I need not have worried. Page after page brings illumination, inspiration, intellectual stimulation even to diehards like me. The generosity of spirit of John Wesley, "the friend of all and the enemy of none" is here displayed again and again. As is the simplicity of his life, the depth of his faith, his determination to go on declaring the good news of the gospel until his last breath. This is a little gem of a book that defies the gravitational pull of oblivion. Day after day for an entire year, it will lift the spirits of twenty-first century men and women and equip them to face the challenges of today's world. No mean feat."

Lord Leslie Griffiths

Also by Stephen J. Poxon

Through the Year with William Booth

Through the Year with Catherine Booth

At the Master's Side

THROUGH THE YEAR WITH

John Wesley

Edited by
Stephen Poxon

MONARCH
BOOKS

Published by Monarch Books
an imprint of
Lion Hudson IP Ltd
Wilkinson House, Jordan Hill Road,
Oxford OX2 8DR, England
Email: monarch@lionhudson.com
www.lionhudson.com/monarch

Hardback ISBN 978 0 85721 823 0
Paperback ISBN 978 0 85721 888 9
e-ISBN 978 0 85721 824 7

First edition 2017

Acknowledgments
Scripture quotations marked *ESV* are from The Holy Bible, English Standard Version® (ESV®) copyright © 2001 by Crossway, a publishing ministry of Good News Publishers. All rights reserved.

Extracts marked *KJV* from The Authorized (King James) Version. Rights in the Authorized Version are vested in the Crown. Reproduced by permission of the Crown's patentee, Cambridge University Press.

Scripture quotations marked *MSG* are taken from The Message. Copyright © by Eugene H. Peterson 1993, 1994, 1995, 1996, 2000, 2001, 2002. Used by permission of NavPress Publishing Group.

Scripture marked *NASB* taken from the New American Standard Bible®, Copyright © 1960, 1962, 1963, 1968, 1971, 1972, 1973, 1975, 1977, 1995 by The Lockman Foundation. Used by permission.

Scripture quotations marked *NIV* taken from the Holy Bible, New International Version Anglicised. Copyright © 1979, 1984, 2011 Biblica, formerly International Bible Society. Used by permission of Hodder & Stoughton Ltd, an Hachette UK company. All rights reserved. "NIV" is a registered trademark of Biblica. UK trademark number 1448790.

Scripture quotations marked *NLT* are taken from the Holy Bible, New Living Translation, copyright © 1996, 2004, 2007 by Tyndale House Foundation. Used by permission of Tyndale House Publishers, Inc., Carol Stream, Illinois 60188. All rights reserved.

Songs on pp. 22, 314, 332, 348 taken from *The Song Book of The Salvation Army, 2015* © Copyright The General of The Salvation Army. Reproduced by permission

A catalogue record for this book is available from the British Library

Printed and bound in Great Britain by Marston Book Services Ltd, Oxfordshire

For Reverend Neil Drayton, Friend and Example

Acknowledgments

It is, quite literally, I am painfully aware, impossible for me to adequately acknowledge the debt I owe to those who have helped me with producing this small glimpse into the life and times of John Wesley. My association with Methodism has, by and large, been pleasant, educational and enriching. I am, therefore, indebted to at least a hundred individual Methodists who have kindly schooled me in some great traditions, and introduced me to the story of Wesley's denomination. Likewise, I now carry deep impressions made upon me by Methodists who have demonstrated holiness and offered me qualities I would like to imitate. Then, there are those who have generously allowed me to borrow or keep books that have proved truly invaluable in my research: volumes about, or by, John Wesley, as well as publications adding to my awareness of this particular branch of Christianity, and treasured hymnals. I do hope it will suffice for me to express here a humble and grateful note of thanks to everyone involved. Perhaps the best way for me to convey my gratitude is to state that I couldn't have produced this book without you.

Introduction

Without question, John Wesley was used of God in a marvellous and mighty way. A stubborn, forthright, complex individual, his unorthodox influence upon the fortunes of England, and his lasting influence upon Christendom was, and is, immense – quite staggering in its proportion.

Wesley, let it be admitted, was, for all his saintly qualities (and there were many), a human being with frailties and flaws. He could be remarkably eccentric, devoutly dogmatic, and, sometimes, horribly mistaken. Yet, the beauty of John Wesley was his utter tenaciousness. Steadfastly convinced of gospel truths, he submitted himself to decades of hardship, deprivation and ostracization in his tireless pursuit of converts and the deepening of their spiritual experience.

Phenomenally intelligent, and an ardent scholar to the end, Wesley nevertheless deliberately and consciously made strident efforts to present a message that was accessible to all: the highly educated, with whom he easily and capably held his own in debate, and the illiterate, believing that each and every individual could become a recipient of grace.

Forced, often, to plough his own furrow in terms of evangelism, Wesley remained undeterred, taking heart from the company of close friends. Blessed with a temperament that was almost uniquely unable to dwell on discouragement, he worked with astounding energy, wit and eloquence to preach, write and witness at every opportunity. Myopic in his devotion to Christ, frustrated and saddened at times by what he regarded as the lesser efforts of some clergy, he nevertheless maintained a spirit of charity, good humour and indefatigable zeal.

Methodical to a tee – obsessive, possibly – and undoubtedly guilty of some catastrophic decisions (not least in his personal life), John Wesley was also kind and generous to a fault. Whereas he could occasionally be scathing in his criticisms, his warmth of heart was perhaps never better demonstrated than by his splendid gesture of inviting paupers to act as pall-bearers at his funeral service, thereby guaranteeing them a fee. Wesley's Christianity – always evangelical – included vast amounts of concern for the poor, and he was years ahead of his time in terms of challenging and motivating the Church at large on questions of social action.

A marvellous theologian, a skilled (if longwinded!) preacher, an evangelist to his fingertips, and most definitely a one-off, we stand in awe of a visionary disciple who was by no means perfect, but consecrated his all to God. A mere fraction of his works are presented within this book – modernized where Wesley's original phraseology would make them incomprehensible – in the hope that "he being dead yet speaketh" (Hebrews 11:4, King James Version).

S. J. P.

JANUARY 1ST

"THOUGH I HAVE BEEN SPEAKING FIGURATIVELY ... I WILL ... TELL YOU PLAINLY ABOUT MY FATHER"

(John 16:25 *NIV*)

I have frequently spoken in public on every subject in this collection and I do not feel there is any one point of Christian doctrine not covered here, for the benefit of each reader. Everyone who reads these pages will clearly see what these doctrines are, which I embrace and teach as the essentials of true religion. Nothing here appears in an unnecessarily elaborate or elegant form of speech, as I write as I generally speak – *ad populum* – to the majority of people, to those who neither relish nor understand the art of speaking, but who are competent judges of Christian truth. I mention this so that readers may spare themselves the effort of seeking for what they will not find. I prefer plain truth for plain people and I therefore abstain from intricate philosophical speculations; and, as far as possible, from any overt demonstration of academic learning, unless in citing the original Scripture when it is helpful and relevant to do so. I try to avoid all words which are not easily understood or used in public life; and, in particular, those kinds of terms that belong mainly to the sphere of intellectual theological study, but which are largely irrelevant to common people – everyday people, that is, who have no need of speaking in such ways, and to whom the gospel appears unadorned and straightforward.[1]

Inclusive Lord, I pray today for ministers and preachers charged with sharing your word with congregations and communities. Bless them with clarity of mind and speech, so that their messages reach many.

1 From *Fifty Three Sermons.*

January 2nd

Don't put it off; do it now! Don't rest until you do

(Proverbs 6:4 *NLT*)

For many years I have wanted to collate and set down in writing, thoughts that have occurred to me either in reading or conversation which might help and encourage people who do not have the advantage of learning, to understand the New Testament. I have, though, been continually deterred from attempting anything of this kind by a deep sense of my own inability; of my lack of learning, experience and wisdom, so I have repeatedly put the thought to one side and procrastinated.

However, having had a loud call from God, I am convinced I must not delay this attempt any longer. My life is nearly over, and I am persuaded to do what little I can in this way, because I can do nothing else; my present weakness makes travelling or preaching impossible. I can, though, still read, and write, and think. May this work be to God's glory![1]

Guiding God, please be close to those who are procrastinating today, for one reason or another. Help them to overcome feelings of inability or even fear. If a particular project is something you would like them to pursue, please direct their thoughts and grant them courage. Direct your disciples!

1 From *Notes on the New Testament.*

Is not this man a burning stick snatched from the fire?

(Zechariah 3:2 *NIV*)

I believe it was just as I was waking, unless it was afterwards, but, either way, I remember all the circumstances as distinctly as though it happened yesterday. Seeing the room was very light, I called to the maid, but as there was no answer, I looked through curtains and saw streaks of fire! I got up and ran to the door, but could get no further because the floor was blazing, so I climbed up on a chest near the window. Someone in the yard saw me, and said he would run to fetch a ladder, but someone else shouted, "There will be no time; but I have another plan. I will stand against the wall and lift a light man on my shoulders." They did this, and he carried me out of the window. Just then the whole roof fell; but it fell inward, otherwise we would all have been crushed.[1]

When they brought me into the house where my father[2] was he cried out, "Come, neighbours, let us kneel down; let us give thanks to God! He has given me all my eight children; let the house go, I am rich enough." The next day, as he was walking in the garden and surveying the ruins of the house, he picked up a leaf of his Polyglot Bible,[3] on which just these words were legible: "*Vade vende omnia quae habes et attolle crucem et sequere*" (Go sell all that thou hast, and take up thy cross and follow me).[4, 5]

Lord, what a marvellously philosophical approach John Wesley's father demonstrated, giving thanks in the aftermath of tragedy! His attitude of gratitude is challenging. This day, I think of those who are coming to terms with shocking news or calamitous circumstances; may they find your peace and presence even in the midst of personal disaster.

1 On the night of 9 February 1709, fire destroyed the Epworth rectory housing the Wesley family in Lincolnshire, England.
2 The Reverend Samuel Wesley (Church of England).
3 A Polyglot Bible contains side-by-side versions of the same text in different languages. Some editions include the Hebrew and Greek original text.
4 Matthew 19:21, *KJV*.
5 From *Rev. John Wesley*.

JANUARY 4TH

HONOUR CHRIST THE LORD AS HOLY, ALWAYS BEING PREPARED TO MAKE A DEFENCE ...FOR THE HOPE THAT IS IN YOU; YET DO IT WITH GENTLENESS AND RESPECT

(1 Peter 3:15 *ESV*)

On Thursday, 20 May 1742, I set out, and the next afternoon, stopped at Newport Pagnell,[1] then rode on until I overtook a serious man with whom I immediately started a conversation. He was quick to share his spiritual and theological opinions, and even though I said nothing to contradict him, he seemed to remain unhappy with me, and was quite anxious to know whether I shared his doctrinal convictions. I told him over and over that it would be advisable to keep our conversation to practical things only in case we became angry with each other. And so we did for two miles till he dragged me into the dispute again before I knew where I was, growing angrier and telling me I was rotten at heart and that I was probably one of John Wesley's followers. I told him "No. I am John Wesley himself." Hearing this, he would gladly have run away outright, but being the better horseman of the two I kept close to his side and tried my best to share my points of view regarding faith and salvation, until we came to Northampton.[2, 3]

What a great picture this is! Lord, there will be those times when people disagree with us, and when we are rejected. Grant two things, Lord; courage to the rejected, and more chances to hear and respond, to those who are initially hostile and don't want to know.

1 Buckinghamshire, England.
2 East Midlands, England.
3 From *John Wesley's Journal (Abridged)*.

January 5th

Commit everything you do to the Lord

(Psalm 37:5 *NLT*)

General Questions which a Christian may reflectively consider before beginning Evening Devotions:

1. How did I apply myself to my morning prayers today?
2. Have I done anything today without careful consideration of its relevance to the glory of God?
3. Did I consider today what business I had to do, and what spiritual qualities that business would require in me?
4. Have I tried to do what good I could today?
5. Have I taken an interest in the welfare of others today, over and above the call of duty?
6. In my pastoral visitation today, have I stopped to think what blessings I might be able to offer to others, and what they might have to offer to me?
7. Have I gossiped unkindly today, or unnecessarily pointed out the faults of others?
8. Have I hurt anyone by word or deed today?
9. Have I considered how my life today might be a means of improving the day?

Questions specifically regarding the love of God:

1. Have I set aside time today to meditate on his mercies?
2. Have I deliberately tried to make today – or parts of today – a day of rest, with moments set aside for worship and adoration?
3. Have I spent my time well when I have not been working; in prayer, reading, and meditation?[1]

Lord of my days, take my life. Let it be consecrated to you.

1 From *John and Charles Wesley: Selected Writings and Hymns.*

January 6th

Let him sit alone in silence

(Lamentations 3:28 *NIV*)

My plan is, in some sense, to forget all that I have read in my life, as if I had never read one author, except the inspired. I feel this may enable me to clearly express the sentiments of my heart, simply following the chain of my own thoughts, without entangling myself with those of other men. I will carry fewer weights upon my mind, and less prejudice, in order to search for myself, or to deliver to others, the naked truths of the gospel…

I am not afraid to share the inmost thoughts of my heart. I am passing through life as an arrow through the air, as a spirit come from God, and returning to God: soon, I shall be here no more; I will drop into eternity! Therefore, only one thing matters to me – the way to Heaven. God himself has taught the way; for this purpose he came from Heaven, in Christ. He has written it down in a book. O give me that book! At any price, give me the book of God! Let me be *homo unius libri.*[1]

Here I am, far from the busy ways of life. I sit down alone: only God is here. In his presence I read his book, to find the way to Heaven.[2]

Still, still with you, Lord. What a privilege. What grace. Help me today to sit alone with you and find you there, in the stillness of your presence.

1 A man of one book.
2 From *Fifty Three Sermons.*

JANUARY 7TH

SIN CAME INTO THE WORLD THROUGH ONE MAN, AND DEATH THROUGH SIN, AND SO DEATH SPREAD TO ALL MEN BECAUSE ALL SINNED

(Romans 5:12 *ESV*)

When humankind was first created, nothing was corrupted, and there was no need for medicinal drugs or the healing arts. Humankind knew no sin, no pain, no sickness, no weakness, and no bodily disorders. The habitations wherein the *Divine Particula Aura*[1] abode, although formed out of the dust of the earth, was not liable to decay – it had no seeds of corruption, and there was nothing to injure it. Heaven and earth and all the hosts of them were mild, benign and friendly towards human nature, and creation was at peace with humankind and humankind was at peace with its Creator. Might well the morning stars sing together, and all the sons of God shout for joy.[2]

But since human beings rebelled against the sovereign of Heaven and earth, how the scene has changed! That which was incorruptible has become corrupted; the immortal has put on mortality,[3] and the seeds of weakness and pain, sickness and death, are now lodged within us, leading to a thousand disorders. And how are these problems increased? The heavens, the earth, and all therein, conspire to punish the rebels against their Creator; the sun and moon shed unwholesome influences from above, the earth exhales poisonous damps from beneath; the beasts of the field, the birds of the air, the fishes of the sea, are in a state of hostility.[4]

Creator God, forgive us for the ways in which we have abused and exhausted the earth's marvellous resources. Bless the work of those who educate and campaign on ecological matters, that we might treat your gift of creation with reverence.

1 The dwelling place of angelic beings – or, more accurately, the 'angelic mind'.
2 See Job 38:7.
3 1 Corinthians 15:53 & Romans 1:23.
4 From *Primitive Physic.*

JANUARY 8TH

YOUR BODIES ARE TEMPLES OF THE HOLY SPIRIT

(1 Corinthians 6:19 *NIV*)

Can nothing be found to lessen those inconveniences, which cannot be wholly removed? To soften the evils of life, and prevent in part the sickness and pain to which we are continually exposed? Without question there may. One preventative of pain and sickness of various kinds seems intimated by the grand Author of Nature in the sentence passed upon us: "In the sweat of thy face shalt thou eat bread, till thou return to the ground."[1]

The power of exercise, both to preserve and restore health, is greater than can be conceived, especially in those who eat that kind of food which experience shows to be most friendly to health and strength … It is certain this [a balanced diet] is preserved among the Americans[2] to this day. Their diseases are exceedingly few; not do they often occur, because of their continual exercise and temperance. But if any are sick, or bitten by a serpent, or bitten by a wild beast, their fathers immediately tell their children what remedy to apply. And it is rare that the patient suffers for long because their medicines are quick and, generally, infallible. Hence it was that ancient civilizations ascribed physical well-being to a divine source; that He who had taught wellbeing to the beasts and birds, would also want to teach it to humankind.[3]

Lord, you have created an abundance of foods that are healthy, and the world is a rich pantry of nutritious options – thank you. You care for us and you know which vitamins and nutrients we need. Grant us wisdom to eat well, with thanksgiving, and to care for our bodies with exercise and diet.

1 Genesis 3:19, *KJV*.

2 Wesley preached in Georgia, and elsewhere in America, from 1735–37, working among Native American Indians. He made little headway but the visit made a tremendous impact upon him personally. He returned from his mission in Georgia asking the question, "I went to America to convert the Indians, but oh, who shall convert me?"

3 From *Primitive Physic.*

Some went out on the sea in ships

(Psalm 107:23 *NIV*)

Tuesday, October 14 [1735] – Mr Benjamin Ingham, of Queen's College, Oxford;[1] Mr Charles Delamotte;[2] my brother, Charles Wesley, and myself, went to Gravesend,[3] in order to embark for Georgia. Our intention in sailing from England was not to avoid God[4] (God having blessed us plentifully), nor to gain riches or honour, but singly this – to save our souls.[5]

Fri. 17 – I began to learn German, in order to converse with the twenty-six Germans on board.[6] On Sunday, we had morning service on deck and I administered the Lord's Supper to six or seven communicants. Mon. 20 – Believing that by denying ourselves might be helpful, we ate only vegetable food, chiefly rice and biscuit. Tues. 21 – We sailed from Gravesend. When we passed the Goodwin Sands, the winds dropped for about an hour, until a gale sprung up and carried us into the Downs.[7]

Our common way of living was this: From four in the morning till five we prayed in private. From five to seven we read the Bible together, sharing insights so that we would not lean to our own understanding. At seven we had breakfast. At eight were public prayers. From nine to twelve I learned German. At twelve, we gave account to each other for how we had used our time, and what we planned to do next. We ate lunch at one.[8]

Lord, for good friends and those who share life's voyage with us, we give thanks. Bless and protect those who travel today. May their journeys in your service be time well-spent, worthwhile, profitable and enjoyable. Go with them.

1 Benjamin Ingham (1712–72), who befriended Wesley at Oxford University. He was an ordained Anglican minister and took part in the 1735 mission in America, developing an interest in the Moravian Church.
2 Charles Delamotte (1724–86), son of a wealthy sugar merchant. He travelled with Wesley as a friend and companion, but was cut out of his father's will as a result of his decision to accompany Wesley to America.
3 Kent, England, on the Thames Estuary.
4 Possibly, a reference to the Old Testament story of Jonah.
5 Wesley was a devout man whose behaviour was impeccable. Yet, he knew something was missing in his personal relationship with Christ, and set sail for America in the hope of discerning what was amiss.
6 Moravians; a Protestant denomination prominent in Germany.
7 A ten-mile stretch of sandbank difficult to sail along and negotiate without a strong wind.
8 From *John Wesley's Journal (Abridged)*.

I was in prison and you came to visit me

(Matthew 25:36 *NIV*)

In November 1729, at which time I came to reside at Oxford,[1] your son [Mr Morgan], my brother, myself, and one more, agreed to spend three or four evenings in a week together, to read over the classics, and on Sunday a book of divinity. The following summer, Mr M. told me he had called at the jail to visit a man who was condemned for killing his wife; and that he believed it would be good if we would visit other prisoners from time to time. On August 24, 1730, my brother and I walked with him to the castle,[2] then agreed to go there again, once or twice a week. He also asked me to visit a poor woman who was sick, and we agreed it would be worth spending an hour or two a week in such visitation, providing the minister of the parish[3] had no objection. I wrote to my father about the ideas, asking his advice, as he had seventy years' life experience to draw upon. I asked my father if we should now stand still or go forward with these proposals.[4, 5]

Lord, today I pray for those in prison, that your light would reach them. I pray too for prison visitors, that your love would flow through their special ministry. Help each of us to follow Wesley's example of consulting experienced Christians when we consider new ideas and projects in ministry.

1 Wesley was admitted to Oxford University in 1720, to study Classics and Logic, returning to Oxford as a tutor in 1729.

2 The debtors' prison at Lincoln Castle, which doubled as a holding place for those awaiting trial on more serious crimes. Wesley's father, Reverend Samuel Wesley, was honest but incompetent when it came to handling his finances, and spent time in the prison in 1705, with a debt of £30.

3 Possibly, Reverend Nathan Drake, minister of St Mary Magdalene Church, which stands between Lincoln Cathedral and Lincoln Castle.

4 An extract from a letter Wesley wrote to a Mr Morgan, making reference to his son, also Mr Morgan.

5 From *John Wesley's Journal (Abridged)*.

January 11th

Love the Lord your God with all your ... mind

(Luke 10:27 *NIV*)

I have endeavoured to make my New Testament commentary notes as short as possible so that the comment may not obscure or swallow up the text; and as plain as possible, all the better to assist the unlearned reader. For this reason I have studiously avoided all use of learned languages and all modes of expression with which people in common life are unacquainted. I purposely avoid going deep into many difficulties, lest I should leave the ordinary reader behind me. I thought I would write down only the barest references to my own personal thoughts, preferring instead to consult none but inspired writers. For example, I thought it might benefit the service of religion were I to simply translate Bengelius's work *Gnomon Novi Testamenti*,[1] rather than write many volumes upon it. Many of his excellent notes I have therefore translated; many more I have abridged. I am likewise indebted to Dr Heylyn's *Theological Lectures*;[2] and Dr Guyse,[3] and to the *Family Expositor* of Dr Doddridge.[4] In using these sources, I resolved to name none of the authors in my text, so that nothing would divert the mind of the reader from keeping close to the point in view. I preferred to focus on the intrinsic value of their lectures.[5]

Lord of the word, thank you for the gifts you have given to scholars and teachers. Bless them as they apply their intellects to excavating biblical truths so that we may all the better learn your ways. Help us, Lord, to take a leaf out of Wesley's book and concentrate on those components of truth in which we best see you.

1 Johann Albrecht Bengel (1687–1752), a Latin scholar noted for his ability to present lucid Christian truth with brevity. His popularity arose because of his skill in condensing rich truths into relatively brief maxims.
2 Dr John Heylyn (1685–1759), an Anglican minister and mystic who exerted a major influence over eighteenth-century theological thought.
3 John Guyse (1680–1761), an English independent minister, lecturer and author.
4 Philip Doddridge (1702–51), an English Nonconformist, lecturer and hymn-writer.
5 From *Notes on the New Testament.*

January 12th

My heart is stirred by a noble theme as I recite my verses for the king; my tongue is the pen of a skilful writer

(Psalm 45:1 *NIV*)

I cannot flatter myself into thinking I have entirely avoided mistakes in writing my commentary, because it is a difficult work. Nevertheless, my conscience is clear in regard to deliberately misrepresenting any single line of Scripture. Likewise, I have not written one line with the purpose of inflaming the heart of one Christian against another (God forbid that I should use the gentle and benevolent words of Jesus in such a poisonous manner). Furthermore, I pray that all unscriptural forms and phrases which divide the Christian world could be forgotten, so that we might all sit down together in agreement as loving, humble disciples, at the feet of the Master, all the better to imbibe his Spirit and adopt his life into our own.

I make the observation that the word of the living God, which directed the Patriarchs in the time of Moses, was committed to writing. Later, successive writings were added; the inspired writings of other prophets. Words of the Son of God, and the actions of the Apostles and evangelists, were also written down. This is what we now call Holy Scripture; this is that "word of God which remaineth for ever;"[1] of which, though "Heaven and earth shall pass away, one jot or tittle shall not pass away."[2, 3]

Lord, it is marvellous and wonderful that you have caused your word to be written, so that it is freely and internationally available. This is a miracle! Grant me time each day to immerse myself in the Bible; instruct me in your ways.

1 See 1 Peter 1:25, *KJV*.
2 See Matthew 5:18, *KJV*.
3 From *Notes on the New Testament.*

THESE THREE REMAIN: FAITH, HOPE AND LOVE.
BUT THE GREATEST OF THESE IS LOVE

(1 Corinthians 13:13 *NIV*)

Wherever I am mistaken, my mind is open to conviction. I sincerely desire to be better informed. I say to God and man, 'What I know not, teach me thou!'[1]

Do you believe you see things more clearly than I do? It is not unlikely that you may. Then treat me as you would like to be treated, by pointing out to me a better way than I have yet known. Show me, with plain proofs from Scripture, but if I am slow to learn, bear with me; take me by the hand and lead me. Please don't be annoyed with me if I ask you not to quicken the pace of my learning; it is better that I learn slowly than not at all. Supposing I was greatly in the wrong? Forcing the issue would not help me at all. It might even make me run from you! If you are angry with me, then perhaps I shall be angry with you too, which leaves little hope of any of us finding the truth, for once anger arises, then smoke dims the eyes of the soul, and nothing can be seen or gained.

For God's sake, let us not kindle in each other this fire of Hell; much less blow it up into a flame. Do we prefer truth without love? We may indeed die without the knowledge of many truths, and still be carried into Paradise. But if we die without love, what will all our knowledge avail?[2] May the God of love prepare us for the knowledge of all truth by filling our hearts with his love![3, 4]

Father God, truth matters, but love must rule. Forgive us when we squabble over doctrine and forget to love, or insist on denominational bias with anger in our hearts. Lord of love, have mercy, and straighten out our priorities.

1 See Job 34:32, *KJV*.
2 See 1 Corinthians 13:2.
3 See 1 Corinthians 13:12.
4 From *Fifty Three Sermons*.

January 14th

We are all as an unclean thing, and all our righteousnesses are as filthy rags; and we all do fade as a leaf; and our iniquities, like the wind, have taken us away

(Isaiah 64:6 *KJV*)

The blessings God has bestowed upon humankind are due entirely to his grace and favour; his free, undeserved favour. None of us has even the least claim to any of his mercies. It was free grace that "formed man of the dust of the ground, and breathed into him a living soul,"[1] and stamped on that soul the image of God,[2] and "put all things under his feet".[3]

That same grace continues to this day; there is nothing we can do, or have, which can deserve the least thing at God's hand. "All our works, thou, O God, hast wrought in us."[4] Whatever righteousness may be found in humans, this is the gift of God.

How may a sinful person atone for even the least of their sins? With their own works? No, because even if those works were numerous and holy, they are God's, not ours. Our hearts are altogether corrupt, and we have "come short of the glory of God,"[5] (the glorious righteousness that was originally imprinted on human souls, in the image of the great Creator). Therefore, we have no righteousness of our own, no works that will accomplish atonement, and our mouths are stopped before God.[6]

"I have no claim on grace; I have no right to plead;
I stand before my maker's face condemned in thought and deed.
But since there died a Lamb who, guiltless, my guilt bore,
I lay fast hold on Jesus' name, and sin is mine no more."[7]

1 See Genesis 2:7, *KJV*.
2 Genesis 1:27.
3 1 Corinthians 15:27 & Ephesians 1:22.
4 See Isaiah 26:12, *KJV*.
5 See Romans 3:23, *KJV*.
6 From *Fifty Three Sermons*.
7 General Albert Orsborn (1886–1967), *The Song Book of The Salvation Army, 2015.*

January 15th

All Scripture is God-breathed

(2 Timothy 3:16 *NIV*)

In the language of sacred writings we observe truth of the utmost depth written in what appears as the utmost ease, to such an extent that even the most elegant human compositions sink into nothing before Scripture, relatively speaking. God speaks not as a human being, but as God, and because his thoughts are inexhaustibly deep, his words are of inexhaustible value. Likewise, the language of God's messengers is exact to the highest degree because the words which were given them – impressed upon their minds – were divinely inspired. As Luther said, "Divinity is nothing but a grammar of the language of the Holy Ghost."[1]

To understand this thoroughly, though, we should make an effort to observe the emphasis which lies upon every word so that we can fully appreciate both the holy affections expressed and the inclinations of every writer; even bearing the latter in mind, we can still discover truths expressed that represent a continued commendation of God's word; the New Testament in particular; the writings of the evangelists and Apostles detailing the history and revelation of Jesus Christ, the institution of the Christian Church, until the consummation of all things.[2]

Thank you, Lord, for progressive revelation of yourself in the pages of the Bible.
Thank you, Lord, for revealing yourself in Christ.
Thank you, Lord, for this encouragement to search the Scriptures.
Thank you, Lord, for the way in which such searching shows us more of your love, your wisdom, and your eternal plan.

1 Martin Luther (1483–1546), German theologian, composer, priest and monk, and the major figure in the Protestant Reformation.
2 From *Notes on the New Testament.*

JANUARY 16TH

IN EVERYTHING SET THEM AN EXAMPLE BY DOING WHAT IS GOOD. IN YOUR TEACHING SHOW INTEGRITY, SERIOUSNESS AND SOUNDNESS OF SPEECH THAT CANNOT BE CONDEMNED, SO THAT THOSE WHO OPPOSE YOU MAY BE ASHAMED BECAUSE THEY HAVE NOTHING BAD TO SAY ABOUT US

(Titus 2:7–8 *NIV*)

Tues. 19 [November 1751] – I began writing a letter to the Comparer of the Papists and Methodists.[1] Heavy work that I would never choose, but sometimes it must be done. It has been well said that God made practical divinity necessary, while the devil made it controversial.[2] It is, however, necessary, and we must 'resist the devil' or he will not 'flee from us'.[3]

Dec. 21, Sat. – I am informed that Mr K.,[4] for some years zealously attached to the Brethren, had now burst his chain. I would like to hear, from his own mouth, how he was delivered. I talked with him, and wrote down his account of matters, so that I might not be mistaken, and a few days later, spoke to him asking, asking him to reassure me that I had not misunderstood anything. His account was abundantly sufficient to pull off the mask from those cruel and deceitful men (I do not speak this of all Brethren, but of those with whom he had to do).[5,6]

Lord, does it grieve you when believers fall out over denominational matters? Yet, sometimes, truth must speak to power, and important points cannot be avoided or brushed under church carpets. At least, Lord, help us to practise holy disagreement at such times, keeping the main thing the main thing.

1 Dr George Lavington (1683–1762), Bishop of Exeter and a fierce critic of Wesley and of Methodism. He maintained that Methodist clergy held Papist principles, an accusation that amounted to a charge of heresy and contained serious political overtones.
2 Possibly a reference to an aphorism popular in the Early Church.
3 See James 4:7.
4 Almost certainly William Peter Knolton.
5 Wesley owed a huge debt to Moravian Brethren members as they had played a major part in his conversion and his understanding of grace. However, he ran into dispute with them on some points of doctrine and behaviour. "Mr K." was a prominent Moravian who left that denomination and aroused Wesley's interest.
6 From *The Journal of John Wesley.*

January 17th

Speaking to one another with psalms, hymns, and songs from the Spirit. Sing and make music from your heart to the Lord

(Ephesians 5:19 *NIV*)

Commit thou all thy griefs
And ways into his hands,
To his sure truth and tender care,
Who Heaven and earth commands.

Who points the clouds their course,
Whom winds and seas obey,
He shall direct thy wandering feet,
He shall prepare thy way.

Thou on the Lord rely,
So safe shalt thou go on;
Fix on his work thy steadfast eye
So shall thy work be done.

No profit canst thou gain
By self-consuming care;
To him commend thy cause, his ear
Attends the softest prayer.

Thy everlasting truth,
Father, thy ceaseless love,
Sees all thy children's wants, and knows
What best for each will prove.

Thou everywhere hast sway,
And all things serve thy might;
Thy every act pure blessing is,
Thy path unsullied light.

When thou arisest, Lord,
What shall thy work withstand?
Whate'er thy children want, thou giv'st;
And who shall stay thy hand?

Give to the winds thy fears;
Hope, and be undismayed:

God hears thy sighs, and counts thy tears,
God shall lift up thy head.

Through waves, and clouds, and storms,
He gently clears thy way:
Wait thou his time, so shall this night
Soon end in joyous day.

Still heavy is thy heart?
Still sink thy spirits down?
Cast off the weight, let fear depart,
Bid every care be gone.

What though thou rulest not?
Yet Heaven, and Earth, and Hell
Proclaim, God sitteth on the throne,
And ruleth all things well!

Leave to his sovereign sway
To choose and to command;
So shalt thou wondering own his way,
How wise, how strong his hand.

Far, far above thy thought
His counsel shall appear,
When fully he the work hath wrought
That caused thy needless fear!

Thou seest our weakness, Lord;
Our hearts are known to thee;
O lift thou up the sinking hand,
Confirm the feeble knee!

Let us in life, in death,
Thy steadfast truth declare,
And publish with our latest breath
Thy love and guardian care.[1]

Father, you know what today will bring to me – give me your songs to sing.

1 Paul Gerhardt: translated from German to English by Wesley in 1739.

Isaiah had said to Hezekiah's servants, "Make an ointment from figs and spread it over the boil, and Hezekiah will recover"

(Isaiah 38:21 *NLT*)

Thus far physic [medicinal treatment] was wholly founded on experiment. The European, as well as the [Native] American, said to his neighbour, Are you sick? Drink the juice of this herb and your sickness will be at an end. Are you experiencing a burning heat? Leap into that river, and sweat until you are well. Has the snake bitten you? Chew and apply that root, and the poison will not hurt you. Ancient peoples, having a little experience joined with common sense, and common humanity, cured both themselves and their neighbours of most of the distempers to which every nation was subject.

In the process of time, people of a philosophical nature were not satisfied with this, and enquired as to how they might *account* for these things – how such medicines wrought such effects. They examined the human body and all its parts; the nature of flesh, veins, arteries, nerves; the structure of the brain, heart, lungs, stomach, bowels – and hence the whole order of medicine came gradually to be inverted. Men of learning began to set experience aside, in order to build upon hypothesis and to build theories of diseases and their cures, substituting these in favour of experiments.[1]

Thank you, Lord of life, for leaps-and-bounds advances in medical knowledge and understanding. Thank you for gifting scientists and medical professionals so that diseases that were once horribly and dangerously commonplace are nowadays eliminated or controlled. We acknowledge you as a healing God, but we give thanks for those gifted with such skills and expertise.

1 From *Primitive Physic.*

January 19th

What we preach is not ourselves, but Jesus Christ as Lord

(2 Corinthians 4:5 *NIV*)

As theories increased, simple medicines were more and more disregarded and disused, until the greater part of them were forgotten. An abundance of new ones were introduced by reasoning, speculative men, which has less and less to do with common observation. Hence, rules for the applications of these were immensely multiplied, until at length medicine became an absolute science, quite out of reach of ordinary people.

Physicians became to be held in admiration, on a pedestal, as people who were something more than human. Honour and wealth accompanied their new status, and it was to their benefit to keep the bulk of mankind at a distance, that they might not pry into the mysteries of their profession. To this end, they increased those difficulties, filling their writing with an abundance of technical terms utterly unintelligible to plain men so that those who understood only how to restore the sick to health were branded with the name Empirics, relying solely on observation and experiment, as though theirs were an inferior method and not quite so sophisticated.[1]

Father God, it is difficult to ignore some parallels with church life, and the profession of the gospel, whereby some preaching is designed to impress with its intelligence but only serves to leave many feeling confused and somewhat worthless. Help those who are gifted intellectually to clearly present the Saviour; to do so intelligently, but inclusively.

1 From *Primitive Physic.*

JANUARY 20TH

BY GRACE ARE YE SAVED THROUGH FAITH

(Ephesians 2:8 *KJV*)

God needs an unbeliever to believe in order to be saved, for "He is a rewarder of them that diligently seek him".[1]

Greeks, Romans, Scythians,[2] and Indians[3] all believed in the being and attributes of God, and in a future state of reward or punishment, and the nature of moral virtue. Unbelievers, though, scarcely accept any such ideas.

Even the Devil believes in God![4] He knows there is a wise and powerful God, gracious to reward, and just to punish. The Devil also believes that Jesus is the Son of God, the Christ, the Saviour of the world. We even find him declaring, "I know thee who thou art; the Holy One of God" (Luke 4:34). The evil one also believes all the words which came out of the mouth of the Holy One.

By what faith, though, are *we* saved? The faith of the primitive? The type of faith exercised by the devil, whereby he believes in the existence of God but remains the great enemy of God? It may be answered, in general, it is a faith in Christ: Christ, and God through Christ, are the proper objects of our faith and belief, faith being the condition of salvation.[5]

This matters, Lord – faith that is not just a general sense of belief in a deity somewhere, faith that believes but doesn't obey or submit, or a saving faith in Christ as Saviour. Confirm my own faith, Lord, and help me as I try to convey this distinction to others.

1 Hebrews 11:6, *KJV*.
2 Iranian Eurasian nomads.
3 Probably Native Americans.
4 See James 2:19.
5 From *Fifty Three Sermons*.

JANUARY 21ST

I KNOW WHOM I HAVE BELIEVED, AND AM CONVINCED THAT HE IS ABLE TO GUARD WHAT I HAVE ENTRUSTED TO HIM UNTIL THAT DAY

(2 Timothy 1:12 *NIV*)

Faith in Christ is immediately distinguished from the faith either of ancient or modern heathens. It is also fully distinguished from the faith of the Devil; it is not barely a speculative, rational thing, a cold, lifeless assent, a train of thought and ideas. Faith in Christ is to do with the head and the heart – as the Scriptures say: "With the heart man believeth unto righteousness";[1] and, "If thou shalt believe in thy heart that God hath raised him from the dead, thou shalt be saved."[2] It is to do with the heart, not merely the intellect.

Christian faith is a full reliance on the blood of Christ; a trust in the merits of his life, death, and resurrection; a dependence upon him as our atonement and our life, as given for us, and living in us – a present salvation attained by those who are partakers. The words of the Apostle to the believers at Ephesus – "Ye are saved by faith"[3] – are for believers of all the ages, and note that the wording is *are*, not *shall be*.[4]

Father, I pray today for those known to me whose faith resides only in the intellect, and has yet to become a heart-warming, life-changing experience. By your Spirit's grace, please minister full salvation.

1 Romans 10:10, *KJV*.
2 Romans 10:9, *KJV*.
3 Ephesians 2:8, *KJV*.
4 From *Fifty Three Sermons*.

January 22nd

Be wise in the way you act toward outsiders; make the most of every opportunity. Let your conversation be always full of grace, seasoned with salt, so that you may know how to answer everyone

(Colossians 4:5, 6 *NIV*)

Fri. 23. [January 1736] – In the evening another storm began. In the morning it increased, and I could not help saying to myself "How is it that you have no faith?" I was unwilling to die. About one in the afternoon, almost as soon as I had stepped out of the great cabin-door, the sea did not break as usual, but came with a full, smooth tide over the side of the ship; the waters covered me and I wondered if I might actually drown. However – thanks be to God – I received no hurt at all and at about midnight, the storm ceased.

Sun. 25. – At noon a third storm began. At four it was more violent than before. At seven I went to see the Germans [Moravians], because I had already been impressed by their serious, humble, and conscientious behaviour on board, helping other passengers and taking no offence if their meekness resulted in them being pushed, struck, or thrown down; no complaints were found in their mouths.[1], [2]

Father, Christian conduct is rarely put to the test in such a way as that of the Moravians was, in a confined space crossing the Atlantic! Nevertheless, grant me your grace today, so that my speech and behaviour may portray something of Jesus, perhaps especially when I have little idea I am being observed or heard.

1 Notes written when Wesley was sailing to America.
2 From *John Wesley's Journal (Abridged).*

January 23rd

He said to his disciples, "Why are you so afraid? Do you still have no faith?"

(Mark 4:40 ***NIV*****)**

At the beginning of their service, as they were reading a psalm, the Moravians were interrupted by a wave breaking over the ship; the mainsail was in pieces, and it seemed as though the great deep was about to swallow us up, at which point a terrible screaming began among the English. The Germans, though, calmly sung on, and I asked one of them afterwards, "Was you not afraid?" He answered, "I thank God, no." I asked, "But were not your woman and children afraid?" He replied, mildly, "No; our women and children are not afraid to die."[1]

Fri. 20 – We had another storm, which did us no harm other than splitting the foresail. My bed was wet, so I slept on the floor, and slept soundly until morning – I believe I shall not find it necessary to sleep in my bed any more.

Thur. 5 – Between two and three in the afternoon, God brought us all safe into the Savannah river. We cast anchor near Tybee Island, where the pine groves, running along the shore, made a pleasant sight.[2]

Fri. 6 – At about eight in the morning, we set foot on American ground. It was a small uninhabited island, over against Tybee. We knelt to give thanks, then took a boat for Savannah. When we were on shore, we called our little flock together for prayers.[3]

Lord, you are with me at every stage of my journey, from here to eternity, and even then, you are with me. Your faithfulness is great!

1 This trusting response made an enormous impact on Wesley, causing him to question his relationship with God and reconsider his personal spiritual experience.

2 South Carolina, US.

3 From *John Wesley's Journal (Abridged).*

January 24th

He that believeth on the Son of God hath the witness in himself

(1 John 5:10 *KJV*)

The well-known Moravian elder, August Gottlieb Spangenberg,[1] came to meet Wesley, and bid him welcome to his new sphere of labour. Wesley asked his advice about the work which lay before him. Spangenburg said, "My brother, I must first ask you one or two questions. Have you the witness within yourself? Does the Spirit of God bear witness with your spirit that you are a child of God?" Wesley was surprised at such questions, and did not know what to answer. Spangenberg observed this, and asked, "Do you know Jesus Christ?" "I know He is the Saviour of the world," replied Wesley. "True," said the other; "but do you know He has saved you?" "I hope He has died to save me," answered Wesley. "Do you know yourself?" asked Spangenberg. "I do," said Wesley; but in his journal afterwards he wrote, "but I fear they were vain words."[2, 3]

What courage, Lord, from Wesley's host! Most of us would opt for simple courtesies when greeting a stranger! Grant me, Lord, a love of souls that ensures I love nothing more than you, whichever company I am in. Thank you for the tremendous impact this conversation was to have, across the centuries and across the world.

1 August Gottlieb Spangenberg (1704–92) a German theologian, and bishop of the Moravian Brethren.
2 Wesley's arrival in America in 1736. These questions really challenged his spiritual condition.
3 From *Rev. John Wesley.*

January 25th

I gave you milk, not solid food, for you were not yet ready for it

(1 Corinthians 3:2 *NIV*)

Nine days after their arrival in America, Wesley and his friends were visited by [Chief] Tomo-Chachi ... and half a dozen other Indians. The young clergymen met them attired in their gowns and cassocks [Wesley had travelled with a group of clergymen]. "I am glad you are come," said Tomo-Chachi, speaking through a woman-interpreter. "When I was in England I desired that some would speak the great word to me; and my nation then desired to hear it; but now we are all in confusion. Yet I am glad you are come. I will go up and speak to the wise men of our nation; and I hope they will hear; but we would not be made Christians as the Spaniards made Christians; we would be taught before we are baptized."[1]

"There is but One – He that sitteth in Heaven – who is able to teach men wisdom," replied Wesley. "Though we have come so far, we know not whether he will please to teach you by us or no. If he teach, you will learn wisdom, but we can do nothing."

The chief's wife, who had accompanied her husband, gave a jar of milk to the missionaries, as emblematic of her wish that they might feed the Indians with milk, for they were but children, and a jar of honey, with the hope that the missionaries would be sweet them.[2]

Gracious Father, prepare my heart and my lips this day so that I am able to speak for you; let me be not lacking with a word in season that will bless someone on your behalf, especially if that someone – like Chief Tomo-Cachi – is seeking you.

1 The Spanish conquest of the Americas included the imposition of religion; the Spanish regarded Native American Indians as heathen savages destined for Hell, and would baptise them – even forcibly – as a means of procuring their salvation. Any resistance to such baptisms was met with violence, as it was seen as the work of Satan.

2 From *Rev. John Wesley*.

January 26th

AND SHE SHALL BRING FORTH A SON, AND THOU SHALT CALL HIS NAME JESUS: FOR HE SHALL SAVE HIS PEOPLE FROM THEIR SINS

(Matthew 1:21 *KJV*)

Verse 21. Jesus – That is, a Saviour. It is the same with Joshua (who was a type of him), which means, "the Lord, salvation". His people – Israel – and all the "Israel" of God; that is, God's entire family throughout the generations.

Verse 23. They shall call his name Emmanuel – According to Hebrew custom and tradition, one's name signifies not merely a title, but what that person should really and effectually be. Therefore, "Unto us a child is born – and his name shall be called Wonderful, Counsellor, the mighty God, the Prince of Peace:"[1] – that is, He shall be all these, though not nominally, but really. Emmanuel was no common name of Christ, but a title pointing to his very nature and actual status; he is God incarnate and dwells, by his Spirit, in the hearts of his people ("God with us").

It is worth noting that Isaiah's prophecy regarding the birth of the Saviour refers only to what Mary, his mother, will call him, whereas Matthew declares that "they" will call him Emmanuel, indicating the intimacy of Mary's knowledge of Jesus long before his fame spread far and wide.[2]

Thank you, Lord, for Wesley's clarification of these points. Thank you for the incarnation. Thank you for Jesus, and all that he is. Thank you for my Saviour.

1 Isaiah 9:6, *KJV*.
2 From *Notes on the New Testament.*

January 27th

Jesus began to explain to his disciples that he must go to Jerusalem and suffer

(Matthew 16:21 *NIV*)

Sun. March 7 [1736] – I entered upon my ministry at Savannah, by preaching on the epistle for the day, 1 Corinthians 13. In the second lesson (Luke 18) was our Lord's prediction of the treatment he himself, and his followers, was to meet from the world.[1] "Verily I say unto you, There is no man that hath left house, or friends, or brethren, or wife, or children, for the Kingdom of God's sake, who shall not receive manifold more in the present time, and in the world to come life everlasting."[2]

I must confess that, despite these declarations from the Lord and the experience of some sincere followers of Christ whom I have talked to or read about, I could hardly believe that attentive, serious people would trample the Lord's words underfoot, and say all manner of evil against him. I must bear witness against myself, that when I saw the number of people crowding into the church, and the deep attention with which they received the word, and the seriousness of their faces, I could barely refrain from giving the lie to experience, reason and Scripture altogether.[3]

Lord, here we have that curious juxtaposition so common to many of us, of great prophetic truth met with great doubt! Oh Lord, thank you for such truths fulfilled in Jesus ... please bear with us when we find things hard to believe. Do not desert us when we grapple with Scripture, but help us through to faith and belief.

1 Luke 18:31–33.
2 Luke 18:28–30.
3 From *John Wesley's Journal (Abridged)*.

January 28th

FRUIT TREES OF ALL KINDS WILL GROW ON BOTH BANKS OF THE RIVER. THEIR LEAVES WILL NOT WITHER, NOR WILL THEIR FRUIT FAIL. EVERY MONTH THEY WILL BEAR FRUIT, BECAUSE THE WATER FROM THE SANCTUARY FLOWS TO THEM. THEIR FRUIT WILL SERVE FOR FOOD AND THEIR LEAVES FOR HEALING

(Ezekiel 47:12 *NIV*)

There have been, from time to time, some lovers of humanity, who have endeavoured to reduce medicine to its ancient standard: who have laboured to recover its basic truths out of all hypotheses, and fine-spun theories, and to make it a plain intelligible thing, as it was in the beginning: having no more mystery in it than this, "Such a medicine removes such a pain."

These have demonstrably shown that neither the knowledge of astrology, astronomy, natural philosophy, nor even anatomy itself, is absolutely necessary to the quick and effectual cure of most diseases that afflict human bodies: nor yet any chemical or exotic or compound medicine, but a single plant or root duly applied, so that everyone of common sense (except in some rare cases) may prescribe either to themselves or their neighbours: and may be very secure from doing harm, even when he can do no good.[1]

Lord, what can I conclude from Wesley's apparent reluctance to embrace great advances in medicine? Two things! Firstly, Lord, I pray for a heart that will keep pace with you and your will for me (even if it is a struggle); and secondly, Lord, I pray for grace to live out a gospel that is plain and intelligible, so that I may assist you in the work of curing souls. So help me, God.

1 From *Primitive Physic.*

January 29th

Believe in the Lord Jesus, and you will be saved –
you and your household

(Acts 16:31 *NIV*)

You are saved from sin. That is the salvation which is through faith. That is the great salvation foretold by the angel, before God brought his first-begotten into the world: "Thou shalt call his name Jesus; for he shall save his people from their sins."[1] Nowhere in Scripture is there limitation or restriction attached to this statement. He will save from sins; from original sin, actual sin, past sin, and present sin. Through faith in Christ, we are saved from the guilt attached to sin and the power sin holds.

All the world is guilty before God, insomuch that, should God "be extreme to mark what is done amiss, there is none that could abide it"[2] No one can be justified in his sight except through the redemption that is in Jesus Christ; "Him God hath set forth to be a propitiation through faith in his blood, to declare his righteousness for (or by) the remission of the sins that are past."[3] Christ has taken away "the curse of the law, being made a curse for us."[4] He has nailed our sins – all of them – to the cross so that there is now no condemnation to them which believe in Christ Jesus.[5] Being saved from guilt, therefore, we are saved from fear.[6]

Saving God, your grace covers every sin – past, present, and future – and such grace is offered without limitation. Thank you for Jesus, the great sin-bearer, and for this offer of freedom from guilt and associated fear.

1 Matthew 1:21, *KJV*.
2 See Psalm 130:3.
3 See Romans 3:25, *KJV*.
4 Galatians 3:13, *KJV*.
5 See Romans 8:1.
6 From *Fifty Three Sermons*.

January 30th

Abide in me, and I in you

(John 15:4 *KJV*)

Author of life divine,
who hast a table spread,
furnished with mystic wine
and everlasting bread,
preserve the life thyself hast given,
and feed and train us up for heaven.

Our needy souls sustain
with fresh supplies of love,
till all thy life we gain,
and all thy fullness prove,
and, strengthened by thy perfect grace,
behold without a veil thy face.[1]

Father God, please accept this hymn as my prayer for this day, and in this way, grant me the privilege of communion in the ordinary comings and goings of life. I need your presence to remain with me in the mundane and routine. I may not partake in an actual service of Holy Communion today, but I pray, nonetheless, that my need and your fullness will meet, wherever I am and whatever I am doing.

1 There is some unresolved dispute about the authorship of this hymn. Often, it is attributed to John Wesley, but sometimes, to his brother Charles. One school of thought maintains this hymn was written by John Wesley for a service of communion. What is beyond dispute is that both John and Charles were gifted communicators; John, mainly, as a preacher and writer, and Charles, mainly, as a hymn-writer.

January 31st

If you look for me wholeheartedly, you will find me
(Jeremiah 29:13 *NLT*)

During the summer [of 1736] Wesley had a long conference with the Chickasaws [Native Americans].[1] The Chickasaw creed was not without a certain poetic beauty of its own.

"We believe," said the spokesman, "that there are four beloved things – the clouds, the sun, the clear sky, and He that lives in the clear sky. We think of them always wherever we are. We talk of them and to them, at home and abroad, in peace, in war, and after the fight, and wherever and whenever we meet together."

"Their belief," says Wedgewood,[2] "that 'He that lived in the clear sky had two with him – three in all' – one cannot but take to imply some reminiscence of Christian teaching [of the Holy Trinity]. Whether He was the Creator of the rest they could not tell … but they believed He made man. They were ignorant whether He loved him. They did not doubt His power to save them from their enemies, but knew not if He would exercise it.

To Wesley's offer of a book that would tell them many things about "the Beloved Ones" above, they returned a faint answer. They were now occupied with war; if ever a more convenient season came, they would hear him.[3]

Lord, the Chickasaws had come so close to finding you, yet their awareness of your love was lacking, and they perceived you to be a capricious deity. Today I pray for those known to me who have some vague notions of your existence, yet are still to be persuaded of your great love and mercy, and your goodwill towards them. Speak to them, I pray.

1 An indigenous people whose territory was in Mississippi, Alabama, and Tennessee.
2 Francis Julia Wedgwood (1833–1913), English novelist, biographer, historian and literary critic; great-granddaughter of the potter Josiah Wedgwood. During Wesley's lifetime, and subsequently, the Wedgwood factory produced a number of porcelain items bearing his image.
3 From *Rev. John Wesley.*

Go ye into all the world, and preach the gospel

(Mark 16:15 *KJV*)

They [the Chickasaw] seem to have felt a certain amount of sympathy with the Christians. The interpreter told Wesley that they had said they knew what he was doing at the funeral of a young girl who had died lately – he had been speaking to the "Beloved Ones" to take up her soul. They believed also, they told Oglethorpe,[1] that the time would come when the black and white man would be one...

This, with one trifling exception, was the sole significant dialogue Wesley ever had with any members of the race he had crossed the Atlantic to convert ... the glowing expectations he had brought with him were chilled, not so much by what they now said as by what he heard and saw of them besides ... They have no religion, no laws, no civil government. They are all, except perhaps the Choctaws,[2] liars, gluttons, drunkards, thieves, dissemblers. They are implacable, unmerciful, murderers of fathers, murderers of their own children – it being a common thing for a son to shoot his own father or mother because they are old and past labour, and for a woman to throw her child into the next river because she will go with her husband to the war.[3]

Father, our efforts in evangelism don't always go according to plan! Forgive us when we misunderstand context or speak too soon, and in your mercy overlook our failings in order to bring some into your Kingdom. Help us not to be discouraged.

1 General James Oglethorpe (1696–1785), British military general, Member of Parliament and philanthropist. He was the founder of a British colony in Georgia and invited Wesley to America as part of his ongoing plan to colonise the area. Oglethorpe regarded Christianity as the only suitable faith for a British colony and proposed Georgia as a suitable destination for outcasts – English debtors, for example, or German Protestants who had been exiled by the Roman Catholic Archbishop of Salzburg – and envisaged Wesley as their pastor.

2 Native Americans from the south-eastern United States.

3 From *Rev. John Wesley*.

February 2nd

Be prepared in season and out of season; correct, rebuke and encourage – with great patience and careful instruction

(2 Timothy 4:2 *NIV*)

Before Wesley went to the university [Oxford], he had acquired some knowledge of Hebrew under his brother Samuel's[1] tuition. At college he continued his studies with all diligence, and was noticed there for his attainments, and especially for his skill in logic, by which he frequently put to silence those who contended with him in after-life. No man, indeed, was ever more dextrous in the art of reasoning. A charge was once brought against him that he delighted to perplex his opponents by his expertness in sophistry; he repelled it with indignation: "It has been my first care," said he, "to see that my cause was good, and never, either in jest or earnest, to defend the wrong side of a question: and shame on me if I cannot defend the right after so much practice, and after having been so early accustomed to separate truth from falsehood, however artfully they are twisted together." Like his father, and both his brothers, he was no inexpert lyricist in his youth: this, however, was a talent he chose not to maximize – the honour of being the sweet singer of Methodism was reserved for his brother Charles.[2, 3]

Lord, thank you for those you have gifted with eloquence, wit, and speed of thought. Bless them as they articulate and maintain a logical defence of Christianity, and enable them to do so with grace and charm.

1 1690–1739.

2 1707–88. Charles expressed his personal theology in outstanding hymns and was superbly gifted at conveying deep theological truths by way of his hymn-writing.

3 From *John Wesley*.

February 3rd

You did not choose me, but I chose you and appointed you

(John 15:16 *NIV*)

While he was an undergraduate, his manners were free and cheerful; a disposition which carried him through years of uninterrupted labour. However, when the time of life arrived at which he might have taken holy orders, he began to reflect seriously upon the importance of the priestly office, and to feel some scruples concerning the motives of someone called to such a position. Confiding in his father,[1] he was advised by the aged clergyman that it might be too soon for him to be ordained. His mother,[2] however, was of the opinion that the sooner John Wesley entered into deacon's office[3] the better, because it might be an inducement to greater application in the study of practical divinity. "And now," said she, "resolve to make religion the business of your life: for, after all, that is the one thing that, strictly speaking, is necessary; all things beside are comparatively little to the purposes of life. I heartily wish you would enter upon a strict examination of yourself, that you may know whether you have a reasonable hope of salvation by Jesus Christ."[4]

Lord of the Church, my prayers today are for those considering the vocation of ordained ministry; guide them as they think about their decision, and let them know whether or not this is what you are calling them to. Father, the Church is in need of priests and ministers, so please speak up to any who are turning a deaf ear to your voice. Bless and help parents if and when they are consulted.

1 Reverend Samuel Wesley (1662–1735).
2 Susanna Wesley (1669–1742).
3 In the Church of England, most people are ordained first as deacon, then as priest.
4 From *John Wesley*.

February 4th

Joseph, the husband of Mary, and Mary was the mother of Jesus who is called the Messiah

(Matthew 1:16 *NIV*)

Verse 16. *The husband of Mary* – Jesus was generally believed to be the son of Joseph. It was needful for all who believed this, to know that Joseph was descended from David,[1] otherwise they would not allow Jesus to be [regarded as] the Christ. A lesser lineage, or a different one, would have disqualified him in their eyes.

Jesus, who is called Christ – The name Jesus respects chiefly the promise of blessing made to Abraham:[2] the name Christ, the promise of the messiah's Kingdom which was made to David.[3]

It may be observed that the word Christ, in Greek, and Messiah, in Hebrew, signifies "Anointed": indicative of the prophetic, priestly and royal characters meeting as one in Jesus. Among the Jews, anointing was the ceremony whereby prophets, priests and kings were initiated into those offices[4] – we find each of these in Christ.[5]

Lord, Wesley's attention to detail is not only impressive, but reassuring, for he creates a picture of Christ that is complete – and what a Christ that is! Help me to remember these important points as I worship the One who is prophet, priest and king; the anointed messiah.

1 "Joseph also went up from the town of Nazareth in Galilee to Judea, to Bethlehem the town of David, because he belonged to the house and line of David" (Luke 2:4, *NIV*).

2 "Your name will be Abraham, for I have made you a father of many nations. I will make you very fruitful; I will make nations of you, and kings will come from you" (Genesis 17:5 ,6, *NIV*).

3 God's promises to David found in 2 Samuel 7, 1 Chronicles 17:11–14 and 2 Chronicles 6:16. This covenant is made between God and David when God promises that the messiah would come from the lineage of David.

4 A ritual act of pouring oil over a person's head or body, used for ceremonial blessings, recorded in the anointing of Aaron, Saul, and David.

5 From *Notes on the New Testament.*

February 5th

In Christ all the fullness of the Deity lives in bodily form

(Colossians 2:9 *NIV*)

We are by nature at a distance from God – alienated from him, and incapable of free access to Him.

Hence, we want a Mediator, an Intercessor; in other words, a Christ in his priestly office. This is in regard to our state in relationship to God.

With respect to ourselves, we come to realize we have a total darkness – a blindness, an ignorance – regarding the things of God.

We therefore find ourselves in need of Christ in his prophetic office, to enlighten our minds and teach us the whole will of God.

We find also within ourselves a strange misrule of appetites and passions.

For these we want Christ in his royal character, to reign in our hearts and subdue all things to himself.[1]

Mediator, mind-enlightener, and monarch! This is Christ, and he is my God. Thank you, Heavenly Father, for sending a Saviour who so completely meets my need. Thank you for such a complete work of salvation.

1 From *Notes on the New Testament.*

February 6th

THERE IS NO FEAR IN LOVE. BUT PERFECT LOVE DRIVES OUT FEAR, BECAUSE FEAR HAS TO DO WITH PUNISHMENT. THE ONE WHO FEARS IS NOT MADE PERFECT IN LOVE

(1 John 4:18 *NIV*)

Being saved from guilt, we are saved from fear. Not a fear of offending, but from that fear attached to torment and punishment; from fear of the wrath of God, whom we now regard not as a severe Master, but as an indulgent Father. "They have not received again the spirit of bondage, but the Spirit of adoption, whereby they cry, Abba, Father; the Spirit itself also bearing witness with their spirits, that they are the children of God."[1] We are also saved from the fear, though not the possibility, of falling away from the grace of God, and coming short of the great and precious promises.

Thus we have "peace with God through our Lord Jesus Christ. We rejoice in the hope of glory of God and the love of God is shed abroad in our hearts, through the Holy Ghost, who is given to us."[2] We are persuaded (though perhaps not at all times with the same strength) that "neither death, nor life, nor things present, nor things to come, nor height, nor depth, nor any other creature, shall be able to separate them from the love of God, which is in Christ Jesus our Lord."[3, 4]

Lord, enable me to stand against those invisible giants seeking to destroy my trusting faith in a loving, pardoning God, fear being one of them. I have no merit of my own in which to stand, yet when I lean hard on grace and truth, fear cannot overcome my belief. Grant me fresh confidence, to your praise and glory.

1 See Romans 8:15.
2 See Romans 5:2.
3 See Romans 8:39, *KJV*.
4 From *Fifty Three Sermons*.

February 7th

You, dear children, are from God and have overcome them, because the one who is in you is greater than the one who is in the world

(1 John 4:4 *NIV*)

Through faith we are saved from the power of sin, as well as from the guilt of it. The Apostle declares, "Ye know that he was manifested to take away our sins; and in him is no sin. Whosoever abideth in him sinneth not' (1 John 3:5).

Again: "Little children, let no man deceive you. He that commiteth sin is of the Devil. Whosoever believeth is born of God. And whosoever is born of God doth not commit sin; for his seed remaineth in him: and he cannot sin, because he is born of God."[1]

Once more: "We know that whosoever is born of god sinneth not: but he that is begotten of God keepeth himself, and that wicked one toucheth him not" (1 John 5:18).

He that is, by faith, born of God sinneth not by any habitual sin, for all habitual sin is sin reigning: but sin cannot reign in the believer; nor can wilful sin, for the person abiding by faith is utterly set against all sin – opposed to it – and abhors it as a deadly poison; nor can sinful desire, for the believer continually desires the holy and perfect will of God, and any tendencies towards ungodliness are stifled at birth.

No believer is able to claim they have never sinned, but set before them is the possibility of not sinning again.[2]

Saving God, these are astonishing claims, yet they are not Wesley's – they are found in your word. Grant me, I pray, an abhorrence of sin, an awareness of its corrupting power, and the strength – through grace – to recognize and then withstand, temptation. Make me, by your Holy Spirit within, a glutton for holiness.

1 1 John 3:7, *KJV*.
2 From *Fifty Three Sermons*.

February 8th

The world was not worthy of them

(Hebrews 11:38 *NIV*)

How happy is the pilgrim's lot
How free from every anxious thought,
From worldly hope and fear!
Confined to neither court nor cell,
His soul disdains on earth to dwell,
He only sojourns here.

This happiness in part is mine,
Already saved from self-design,
From every creature love;
Blest with the scorn of finite good,
My soul is lightened of its load,
And seeks the things above.

The things eternal I pursue,
A happiness beyond the view
Of those that basely pant
For things by nature felt and seen;
Their honours, wealth, and pleasures mean
I neither have nor want.

I have no sharer of my heart,
To rob my Saviour of a part,
And desecrate the whole;
Only betrothed to Christ am I,
And wait His coming from the sky,
To wed my happy soul.

I have no babes to hold me here;
But children more securely dear
For mine I humbly claim,
Better than daughters or than sons,
Temples divine of living stones,
Inscribed with Jesus' Name.

No foot of land do I possess,
No cottage in this wilderness,
A poor wayfaring man,
I lodge awhile in tents below;
Or gladly wander to and fro,
Till I my Canaan gain.

Nothing on earth I call my own;
A stranger, to the world unknown,
I all their goods despise;
I trample on their whole delight,
And seek a country out of sight,
A country in the skies.

There is my house and portion fair,
My treasure and my heart are there.
And my abiding home;
For me my elder brethren stay,
And angels beckon me away,
And Jesus bids me come.

"I come," Thy servant, Lord, replies,
"I come to meet thee in the skies,
And claim my heavenly rest";
Now let the pilgrim's journey end,
Now, O my Saviour, Brother, Friend.
Receive me to Thy breast![1]

Lord, these words are ancient and outdated, yet their meaning is very much up-to-date. Help me, I pray, to take this hymn to heart and carry the experiences and things of this world lightly, regarding my time here as little more than a temporary sojourn. Grant me your perspective, Lord, as you granted it to Wesley.

1 From *Hymns for Those That Seek and Those That Have Redemption in the Blood of Jesus*, 1747.

February 9th

There were fourteen generations in all from Abraham to David, fourteen from David to the exile to Babylon, and fourteen from the exile to the Messiah

(Matthew 1:17 *NIV*)

Verse 17. *So all the generations* – Observe that, in order to complete the three fourteens, David ends the first fourteen, and begins the second: (which reaches to the captivity ;) and Jesus ends the third fourteen.

When we consider such a series of generations, it is a natural and obvious reflection., how "like the leaves of a tree one passeth away, and another cometh!"[1] Yet "the earth still abideth"[2] and with it, the goodness of the Lord, which runs on from generation to generation, the common hope of parents and children.

Of all those who have lived upon the earth – even the most conspicuous and famous – how many whose names perished with them! How many are there of whom only names remain! Thus, we are, likewise, passing away! Thus, we too shall be forgotten! Happy are we, therefore, if, though forgotten on earth, we are remembered by God; if our names are found written in the book of life![3], [4]

Father, yet again, I notice Wesley's perspective on this earthly life, and his focus on the importance of one's eternal destiny. I thank you, Lord, for my salvation, and I pause to pray today for those known to me who have not yet received your grace in their lives. Open their eyes, I ask.

1 See Ecclesiastes 1:4 and Homer's *Iliad.*
2 See Ecclesiastes 1:4.
3 Frequent references to this book are made throughout Scripture, perhaps especially in Revelation.
4 From *Notes on the New Testament.*

February 10th

When Jesus was born in Bethlehem of Judaea in the days of Herod the king, behold, there came wise men from the east to Jerusalem

(Matthew 2:1 *KJV*)

Verse 1. *Bethlehem of Judea* – There was another Bethlehem in the tribe of Zebulon.

In the days of Herod – Commonly called Herod the Great, born at Ascalon. The sceptre was now on the point of departing from Judah. Among his sons were Archelaus, mentioned in verse 22; Herod Antipas, mentioned in chapter 14; and Philip, mentioned in Luke 3. Herod Agrippa, mentioned in Acts 12, was his grandson.

Wise men – Probably, they were Gentile philosophers, who, with divine assistance, had improved their knowledge of natural phenomena as a means of leading to the knowledge of the one, true God. It is not unreasonable to suppose that God had favoured them with some extraordinary revelations of himself, as he did Melchisedec,[1] Job, and several others, who were not of the family of Abraham (to which he never intended to confine his favours). The title given to the wise men in the original language was given to all philosophers in ancient times; men of learning; those who were particularly involved with studying the movements of the stars and heavenly bodies.

From the East – So Arabia is frequently called in Scripture. It lay to the east of Judea, and was famous for gold, frankincense, and myrrh.[2]

Lord, thank you for Wesley's attention to detail here, mixing news of divine revelation with practical information. Here is the heart of the Incarnation; God made man. Thank you, Lord, for Jesus, who stepped out of eternity into time and space; into dates and details, for me.

1 See Hebrews 7.
2 From *Notes on the New Testament.*

February 11th

Some of you are saying, "I am a follower of Paul." Others are saying, "I follow Apollos," or "I follow Peter," or "I follow only Christ"

(1 Corinthians 1:12 *NLT*)

Two books which he [Wesley] read in the course of his preparation [for ordained ministry] laid strong hold upon him. The first was the famous treatise *De Imitatione Christia*,[1] commonly ascribed to Thomas a Kempis.

The theological views expressed in this book revolted him at first, and he consulted his parents as counsellors. "I cannot think," said he, "that when God sent us into the world, he had irreversibly decreed that we should be perpetually miserable in it. If our joy in taking up the Cross implies our saying farewell to all joy and satisfaction,[2] how is it reconcilable with what Solomon expressly affirming religion, that her ways are ways of pleasantness, and all her paths are peace?"[3]

Another of the tenets of Thomas a Kempis is that mirth or pleasure is useless, if not sinful; and that nothing is to be regarded as an affliction to a good man – that he ought to thank God even for sending him misery. "This, in my opinion," says Wesley, "is contrary to God's design in afflicting us; for though he chasteneth those whom he loveth,[4] yet it is in order to humble them." Wesley's mother agreed with him that Thomas a Kempis had more zeal than knowledge, and was one of those men who would unnecessarily strew the way of life with thorns.[5, 6]

Thank you, Lord, for writers who leave behind their spiritual thoughts and impressions. Help me to sift wheat from chaff and, however respected or revered the author, and only to cling to that which emanates from the Author of life, the living Word.

1 *The Imitation of Christ.*
2 It is possible to infer this from some of the writings of Thomas a Kempis.
3 Proverbs 3:17, *KJV*.
4 See Hebrews 12:6, *KJV*.
5 Possibly, a reference to Proverbs 15:19.
6 From *John Wesley*.

FEBRUARY 12TH

EVERYTHING SHOULD BE DONE IN A FITTING AND ORDERLY WAY

(1 Corinthians 14:40 *NIV*)

Sun. April 4 [1736] – About four in the afternoon I set out for Frederica,[1] in a pettiawga – a sort of flat-bottomed barge. The next evening we anchored near Skidoway Island,[2] where the water, at flood, was twelve or fourteen feet deep. I wrapped myself up from head to foot in a large cloak, to keep off the sand flies, and lay down on the quarter-deck. Between one and two I awoke, and was under water, having fallen fast asleep. My mouth was full of water. Leaving my cloak on deck, I swam round to the other side of the pettiawga, where a boat was tied, so I climbed up the rope and survived the incident without any more hurt than wet clothes.

Sat. 17 – Not having found, as yet, any doors of opportunity opening for our main mission, we began to consider ways in which we might be useful to the little flock at Savannah, and we agreed:

- To advise the more serious among them to form themselves into a sort of little society, and to meet once or twice a week in order to reprove, instruct and exhort each other.
- To choose from them a smaller number to join with us every Sunday in the afternoon for conversation and more intimate friendship.

Mon. May 10 – I began visiting my parishioners in order, from house to house, for which I set apart time from twelve till three in the afternoon, when it is too hot to work.[3]

Father, how fascinating it is to sense here, the very first origins of Methodism – a methodical plan of organized action in spiritual service. Bless those, Lord, who, like Wesley, love to organize and are gifted in such ways. Bless, too, those who struggle to be organized! Use us all for your Kingdom's sake.

1 Delaware, US.
2 Or Skidaway, Georgia, US.
3 From *John Wesley's Journal (Abridged)* .

FEBRUARY 13TH

AN ARGUMENT STARTED AMONG THE DISCIPLES

(Luke 9:46 *NIV*)

Oglethorpe and Wesley seem not to have entirely understood each other as to the object of his [Wesley's] journey … He had come to America to preach to the Indians; Oglethorpe wanted him for the position of parish priest at Savannah. Wesley made several attempts to leave Savannah for an expedition [a preaching tour], but was prevented from doing so by the impossibility of finding a substitute for his duties there, but what is most noteworthy in this failure is that he could not find any Indians on the continent of America who had the least desire of being instructed! There were about as many Indians in America desirous of Christian instruction as there were colliers in Kingswood[1] or miners in Cornwall.[2] The evil influence of delusion breeds delusion, and people recoil to equally unfavourable attitudes, resisting correct judgment, a situation not helped by the fact that Wesley never seemed to have attempted the arduous task of learning the [native] language.[3], [4]

Lord, this appears to read as something of a catalogue of errors; colleagues at loggerheads, misunderstanding what was expected of each other, an almost entirely unreceptive audience, and problems in communication.
How wonderful it is, then, that you use ordinary people in your service, with all our faults, failings and fall-outs! Thank you, Lord, for persevering with us.
Please keep doing so!

1 Bristol, England. Kingswood Colliers were renowned for being unruly.
2 South-west England. Tin, silver, and zinc miners.
3 This point is intriguing, as Wesley had a gift for learning languages. This reluctance may possibly have been indicative of his sense of discouragement and pessimism.
4 From *Rev. John Wesley.*

February 14th

Let us lift up our heart with our hands unto God in the heavens

(Lamentations 3:41 *KJV*)

We lift our hearts to thee,
O Day Star from on high!
The sun itself is but thy shade,
Yet cheers both earth and sky.

O let thine orient beams
The night of sin disperse,
The mists of error and of vice
Which shade the universe.

How beauteous nature now:
How dark and sad before!
With joy we view the pleasing change,
And nature's God adore.

O may no gloomy crime
Pollute the rising day;
Or Jesus' blood, like evening dew,
Wash all the stains away.

May we this life improve,
To mourn for errors past;
And live this short, revolving day
As if it were our last.

To God the Father, Son,
And Spirit, One in Three,
Be glory; as it was, is now,
And shall forever be.[1]

Father God, king of my heart, hear my prayer today.

1 From *Collection of Psalms and Hymns*, 1741.

February 15th

Not having mine own righteousness, which is of the law, but that which is through the faith of Christ, the righteousness which is of God by faith

(Philippians 3:9 *NIV*)

Does not preaching salvation by faith lead men into pride? Accidentally, it may. Every believer should, therefore, be cautioned, in the words of the great Apostle, "Because of unbelief," the first branches "were broken off: and thou standest by faith. Be not high-minded, but fear. If God spared not the natural branches, take heed lest He spare not thee."[1]

We remember, too, those words of St Paul, foreseeing and answering this very objection (Romans 3:27), "Where is boasting then? It is excluded. By what law? Of works? Nay: but by the law of faith."

It is by grace that we are saved, and our salvation is received by faith; faith is a consequence of grace, but we are not saved because we believe, but only because of God's good favour. All our works, all our righteousness, merit nothing in terms of salvation, for salvation is not of works. God commends to us the riches of his mercy, leaving us no reason to boast.[2, 3]

God of grace, how tempting it is to imagine that my good works will somehow influence your plan for my salvation! How humbling it is to realize that there is nothing I can do to save myself. Yet, how wonderful it is to remember the absolute efficacy of Christ's saving work on Calvary; keep this high in my heart and at the front of my mind: Jesus, only Jesus.

1 See Romans 11:19, 20.
2 See Ephesians 2:4 & Romans 5:8.
3 From *Fifty Three Sermons.*

FEBRUARY 16TH

YOU TRY MANY MEDICINES IN VAIN

(Jeremiah 46:11 *NIV*)

People sometimes enquire about the numbers of books on medicine that now exist, wondering if there aren't too many. Yes, there are – ten times over, especially considering how little many of them actually have to say. Besides this, they are too expensive for poor men to buy, and too hard for plain men to understand. I have not seen one yet which contains only safe, and cheap, and easy medicines. Many of them are dangerous, and a prudent man would never deal with them. There is a further objection; they consist of too many ingredients whereas experience shows that one thing will cure most disorders. Why, then, add another nineteen? Only to increase the doctor's bill?

How often, when medicines are compounded, is the virtue of both utterly destroyed? This practice caused the great Boerhaave[1] to caution against mixing medicines without evident necessity, and without full proof of the effects they will produce when joined together. Medicines, when taken separately, are safe and powerful. When compounded, they not only lose their former powers, but form a strong and deadly poison.[2]

Lord, this seems an odd train of thought for a clergyman! Nevertheless, there is a spiritual parallel of keeping things simple and uncomplicated – a gospel message that stands perfectly well on its own, and has no need of additions. Thank you for such an all-sufficient gospel, meeting every need.

1 Herman Boerhaave (1668–1738), Dutch botanist, chemist, Christian humanist and physician whose guiding principle was '*Simplex sigillum very: The simple is the sign of the true*'.

2 From *Primitive Physic.*

February 17th

THE JAILER TOOK THEM AND WASHED THEIR WOUNDS; THEN IMMEDIATELY HE AND ALL HIS HOUSEHOLD WERE BAPTIZED

(Acts 16:33 *NIV*)

Is there a danger that speaking of the mercy of God as the only means of salvation will only encourage people in their sin? Indeed it may, and will: many will "continue in sin that grace may abound"[1]: but their blood is on their own head because the goodness (mercy) of God ought to lead them to repentance; and so it will, those who are sincere of heart.

When they discover there is forgiveness in Christ, they will cry aloud regarding their sins, and if they earnestly cry, and faint not; if they seek him and refuse to be comforted until he answers their prayers, He will come to them.

Furthermore, Christ Jesus can do so much work in a short time. Many are the examples, in the Acts of the Apostles, of God working faith in men's hearts, like lightning falling from Heaven. In the same hour that Paul and Silas began to preach, the jailer repented, believed, and was baptized, as were three thousand, by St Peter, on the day of Pentecost, who all repented and believed as he preached.[2]

Blessed be God, there are now many living proofs that he is still "mighty to save".[3, 4]

Lord Jesus, you paid such a great price for my sins; why would I wish to continue in sin when I realize something of what it cost you to arrange my forgiveness? Thank you, Lord, that you do not delay grace.

1 Romans 6:15, *KJV*.
2 Acts 2:41.
3 From Zephaniah 3:17.
4 From *Fifty Three Sermons*.

FEBRUARY 18TH

THE LAND YOU HAVE GIVEN ME IS A PLEASANT LAND

(Psalm 16:6 *NLT*)

When they commenced work in Georgia the brothers separated. Charles went with Ingham[1] to Frederica, a settlement on the west side of the island of Alatamaha,[2] and he was the first to make the painful discovery that their mission was a failure.

[John] Wesley, however, at first was pleased with his situation; he thought the place was pleasant and healthful, and even wrote to his other saying he should be heartily glad if any poor and religious men or women of Epworth[3] or Wroote[4] would come out to him; inviting them with a promise of land enough, and of provisions till they could live upon its produce.

He was satisfied, too, with his reception, and the effect he produced. The people crowded to hear him, and when he saw their "deep attention and the seriousness which sate upon all their faces," he hoped that his preaching would not be in vain.[5]

Lord, life doesn't always go according to plan, and not everything in the human experience is pleasant. Nevertheless, there are those times – days, months, years, even – when things go well and run smoothly. Thank you, Lord, for such times. Help me to remember in the darkness they which you have taught me in the light.

1 Benjamin Ingham (1712–72), a companion of the Wesley brothers on their American expedition. He was an ordained Anglican minister with a keen, active interest in the Moravian Church and, subsequently, Methodism.
2 Georgia, US.
3 Lincolnshire, England: birthplace of John & Charles Wesley.
4 North Lincolnshire, England, where John Wesley was an Anglican curate.
5 From *Rev. John Wesley.*

February 19th

For the law was given through Moses; grace and truth came through Jesus Christ

(John 1:17 *NIV*)

Yes, they welcomed him and heard him gladly when first he came among them, and if he had only had more tact, if he had only remembered Dr Burton's[1] warning, that the people among whom he was going were "babes in the progress of their Christian life, to be fed with milk instead of strong meat;"[2] above all, if he had only had a saving knowledge of the redemption wrought for us and in us by our Saviour Christ, his would have been a very different work in America.[3]

As it was, he bewildered and alarmed the people by his hard and fast rules of life, his asceticism, his scrupulous adherence to the letter rather than the spirit of Church laws, and his want of tact and of the power to yield, when it was really unnecessary to be unyielding.[4]

Gracious God, grant me that lovely balance whereby truth and grace are experienced – and then shared – in equal measure. Teach me the benefits of truth smothered in grace, that my witness may all the more represent Jesus.

1 Dr John Burton (1696–1771), Oxford scholar, lecturer and writer; one of the founders of the Georgia Colony, invited there by General Oglethorpe.

2 See 1 Corinthians 3:2 & Hebrews 5:12.

3 Wesley's understanding of the gospel had yet to evolve to a position whereby he understood salvation by grace. His emphasis was still on works.

4 From *Rev. John Wesley.*

FEBRUARY 20TH

PRECIOUS IN THE SIGHT OF THE LORD IS THE DEATH OF HIS SAINTS

(Psalm 116:15 *ESV*)

Servant of God, well done!
Thy glorious warfare's past;
The battle's fought, the race is won,
And thou art crowned at last.

Of all thy heart's desire
Triumphantly possessed;
Lodged by the ministerial choir
In thy Redeemer's breast.

In condescending love,
Thy ceaseless prayer He heard;
And bade thee suddenly remove
To thy complete reward.

Ready to bring the peace,
Thy beauteous feet were shod,
When mercy signed thy soul's release,
And caught thee up to God.

With saints enthroned on high,
Thou dost thy Lord proclaim,
And still to God salvation cry,
Salvation to the Lamb!

O happy, happy soul!
In ecstasies of praise,
Long as eternal ages roll,
Thou seest thy Saviour's face.

Redeemed from earth and pain,
Ah! when shall we ascend,
And all in Jesus' presence reign
With our translated friend?

Come, Lord, and quickly come!
And, when in thee complete,
Receive thy longing servants home,
To triumph at thy feet.[1]

Lord of life and death, I thank you for the wonderful promise of eternal in your loving presence, but I pray today for those experiencing bereavement. However comforting the gospel is for the believer, the pain of loss is still very real; please draw alongside those who are missing loved ones.

1 Wesley wrote this hymn in 1770, commemorating the death of his friend Reverend George Whitefield (1714–70), an Anglican cleric and one of the founders of Methodism.

February 21st

A soft answer turneth away wrath

(Proverbs 15:1 *KJV*)

Thur. June 17 [1736] – An officer of a man-of-war,[1] walking just behind us, with two or three of his acquaintances, cursed and swore exceedingly; but when I reproved him, he seemed to be very moved, and gave me many thanks.

Tues. 22 – Observing much coldness in M.—'s behaviour, I asked him the reason for it. He answered, "I like nothing you do. All your sermons are satires of people, and therefore I will never listen to you again; all those people are known to me, and I don't want to hear them abused. Besides, they say, they are Protestant, but they can't even tell which religion you belong to – they have never heard of such a religion as yours before and they don't know what to make of it. And then your private behaviour; all the quarrels you have had since you came here. There is not a man or woman in the town who cares what you have to say. Nobody will come to hear you."

He was too overheated to hear my answer, so I had no option but to thank him for his openness and walk away.[2]

What an astonishing conversation! Lord, if and when I need to speak words of truth to anyone, please remind me to do so with gentle humility and courtesy. Likewise, if I am on the receiving end of criticism, remind me of Wesley's example: the futility of angry retaliation and the better option of quietly walking away. Help me, too, like John Wesley, to give thanks for points made which may well be true, even if they are hard to swallow!

1 British slang for a powerful warship or frigate.
2 From *John Wesley's Journal (Abridged).*

February 22nd

See Matthew 2:2–6

(KJV)

Verse 2. *To do him homage* – To pay him that honour, by bowing to the earth before him, which the eastern nations used to pay to their monarchs.[1]

Verse 4. *The chief priests* – That is, not only the high priest and his deputy, with those who formerly had borne that office; but also the chief man in each of those twenty-four courses into which the body of those priests were divided, 1 Chronicles 24:4–18. The scribes were those whose business it was to explain the scriptures to the people. They were the public preachers, or expounders of the law of Moses, the chief of whom were called doctors of the law.

Verse 6. *Thou art in no wise the least among the princes of Judah* – That is, among the cities belonging to the princes or heads of the thousands in Judah.[2] When this and several other quotations from the Old Testament are compared with the original, it appears the Apostles did not always think it necessary to exactly transcribe the passages they cited; but contented themselves with giving the general sense. For example, the words of the prophet Micah, "Though thou be little" are rendered (paraphrased) as "Art thou little?" but the meaning is entirely the same.[3]

Three things, Lord:
Teach me too to bow in your presence.
Help me too to study your law, and apply it to my life.
Thank you that you often surprise us by appearing among the least and lowest; remind me to expect to find you there.

1 Not necessarily an act of worship, but a mark of honour and respect.
2 In terms of population, Judah was small and, therefore, an unlikely venue for the advent of the messiah.
3 From *Notes on the New Testament.*

February 23rd

Let the wise listen and add to their learning,
and let the discerning get guidance

(Proverbs 1:5 *NIV*)

The treatise *De Imitatione* appears to have offended Wesley's reason, as well as the instincts of hilarity and youth. Jeremy Taylor's Rules of Holy Living and Dying[1] soon became pre-eminent in Wesley's estimation and affected him exceedingly. "Instantly," he said, "I resolved to dedicate all my life to God – all my thoughts and actions – being thoroughly convinced there was no medium; but that every part of my life (not some only) must either be a sacrifice to God, or myself – that is, in effect to the Devil."

The *Imitation*, which he had found repulsive at first, appeared so no longer now: Bishop Taylor had prepared the way for the ascetic author, and he began to find in the perusal sensible comfort, such as he was an utter stranger to before.

His father, who had once thought him wanting in theopathy,[2] and probably for that reason had advised him to delay his ordination, perceived the change with joy. "God fit you for your great work!" he said to him. "Fast, watch, and pray; believe, love, endure, and be happy, towards which you shall never lack the most ardent prayers of your affectionate father."[3]

Help me, Lord, to be willing to change and adapt my ideas – and prejudices! – if I am shown a better way. Grant me that flexibility of heart and mind so that I may absorb all you have for me.

1 *Holy Living* and *Holy Dying*: two books originally published as *The Rules and Exercises of Holy Living* and *The Rules and Exercises of Holy Dying*. Jeremy Taylor (1613–67), an Anglican cleric.
2 The ability to receive divine illumination and/or correction.
3 From *John Wesley*.

FEBRUARY 24TH

IN CHRIST GOD FORGAVE YOU

(Ephesians 4:32 *NIV*)

Jeremy Taylor had remarked that we ought, "in some sense or other, to think ourselves the worst in every company where we come". The duty of absolute humility Wesley at once acknowledged; but he denied that this comparative humility, as he called it, was in our power; it could not be reasonable, or sincere, and therefore it could not be a virtue.

The bishop [Taylor] had affirmed that we know not whether God has forgiven us. Wesley could not assent to this position. "If," said he, "we dwell in Christ and Christ in us, which we will not do unless we are regenerate, certainly we must be sensible [aware] of it. If we can never have any certainty of our being in a state of salvation, then every moment should be spent, not in joy, but in fear and trembling; and then undoubtedly in this life we are of all men most miserable. God deliver us from such a fearful expectation! Humility is undoubtedly necessary to salvation, and if all these things are essential to humility, who can be humble. Our sins will never be brought up against us unless we apostatise; and I am not satisfied what evidence there can be of our final perseverance till we have finished our course, but I am persuaded we may know if we are *now* in a state of salvation.[1]

Saving God, preserve me from apostasy, I pray. Grant me faith for salvation, even when I am tempted to doubt. Grant strength to those whom today are wavering, or under attack, that their faith may hold fast, by your grace. Bless me with discernment so that I can sense the difference between your truth and the devil's lies.

1 From *John Wesley.*

WHEN I WAS A CHILD, I SPOKE LIKE A CHILD, I THOUGHT LIKE A CHILD, I REASONED LIKE A CHILD

(1 Corinthians 13:11 *ESV*)

[Susanna Wesley's] son John was the fifteenth of her scholars.[1] If the others prayed hard to be saved for heaven, John was literally snatched from the fires of hell. For the vicarage went up in flames when he was but a child. All the others were brought safely outdoors, but Johnny had been left behind in the confusion. It was some time before his absence was noted and the vicar rushed into the flames to save him.[2] Wesley never forgot how close he had been to falling into the arms of the devil. His own experience, he felt, was a living proof of redemption.

At ten he entered the Charterhouse School[3] and applied himself to his studies with the conscience of a young man whose father was the Vicar of Epworth and whose mother knew Latin and Greek. He carried the weight of the world's sin upon his little shoulders. It mattered not that other, "less innocent" souls were passing through a carefree childhood at Charterhouse. The son of Susanna Wesley felt that his ten years were merely added on to the accumulated responsibilities of the human race. Just as a child may inherit the ugly physical features of his ancestors, so too – believed Wesley – he himself had inherited the ugly moral imperfections of all mankind.[4]

Lord, it is difficult to avoid a sense of sadness here, at a child weighed down with concerns and responsibilities no child should have to consider. I'm all for religious instruction and upbringing, Lord, but I feel childhood is precious and all-too-short anyway. I pray for Christian parents, that their influence may be strong, yet gentle
… and I pray for the children of Christian parents too!

1 Wesley was one of nineteen children and his mother regarded them as little Christian "soldiers" to be trained in theology, holiness, and spiritual matters.
2 See January 3rd.
3 An independent boarding and day school in Surrey, England, founded in 1611.
4 From *Living Biographies of Religious Leaders*.

February 26th

The Lord God said, "It is not good for the man to be alone"

(Genesis 2:18 *NIV*)

There was no childhood for John. At seventeen he already felt like an old man. He entered Christ Church, Oxford, hewed his conduct to the line of God, and wrote to his mother about his daily schedule of meditations and prayer. He might have formulated the golden rule, "Do unto the Lord what you would have the Lord do unto you."

He took his degree, entered Lincoln College as a Fellow, prepared himself in the "honest art of logic" and, following in the footsteps of his father, accepted a vicarage in a country parish.[1]

But he discovered that he had no taste for tending a flock. Compared to the arduous study of God in his chambers at Oxford, the simple life of a village priest was a wasted time of idleness and indignity. He returned to Oxford, determined to become a religious recluse. Nobody but the Lord God was fit company for the impulsive and ambitious young Don. He would have no communication with the world. His desire was to commune alone with the world's Creator. But one day a stray remark was tossed into his ear – a simple statement made by one of the most insignificant of his handful of acquaintances. "Mr Wesley," remarked this man, "it seems to me that to serve God, you must find companions. The Bible knows nothing of solitary religion."[2]

Lord, today I think of those who are on their own – whether by choice or circumstance. Truly, the person who is alone with God is never really alone, but good friendships and relationships are beyond price, and I pray for those whose loneliness is a heavy burden and a cause of sadness.

1 Wroote, Lincolnshire, England.
2 From *Living Biographies of Religious Leaders*.

February 27th

We are more than conquerors through him who loved us

(Romans 8:37 *NIV*)

O My Father, my God, I am in your hand; and may I rejoice above all things in being so. Do with me what seems good in your sight; only let me love you with all my mind, soul, and strength.

I magnify you for granting me to be born in your Church, and of religious parents; for washing me in your baptism, and instructing me in your doctrine of truth and holiness; for sustaining me by your gracious providence, and guiding me by your blessed Spirit; for admitting me, with the rest of my Christian brethren, to wait on you at your public worship; and for so often feeding my soul with your most precious body and blood, those pledges of love and sure conveyances of strength and comfort.

O, be gracious unto all of us, whom you have this day (or at any time) admitted to your holy table. Strengthen our hearts in your ways against all our temptations, and make us *more than conquerors* in your love.[1]

Father God, what a gloriously comprehensive prayer this is, offering notes of worship, submission and gratitude, speaking of humility, and calling upon you for daily strength. I adopt this prayer as my own, today, for my life and my pilgrimage. Lord, in your mercy, hear my prayer.

1 From *John and Charles Wesley: Selected Writings and Hymns.*

February 28th

I seek you with all my heart; do not let me stray from your commands

(Psalm 119:10 *NIV*)

O my Father, my God, deliver me, I beseech you, from all violent passions; I know how greatly obstructive these are of both the knowledge and the love of you. Oh, let none of them find a way into my heart, but let me ever possess my soul in meekness. O my God, I desire to fear them more than death; let me not serve these cruel tyrants, but reign in my breast; let me be ever your servant, and love you with all my heart.

Deliver me, O God, from too intense an application to even necessary business. I know how this dissipates my thoughts from the one end of all my business, and impairs that lively perception I would ever retain of your standing at my right hand. I know the narrowness of my heart, and that an eager attention to earthly things leaves it no room for the things of heaven. Oh, teach me to go through all my employments with so truly disengaged a heart that I may still see you in all things, and see you therein as continually looking upon me, and searching me; that I may never impair that liberty of spirit necessary for the love of you.[1]

Amen.
Amen.
Amen.

1 From *John and Charles Wesley: Selected Writings and Hymns.*

March 1st

For my thoughts are not your thoughts, neither are your ways my ways, saith the Lord. For as the heavens are higher than the earth, so are my ways higher than your ways, and my thoughts than your thoughts

(Isaiah 55: 8, 9 *KJV*)

What then shall I say of predestination? If it was inevitably decreed from eternity that a determinate part of mankind should be saved, and none beside them, a vast majority of the world were only born to eternal death, without so much as a possibility of avoiding it.

How is this consistent with either the divine justice or mercy?

Is it merciful to ordain a creature to everlasting misery?

Is it just to punish man for crimes which he could not but commit?

That God should be the author of sin and injustice (which must, I think, be the consequence of maintaining this opinion) is a contradiction of the clearest ideas we have of the divine nature and perfections.

[Wesley's] mother, to whom these feelings were imparted, agreed with him that the Calvinistic doctrine of predestination[1] was shocking, and ought utterly to be abhorred … She wondered why men would amuse themselves with searching into the decrees of God, which no human heart could fathom, and not rather employ their time and powers in making their own election sure. "Such studies," she said, "tended more to confound than to inform their understanding."[2]

Lord God, whose ways are above mine, I do not wish to skate over important theological research, but I can't help feeling John Wesley's mother speaks a great deal of good sense here. Enlighten my understanding, I pray, but help me too, to remember her advice.

1 John Calvin (1509–64), hugely influential French theologian and pastor whose doctrine of election remains a controversial and divisive theological opinion.

2 From *John Wesley.*

March 2nd

See Matthew 2:11–16

Verse 11. *They presented to him gifts* – It was customary to offer some present to any eminent person whom they visited. And so it is, as travellers observe, in the eastern countries to this day.

Gold, frankincense, and myrrh – Probably these were the best things their country afforded, and the presents ordinarily made to great persons. This was a most seasonable providential assistance for a long and expensive journey into Egypt, a country where they were entirely strangers, and were to stay for a considerable time.

Verse 15. *That it might be fulfilled* – That is, whereby was fulfilled. The original word frequently signifies, not the design of an action, but the consequence or event of it.

Out of Egypt I have called my son – which was now fulfilled as it were anew; Christ being in a far higher sense the Son of God, than Israel, of whom the words were originally spoken.

Verse 16. *Then Herod, seeing that he was deluded by the wise men* – So did his pride teach him to regard this action, as if it were intended to expose him to the derision of his subjects.[1]

Lord, I love Wesley's insights into verses of Scripture that I confess I have taken for granted. These comments speak to me, and aid my worship. Help me to apply these facets of knowledge to my daily devotion, I pray.

1 From *Notes on the New Testament.*

March 3rd

I have placed before you an open door that no one can shut

(Revelation 3:8 *NIV*)

Wed. 30 [July 1736] – I hoped a door was opened for going up immediately to the Choctaws, the least polished, that is, the least corrupted, of all the Indian nations.[1] But upon my informing Mr Oglethorpe of our design, he objected, not only [because of] the danger of being intercepted or killed by the French there;[2] but much more, the inexpediency of leaving Savannah destitute of a minister.[3] These objections I related to our brethren in the evening, who were all of the opinion, "We ought not to go yet."[4]

Lord, it is not difficult to sense a note of frustration and disappointment in Wesley's notes today. I therefore pray for all those who are experiencing similar emotions today; when plans are thwarted and hopes dashed. Help them, Lord, not to be discouraged and not to give up. Help them to trust your timing.

1 The Choctaw were a tribe; not, strictly speaking, a nation, although they did have their own system of government and their own language.

2 The French had entered into a relatively peaceful alliance with the American Indians after the Franco-Indian War (1754–63). As this alliance was mutually beneficial to both French settlers and protected Native Americans, it is likely any British or European interference would have met with hostile resentment and probably military conflict.

3 Mr (General) Oglethorpe's perception of John Wesley as a pastor to his Georgia Colony had not been well received by the latter. Wesley could not be restricted to a single "parish", setting the pattern for his lifelong itinerant ministry.

4 From *John Wesley's Journal (Abridged)*.

March 4th

PRAY ... FOR KINGS AND ALL WHO ARE IN AUTHORITY SO THAT WE CAN LIVE PEACEFUL AND QUIET LIVES MARKED BY GODLINESS AND DIGNITY

(1 Timothy 2:2 *NLT*)

Thur. July 1 [1736] – The Indians had an audience; and another on Saturday, when Chicali, their head-man,[1] dined with Mr Oglethorpe. After dinner, I asked the grey-headed old man what he thought he was made for. He said, "He that is above knows what he made us for. We know nothing. We are in the dark. But white men know much. And yet white men build great homes, as if they were to live for ever. But white men cannot live for ever. In a little time, white men will be dust as well as I." I told him, "If red men will learn the good book, they may know as much as white men. But neither we nor you can understand that book, unless we are taught by him that is above: and he will not teach, unless you avoid what you already know is not good." He answered, "I believe that. He will not teach us while our hearts are not white. And our men do what they know is not good: they kill their own children. And our women do what they know is not good: they kill the child before it is born.[2] Therefore he that is above does not send us the good book."[3]

Lord, today I pray for community leaders; chosen and elected leaders, people who have influence. Grant them wisdom in their policy-making. Use them to help people in humane ways. I think of those in my area, and lift them to you in prayer.

1 *Meeko, which translates as Chief.*

2 Abortion was an acceptable practice in many areas of Native American culture because of the belief that the soul of a person did not inhabit the body until the first breath had been drawn, after birth.

3 From *John Wesley's Journal (Abridged).*

March 5th

Learn what this means: "I desire mercy, not sacrifice." For I have not come to call the righteous, but sinners

(Matthew 9:13 *NIV*)

The objection is sometimes made: "If a man cannot be saved by all that he can do, this will drive men to despair." And so it ought; for none can trust in the merits of Christ, till he has utterly renounced his own. He that "goeth about to establish his own righteousness"[1] cannot receive the righteousness of God. The righteousness which is of faith cannot be given while he is trusting that which is of the law.

But this it is said, is an uncomfortable doctrine. The Devil spoke like himself – that is, without either truth or shame – when he dared to suggest to men that it is such. It is the only comfortable one, it is "very full of comfort," to all self-destroyed, self-condemned sinners. That "whosoever believeth on Him shall not be ashamed: that the same Lord over all is rich unto all that call upon Him":[2] here is comfort, high as heaven, stronger than death!

What!

Mercy for all?

For Zacchaeus, a public robber? For Mary Magdalene, a common harlot?

I think I hear someone say, "Then I, even I, may hope for mercy!" And so you may, afflicted one, whom no one can comfort. God will not cast out your prayer.[3]

Thank you, Lord, for such a depth of mercy. I may not understand it, and I certainly don't deserve it, but help me to trust that this is your gracious gift, and is utterly reliable in this world and the next.

1 Romans 10:3, *KJV*.
2 See Romans 10:11, 12, *KJV*.
3 From *Fifty Three Sermons*.

March 6th

I will be merciful toward their iniquities, and I will remember their sins no more

(Hebrews 8:12 *ESV*)

'Be of good cheer, thy sins are forgiven thee'[1]: so forgiven, that they shall reign over you no more; and the Holy Spirit shall bear witness that you are a child of God.

O glad tidings! Tidings of great joy, which are sent to all people! "Everyone that thirsteth, come ye to the waters: come ye, and buy, without money and without price."[2] Whatsoever your sins be, "though red like crimson,"[3] though more than the hairs of your head, "return ye unto the Lord, and he will have mercy upon you; and to our God, for he will abundantly pardon.'[4]

When no more objections occur, then we are simply left with the conclusion that salvation by faith ought either to be preached as our first doctrine, or not preached at all. So then, "whosoever believeth on him shall be saved"[5] is, and must be, the foundation of all our preaching; that is, must be preached first.[6]

Every sin!

1 See Matthew 9:2, *KJV*.
2 Isaiah 55:1, *KJV*.
3 Isaiah 1:18.
4 See 2 Chronicles 30:9, *KJV*.
5 See John 3:16 & Romans 10:11, *KJV*.
6 From *Fifty Three Sermons.*

March 7th

Keep your spiritual fervour

(Romans 12:11 *NIV*)

Deliver me, O God, from a slothful mind, from all luke-warmness, and all dejection of spirit. I know these will deaden my love for you; mercifully free my heart from them, and give me a lively, zealous, active, and cheerful spirit, that I may vigorously perform whatever you command, thankfully suffer whatever you choose for me, and be ever ardent to obey in all things your holy love.

Deliver me, O God, from all idolatrous love of any creature. I know infinite numbers have been lost to you by loving those creatures for their own sake, which you permit – command – to love subordinately. Preserve me from all such blind affection; be a guard to all my desires. You require me to love you with all my heart: undertake for me, I beseech you, and be my security, that I may never open my heart to anything but out of love to you.

Above all, deliver me, O my God, from all idolatrous self-love. I know, O God (blessed be your infinite mercy for giving me this knowledge) that this is the root of all evil. I know you made me not to do my own will but yours.[1]

Lord, in this prayer of Wesley's, I see a clue regarding how and why you were able to use him to such great effect. I would like to borrow his prayer for myself, today.

1 From *John and Charles Wesley: Selected Writings and Hymns.*

March 8th

For we are co-workers in God's service

(1 Corinthians 3:9 *NIV*)

Mon. Aug. 2 [1736] – I set out for the Lieutenant-Governor's seat,[1] about thirty miles from Charlestown, to deliver Mr Oglethorpe's letters. It stands very pleasantly, on a little hill, with a vale on either side, in one of which is a thick wood; the other is planted with rice and Indian corn. I planned to return via Mr Skeen's,[2] who keeps about fifty Christian workers,[3] but my horse was tiring, so I returned the straight way to Charlestown.

I had sent the boat we came in back to Savannah, expecting a passage there myself in Colonel Bull's.[4] However, as his was not sailing soon, I went to Ashley Ferry, intending to walk to Port Royal.[5] Mr Belinger,[6] though, not only provided me with a horse, but rode with me himself ten miles, and sent his son with me to Cumbee Ferry, twenty miles farther; where, having hired horses and a guide, I came to Beaufort (or Port Royal) the next evening. We took a boat in the morning; but, the wind being contrary, and very high, did not reach Savannah until Sunday afternoon.[7]

As I read this list of names, Lord, I realize, with thanksgiving, just how many people help me day by day; colleagues, friends, neighbours and family. I pray your blessing on them each as I appreciate their support and company in everyday matters.

1 Possibly John Reynolds, a British Royal Navy officer who served as Royal Governor of Georgia.
2 Possibly Major Skeen, a military officer in some position of authority in the Georgia Colony.
3 Almost certainly black slaves or servants.
4 Colonel William Bull, a military officer largely responsible for planning and supervising the building of houses for colony officials, including enforced land clearance.
5 Port-Royal: an island in South Carolina served by ferry routes.
6 Landowner and supplier of livestock to the colony. His surname was sometimes spelt Bellinger.
7 From *John Wesley's Journal (Abridged)*.

March 9th

Christ's one act of righteousness brings a right relationship with God

(Romans 5:18 *NLT*)

To whom are we not to preach the gospel of faith? For whom should we make an exception? The poor? No; they have a particular right to have the gospel preached to them. The unlearned? No. God has revealed these things unto the unlearned and ignorant from the beginning. The young? By no means. "Suffer these," in any wise, to come unto Christ, "and forbid them not."[1] Sinners? Least of all. "He came not to call the righteous, but sinners to repentance."[2] If any, we should make an exception for the rich, the learned, the reputable, and the moral. It is true that they often exempt themselves from hearing; yet we must speak the words of our Lord because our commission runs, "Go and preach the gospel to every creature."[3] "As the Lord liveth, whatsoever the Lord saith unto us, that we will speak."[4]

More especially, we will speak that "by grace are ye saved through faith":[5] because, never was the maintaining of this doctrine more reasonable than it is today. Nothing but this can effectually prevent the increase of the Romish doctrine among us. It is endless to attack, one by one, all the errors of that Church.[6] But salvation by faith strikes at the root, and all fall at once where this is established.[7]

Lord, the riches of your gospel are available to everyone, in equal measure. Today, I pray for anyone who might feel excluded, and for those who exclude themselves; those who feel they aren't good enough, and those who feel they don't need forgiveness. In your mercy, reveal the cross of Christ to those for whom I pray.

1 See Matthew 19:14, *KJV*.
2 See Luke 5:32, *KJV*.
3 See Mark 16:15, *KJV*.
4 See 1 Kings 22:14 & 2 Chronicles 18:13, *KJV*.
5 Ephesians 2: 8, 9, *KJV*.
6 Wesley, an Anglican, was an outspoken critic of Roman Catholic doctrines which taught that salvation could in some way be earned by works.
7 From *Fifty Three Sermons*.

March 10th

The Lord is good

(Psalm 100:5 *NIV*)

May my soul be fixed against its natural inconstancy; by this may it be reduced to an entire indifference as to all things else, and simply desire what is pleasing in your sight. May this holy flame ever warm my breast, that I may serve you with all my might; and let it consume in my heart all selfish desires, that I may in all things regard not myself but you.

O my God, let your glorious name be duly honoured and loved by all the creatures you have made. Let your infinite goodness and greatness be ever adored by all angels and people. May your Church, the catholic seminary of love divine, be protected from all the powers of darkness. Oh, vouchsafe to all who call themselves by your name one short glimpse of your goodness. May they once taste and see how gracious you are, that all things else may be tasteless to them; that their desires may be always flying up towards you, that they may render to you love, and praise, and obedience, pure and cheerful, constant and zealous, universal and uniform, like that the holy angels render to you in heaven.[1]

What a prayer! Help me this day, my God, even if just briefly, to worship you as the angels do, with a greater awareness of your "goodness and greatness".

1 From *John and Charles Wesley: Selected Writings and Hymns.*

March 11th

I PRAY THAT YOU, BEING ROOTED AND GROUNDED IN LOVE, MAY … COMPREHEND THE LENGTH AND WIDTH AND HEIGHT AND DEPTH OF HIS LOVE

(Ephesians 3:17, 18 *NIV*)

Eternal depth of love divine,
In Jesus, God with us, displayed;
How bright thy beaming glories shine!
How wide thy healing streams are spread!

With whom dost thou delight to dwell?
Sinners, a vile and thankless race:
O God, what tongue aright can tell
How vast thy love, how great thy grace!

The dictates of thy sovereign will
With joy our grateful hearts receive:
All thy delight in us fulfil;
Lo! all we are to thee we give.

To thy sure love, thy tender care,
Our flesh, soul, spirit, we resign:
O fix thy sacred presence there,
And seal the abode for ever thine.

O King of glory, thy rich grace
Our feeble thought surpasses far;
Yea, even our crimes, though numberless,
Less numerous than thy mercies are.

Still, Lord, thy saving health display,
And arm our souls with heav'nly zeal;
So fearless shall we urge our way
Through all the powers of earth and Hell.[1]

Lord, in your mercy, hear and answer prayer.

1 Nikolaus L. von Zinzendorf. Translated from the German by Wesley in *Hymns and Sacred Poems*, 1739.

March 12th

We may be mutually encouraged by each other's faith

(Romans 1:12 *ESV*)

It seems to have been one of the Kirkham sisters[1] who introduced [Wesley], in the spring of 1725, to Thomas a Kempis. John was, he says, at first angry with a Kempis for being "too strict". "Yet," he continues, "I had such comfort in reading him, such as I was an utter stranger to before; and meeting likewise with a religious friend, which I never had till now, I began to alter the whole form of my conversation and to set in earnest upon a new life."

It was at this time, too, that he "became convinced that there is no medium; but that *every* part of my life (not *some* only) must either be a sacrifice to God, or myself – that is, in effect, to the devil." It was this conviction that led him to fear being a "half Christian"...

John now set aside an hour or two a day for religious retirement, communicated every week,[2] watched against all sin, whether in word or deed, and began to aim at, and pray for, inward holiness. "I began to see," he concludes, "that true religion was seated in the heart, and that God's law extended to all our thoughts, as well as to words and actions."[3]

Thank you, Lord, for good friends; those with whom I may discuss serious matters of life and spirituality, and with whom I may risk honesty and vulnerability. Thank you for all that friendships teach and give. Thank you too for "friendships" with writers, such as Wesley's with Thomas a Kempis, whereby I may learn from their written thoughts. Make me a good friend to others, I pray.

1 As Wesley approached the time of his ordination, he began to gravitate towards the social company of families who could provide him with intellectual, spiritual, and cultural stimulation. One such family was the Kirkhams, and he spent time in serious conversation with the three Kirkham sisters.

2 Took Holy Communion.

3 From *John Wesley, Anglican.*

A TIME TO LAUGH

(Ecclesiastes 3:4 *NIV*)

He ... began to pray for inward holiness, of the necessity of which Bishop Taylor had convinced him, and to aim at it with his utmost endeavours. This prepared in heart as well as knowledge, he was ordained in the autumn of the year 1725 by Dr Potter, then Bishop of Oxford,[1] and afterwards primate. In the ensuing spring he offered himself for a fellowship at Lincoln College. Even in college elections there is play enough for evil passions, and too much licence allowed them. Though Wesley was not yet eccentric in his habits of life, the strictness of his religious principles was sufficiently remarkable to afford subject for satire; and his opponents hoped to prevents his success by making him ridiculous.

Upon this occasion his father told him it was a callow virtue that could not bear being laughed at. His mother encouraged him in a different manner. "If," said she, "it be a weak virtue that cannot bear being laughed at, I am sure it is a strong and well-confirmed virtue that can stand the test of a brisk buffoonery. Many people, though well inclined, have yet made shipwreck of faith and a good conscience, merely because they could not bear raillery. I would therefore advise those who are in the beginning of a Christian course, to shun the company of profane wits, as they would the plague or poverty; and never to contract an intimacy with any but such as have a good sense of religion."[2]

Lord, as I thanked you for good friendships yesterday, I now pray that those friendships will help me, will knock off my rough edges, and will inform and edify me, spiritually. Teach me the value of taking a joke against myself!

1 Bishop of Oxford, 1725–37. Archbishop of Canterbury, 1737–47.
2 From *John Wesley*.

March 14TH

Almost thou persuadest me to be a Christian

(Acts 26:28 *KJV*)

Many there are who go thus far; ever since the Christian religion was in the world, there were many in every age and nation who were almost persuaded to be Christians…

In confessing their status as *almost* Christians, we acknowledge what we might call heathen honesty. That is to say, heathens who have been taught not to be unjust, not to take away their neighbour's gods; not to oppose the poor, neither to use extortion, not to cheat the poor or rich, or to defraud anyone and, if were possible, to owe no one anything.

In these ways, and in adopting such behaviours, the heathen allow scope for justice and truth in their behaviour. There is also a sort of love and assistance which they expect from one another. They expect whatever assistance anyone can give another, without prejudice. They extend this form of conduct and principle towards feeding the hungry, clothing the naked, and giving away those things they do not need.

Thus, in the lowest account of it, so far as heathen honesty goes, the inference is that they behave as those who are *almost* Christians.[1]

Thank you, Lord, for people of goodwill who engage in acts of kindness and charity even if they do not name you as Saviour. Bless their efforts and reward their altruism, I pray, but show them the way of faith and salvation too.

1 From *Fifty Three Sermons.*

March 15th

I urge Euodia and I urge Syntyche to live in harmony in the Lord

(Philippians 4:2 *NASB*)

Tues. Nov. 23 [1736] – Mr Oglethorpe sailed for England, leaving Mr Ingham, Mr Delamotte, and me, at Savannah; but with less prospect of preaching to the Indians than we had the first day we set foot in America. Whenever I mentioned it, it was immediately replied, "You cannot leave Savannah without a minister."

To this my plain answer was, "I never promised to stay here one month. I openly declared both before coming here, and at every point since, that I neither would, nor could, take charge of the English any longer until I could go among the Indians."

It was said, "But did not the trustees of Georgia appoint you to be minister of Savannah?" I replied, "They did; but it was not done by my solicitation: it was done without either my desire or knowledge. Therefore, I feel no obligation to continue with the English in Savannah any longer until a door pens to the heathen; this I expressly declared at the time I consented to this appointment."[1], [2]

Lord, in your mercy, give your people good grace to handle misunderstandings and disagreements in a Christ-like manner. We will not always see eye-to-eye, but with your help we can negotiate our discussions with goodwill.

1 Wesley was expected to serve as minister to the English colony in Georgia. He, however, regarded his missions as for the Native Americans.

2 From *John Wesley's Journal (Abridged)*.

March 16th

He makes wars cease to the ends of the earth. He breaks the bow and shatters the spear; he burns the shields with fire

(Psalm 46:9 *NIV*)

Even though I had no obligation not to leave Savannah, I could not resist the request of the more serious parishioners "to watch over their souls yet a little longer, till someone came who might supply my place".

I did this willingly, because the time was not yet come to preach the gospel of peace to the heathens; all their nations being in a ferment, and Paustoobee and Mingo Mattaw[1] having told me, in my own house, "Now our enemies are all about us, we can do nothing but fight, but if we are ever at peace, then we would hear the great word."[2]

Heavenly Father, how sad it is to read here of Wesley's plans for mission and evangelism being thwarted by tribal conflicts. Please, Lord, quell such conflicts around the world wherever they hinder your ways of peace and love. Likewise, let no such troubles disturb my heart as I seek to reach others with the gospel; give me the grace to forgive those with whom I have arguments, if it means they may be won for the Kingdom.

1 Native American chiefs.
2 From *John Wesley's Journal (Abridged)*.

March 17th

When you pass through the waters, I will be with you; and when you pass through the rivers, they will not sweep over you

(Isaiah 43:2 *NIV*)

Wed. Dec. 23 [1736] – Mr Delamotte and I, with a guide, set out to walk to the Cowpen.[1] When we had walked two or three hours, our guide told us plainly, he did not know where we were. However, believing it could not be far off, we thought it best to go on. In an hour or two we came to a cypress swamp, which lay directly across our way: there was not time to walk back to Savannah before night; so we walked through it, the water being about breast high.

By the time we had gone a mile beyond it, we were out of all path; and it being now past sunset, we sat down, intending to make a fire, and to stay there till morning; but finding our tinder wet, we were at a standstill. I advised to walk on still; but my companions, being faint and weary, were for lying down, which we did at about six o'clock; the ground was as wet as our clothes, which, it being a sharp frost, soon froze together; however, I slept till six in the morning. There fell a heavy dew in the night, which covered us over as white as snow. Within an hour after sunrise, we came to a plantation; and in the evening, without any hurt, to Savannah.[2]

Lord, you carry your people through deep waters, when life is tough and we think we might drown beneath our problems. Thank you. I pray today for those who feel as though they might be "going under" and are calling to you for help and guidance. Bring them safely through, I ask.

1 Cowpens, South Carolina, US.
2 From *John Wesley's Journal (Abridged).*

March 18th

Write down the revelation and make it plain

(Habakkuk 2:2 *NIV*)

Susanna[1] wrote to him … noticing his "alteration of temper" and recommending a "strict examination" of himself. From now on, there appear in his diary regular records of his shortcomings and of the resolutions with which he tried to meet them.

On the eve of his ordination in September 1725, he notes boasting, greed of praise, intemperate sleep, distractions, lying, heat in arguing as his salient faults. Such lists were to appear frequently in future years, particularly on Saturday evenings when he reviewed the past week, and prepared for the next.

On 1 December 1725, for example, he wrote: "Breach of vows: hence careless of fixing days of mortification, etc. Pride of my parts of holiness: greedy of praise: peevishness: idleness. Intemperance in sleep: sins of thought: hence useless and sinful anger. Breach of promise: dissimulation: lying: rash censures: condemning others: disrespectful of governors: desire to seem better than I am."

"Resolution: to fast every Wednesday in the month."[2]

One day at a time, Lord. Help me, I pray, one day at a time.

1 John Wesley's mother.
2 From *John Wesley, Anglican.*

MARCH 19TH

WHETHER YOU EAT OR DRINK, OR WHATEVER YOU DO, DO ALL TO THE GLORY OF GOD

(1 Corinthians 10:31 *ESV*)

For the sake of those who desire, through the blessing of God, to retain their health ... I have added a few plain, easy rues, chiefly transcribed from Dr Cheyne.[1]

- The air we breathe is of great consequence to our health. Those who have been long abroad in easterly or northerly winds, should drink some thin and warm liquor going to bed, or take toast and water.
- Tender people should surround themselves with people who are sweet, and healthy.
- Everyone that would preserve health, should be as clean and sweet as possible in their houses, clothes and furniture.

The great rule of eating and drinking is to suit the quality and quantity of the food to the strength of our digestion; to always take such a sort and such a measure of food as sits lightly and easily on the stomach. All pickled, or smoked, or salted food, and all high-seasoned, is unwholesome. Nothing is more conducive to health than abstinence and plain food, and labour. For studious people, about eight ounces of animal food and twelve ounces of vegetables in twenty-four hours is sufficient.[2]

Lord, whether Wesley's advice is right or wrong, my prayers today are for those known to me whose health is failing them, for whichever reason. Help them to find remedies that work, either medicinal or dietary, so that their health may improve. Grant them, too patience and strength in affliction.

1 George Cheyne (1671–1743), physician, psychologist, philosopher, mathematician. Wesley was heavily influenced by his writings, especially in regard to diet and wellbeing.

2 From *Primitive Physic.*

March 20th

I will give you pastors according to mine heart, which shall feed you with knowledge and understanding

(Jeremiah 3:15 *KJV*)

Brethren and fathers, let it not be regarded as forwardness, vanity, or presumption, that one who is of little esteem in the Church takes it upon himself to address a body of people, to many of whom he owes the highest reverence. I owe a still-higher regard to him who I believe requires this from me; to the great Bishop of our souls; before whom both you and I must shortly give an account of our stewardship. It is a debt I owe to love, to real, disinterested affection, to declare the burden of my soul. And may the God of love enable you to read these lines in the same spirit wherewith they were wrote!

I do not speak from a spirit of anger or resentment. I know well, "the wrath of man worketh not the righteousness of God."[1] I would not utter one word out of contempt; a spirit justly abhorred by God and man. Neither of these can consist with that earnest, tender love which is the motive of my present undertaking. In this spirit I desire to cast my bread upon the waters; it is enough if I find it again after many days.[2]

Love does not forbid, but rather requires, plainness of speech. Let me earnestly entreat you, for the love of God, for the love of your own soul, for the love of the souls committed to your charge, and of the whole Church of Christ, to avoid any bias in your mind, by thinking who it is that speaks; but impartially consider what is spoken. And if it be false or foolish, reject it; but do not reject "the words of truth and soberness."[3, 4, 5]

Lord, I love the spirit of humility and grace evident in Wesley's approach to this address. Please clothe me with the same attitude in all my dealings with clergy. Bless them, Lord, as they go about their calling. Help me to help them.

1 James 1:20, *KJV*.
2 See Ecclesiastes 11:1.
3 Acts 26:25, *KJV*.
4 From an address Wesley gave to clergy.
5 From *Wesley's Works*.

PREACH THE WORD

(2 Timothy 4:2 *NIV*)

My first idea was to offer a few thoughts to Clergy of our own Church only.[1] But I see no cause for being so "straitened in my own bowels."[2] I am a debtor to all; and though I primarily speak to them with whom I am connected, I would not exclude any, of whatsoever denomination, whom God has called to "watch over the souls of others, as they that must give account."[3] There are two important things to consider: First, What manner of men ought we be. Secondly; are we such? If we are "overseers over the Church of God, which he hath bought with his own blood,"[4] what manner of men ought we to be, in gifts as well as in grace. To begin with gifts; those that are natural. Ought not a minister to have a good understanding, a clear apprehension, a sound judgment, and a capacity of reasoning; is not this necessary for the work of the ministry? Otherwise, how will he understand the various states of those under his care; or steer them through difficulties and dangers? Can a fool cope with those who know not God, and with the spirits of darkness? No, for he will neither be aware of the devices of Satan, nor the craftiness of his children. Is it not expedient that a guide of souls should have liveliness and readiness of thought? Or how will he be able to "answer a fool according to his folly"?[5] Reasoning is not the weapon to be used with them [fools]. You cannot deal with them thus. They scorn being convinced. To a sound understanding, and a lively turn of thought, should be joined a good memory; so that you may make whatever you discover in reading or conversation your own, lest we be "ever learning, and never able to come to the knowledge of the truth." Every Teacher fitted for his work, "is like a householder who bringeth out of his treasures things new and old."[6,7]

Lord, I pray for my minister.

1 The Church of England.
2 See 2 Corinthians 6:12.
3 See Hebrews 13:17.
4 See Acts 20:28.
5 Proverbs 26:5, *KJV*.
6 See Matthew 13:52, *KJV*.
7 From *Wesley's Works*.

March 22ND

Avoid foolish controversies

(Titus 3:9 *NIV*)

Lincoln College, 25 January 1727. Dear Mother, I am shortly to take my Master's degree. I have drawn up for myself a scheme of studies from, which I do not intend, for some years at least, to vary. I am persuaded by your opinion that there are many truths it is not worthwhile to know. Curiosity, indeed, might be a sufficient reason for our spending time upon them, if we had half a dozen centuries of life to come; but methinks it is poor stewardship to spend a considerable part of the small pittance now allowed us in what makes neither a quick nor a sure return. Two days ago I was reading a dispute between those celebrated masters of controversy, Bishop Atterbury[1] and Bishop Hoadly,[2] but I must admit to breaking off from reading in the middle because I could not imagine that reaching the end of the controversy would be worth the difficulty of doing so. I thought the labour of twenty or thirty hours, if I was sure of succeeding, which I was not, would be ill rewarded by that important piece of knowledge whether Bishop Hoadly had misunderstood Bishop Atterbury or not.[3] About a year and an half ago I stole out of company with a young gentleman with whom I was friendly. As we took a turn in an aisle of St Mary's Church[4] in expectation of a young lady's funeral with whom we were both acquainted, I asked him if he really thought himself my friend; and if he did, why he would not do me all the good he could. He began to protest; in which I cut him short by asking him to let me have the pleasure of making him a whole Christian, to which I knew he was at least half persuaded already; he could not do me a greater kindness. He turned exceedingly serious, and kept something of that disposition ever since. A fortnight ago yesterday, he died of a consumption. I saw him three days before he died; and, on the Sunday following, did him the last good office I could here, by preaching his funeral sermon; which was his desire when living.[5]

Oh, Lord! People die while we argue! Forgive our odd priorities.

1 Francis Atterbury (1663–1732), politician and High Church Bishop. He was noted for his witty and eloquent preaching.
2 Benjamin Hoadly (1676–1761), English bishop.
3 Bishops Atterbury and Hoadly would preach and publish sermons attacking each other's points of view.
4 The University Church of St Mary the Virgin, Oxford, England.
5 From *The Letters of John Wesley*.

Your strength will equal your days

(Deuteronomy 33:25 *NIV*)

Into thy gracious hands I fall,
And with the arms of faith embrace;
O King of glory, hear my call!
O raise me, heal me by thy grace!

Arm me with thy whole armour, Lord,
Support my weakness with thy might;
Gird on my thigh thy conquering sword,
And shield me in the threatening fight.

From faith to faith, from grace to grace,
So in thy strength shall I go on,
Till Heaven and earth flee from thy face,
And glory end what grace begun.[1]

Father, accept this as my prayer today. I need to know that you will hold me, and support me, come what may. I need to know that you will protect me. I need to know that your strength is limitless on my behalf. Bless me with such knowledge this day.

1 Wolfgang C. Dessler. Translated from German by Wesley for *Hymns and Sacred Poems*, 1739.

March 24th

The righteous choose their friends carefully

(Proverbs 12:26 *NIV*)

"When it pleased God," he says, "to give me a settled resolution to be, not a nominal, but a real Christian (being then about twenty-two years of age), my acquaintances were as ignorant of God as myself. But there was this difference: I knew my own ignorance; they did not know theirs. I faintly endeavoured to help them, but in vain. Meantime I found, by sad experience, that even their harmless conversation, so called, damped all my good resolutions. But how to get rid of them was the question which I revolved in my mind again and again. I saw no possible way, except it pleased God to remove me to another college. He did so, in a manner utterly contrary to all human probability. I was elected fellow of a college,[1] where I knew not one person ... Entering now, as it were, into a new world, I resolved to have no acquaintance by chance, but by choice, and to choose such only as I had reason to believe would help me on my way to Heaven.[2]

Thank you, Lord, for friendships in a world where many are lonely. I pray for those at school or university, as Wesley was, who are choosing and making friendships. Guide them in wisdom so that the friendships they choose will be edifying.

1 28 March 1726, Wesley was admitted to a fellowship of Lincoln College, Oxford.
2 From *John Wesley.*

March 25th

Whatever else you do, develop good judgment

(Proverbs 4:7 *NLT*)

I observed the temper and behaviour of all that visited me [at Lincoln College]. I saw no reason to think that the greater part of these truly loved or feared God. Such acquaintance, therefore, I did not choose: I could not expect they would do me any good. Therefore, when any of these came, I behaved as courteously as I could: but to the question, "When will you come to see me?" I returned no answer. When they had come a few times, and found I still declined returning the visit, I saw them no more. And I bless God this has been my invariable rule for about threescore years.[1]

Lord, I admire Wesley's resolve in this matter. Grant me, I pray, the courage of my convictions regarding friendships or any other important decisions. Help me to know what you would like me to do, then help me to stick to it.

1 From *John Wesley.*

MARCH 26TH

SUPPOSE ONE OF YOU WANTS TO BUILD A TOWER.
WON'T YOU FIRST SIT DOWN AND ESTIMATE THE COST
TO SEE IF YOU HAVE ENOUGH MONEY TO COMPLETE IT?

(Luke 14:28 *NIV*)

Lincoln College, March 19, 1727.

Dear Mother,

One advantage at least my degree has given me: I am now at liberty, and shall be in a great measure for some time, to choose my own employment; and as I believe I know my own deficiencies best and which of them are most necessary to be supplied, I hope my time will turn to somewhat better account than when it was not so much in my own disposal.

On Saturday next I propose beginning an entirely different life, with relation to the management of my expenses, from what I have hitherto done. I expect then to receive a sum of money,[1] and intend immediately to call in all my creditors' bills (that they may not grow by lying by, as it sometimes happens), and from that time forward to trust no man, of what sort or trade so ever, so far as to let him trust me.[2]

Thank you, Lord, for my income in a world where many struggle to find one. Grant me wisdom, I pray, regarding what to keep, what to share, and how you would best have me use my finances. I thank you, Lord, for your provision. Thank you too, for Wesley's systematic and sensible example.

1 Probably an allowance remunerate with his fellowship of Lincoln College.
2 From *The Letters of John Wesley.*

March 27th

Learn to do right; seek justice. Defend the oppressed.
Take up the cause of the fatherless

(Isaiah 1:17 *NIV*)

One of the ladies to whom he was introduced on his first landing, assured him that he would see as well dressed a congregation on Sunday as most which he had seen in London. "I did do," he said afterwards, "and soon after took occasion to expound those Scriptures which relate to dress, and to press them freely upon my audience in a plain and close application. All the time that I afterwards ministered at Savannah, I saw neither gold in the Church nor costly apparel; but the congregation in general was almost constantly clothed in plain clean linen or woollen. All was smooth and fair and promising; many seemed to be awakened; all, all were full of respect and commendation." He taught one school, and Delamotte another.[1] Some of Delamotte's boys, who wore shoes and stockings, thought themselves superior to the poor fellows who were barefoot. Delamotte was at a loss how to remedy this evil, but Wesley proposed to change schools for a time, that he might try to cure it. To effect this he one day went into the school without his shoes and stockings. The boys stared at him and at each other, but he said nothing, and only kept them to their work as usual. Before the week was over the boys who had no shoes and stockings took courage, and many more of them came to the school.[2]

Lord, this is a challenging example of solidarity with the poor and marginalized. Bless those organizations who today stand up for the rights of the downtrodden around the world; amplify their voice.

1 Schools for orphaned children.
2 From *Rev. John Wesley.*

March 28th

My dear brothers and sisters, stand firm. Let nothing move you

(1 Corinthians 15:58 *NIV*)

On another occasion, one of the richer colonists gave a ball, and Wesley arranged that the public prayers should begin at the same time: consequently, the Church was full, while the ballroom was so empty that the dancing could not proceed. But this made people angry, and it seemed unnecessary that he should have excited their feelings in this way.[1]

Heavenly Father, this is a tricky one! Do we opt for peace and goodwill even if it means compromise, or do we, like Wesley, stick to our guns on points of morality and principle, even if it means unpopularity? Grant your people a divine mixture of wisdom and courage on matters large and small, helping us to choose our battles wisely and bravely.

1 From *Rev. John Wesley.*

March 29th

I will put my Spirit within you, and cause you to walk in my statutes and be careful to obey my rules

(Ezekiel 36:27 *ESV*)

In his strict following of the rubric,[1] in opposition to the practice of the English Church,[2] he insisted upon baptizing children by immersion, and refused to baptize them if their parents would not consent to that method. He would not allow some to be sponsors, because they were not communicants, and would not allow one who had been baptized by a Dissenter,[3] but who was a very holy man, to come to Holy Communion unless he would consent to being re-baptized by himself, while, on the other hand, it was said that he allowed those who had been baptized by the Roman Catholics to come.[4]

Enable me, Lord, to discover that happy balance that hovers somewhere between strict regulation and flexible spirituality. I pray for your Spirit's guidance in assisting me to spot the difference between the standards you expect and rules that are, frankly, unhelpful. Help!

1 Associated with the *Book of Common Prayer*, referring to instructions for the liturgical content of Anglican services.
2 As distinct from the Anglican Church, and following many points of Roman Catholic theology.
3 A member of a Nonconformist (free) church.
4 From *Rev. John Wesley.*

March 30th

Go into all the world and preach the gospel

(Mark 16:15 *NIV*)

A trip to London brought John Wesley his first mission "among the people". He met one of Marlborough's[1] soldiers – John Oglethorpe – a man whose social conscience was as keen as his sword. Oglethorpe proposed the founding of the colony in Georgia in the New World[2] and the settling of this colony with the outcasts of the Old World[3] – English debtors who had been huddled in filthy prisons,[4] German Protestants who had been exiled from Salzburg by the [staunchly Roman Catholic] Archbishop,[5] [and] other similar stepchildren of the human family. He asked Wesley to become pastor of the "regathered flock" in this new colony, and also to serve as missionary among the Indians.[6] And the young Oxford don eagerly accepted the offer. He took passage on the *Simmonds*;[7] and the trip, which lasted a hundred days, had its romantic as well as its religious side. The young ladies on board were especially moved to prayers by this handsome young pastor. And several of them fell madly in love with his "Christians perfections."[8, 9]

Bless those, Lord, whose call in these days is to carry your gospel overseas. Help them as they encounter different cultures, different foods, and different languages. Guide their efforts, and reassure them of your international presence.

1 The Duke of Marlborough.
2 A name used for areas of the earth's Western hemisphere: the Americas, the Caribbean, and Bermuda.
3 The parts of the world known to Europeans before contact with the Americas.
4 Debtors' Prisons existed for people unable to repay loans and debts.
5 Prince-Archbishop von Kuenburg.
6 A charter agreed by King George II in 1732 authorized the creation of a British colony on land between South Carolina and Florida.
7 An ocean-going vessel of two hundred and twenty tonnes.
8 A series of theological teachings, sermons and lectures whereby John Wesley taught that Christian perfection was not only desirable, but possible, as a spiritual state.
9 From *Living Biographies of Religious Leaders*.

MARCH 31ST

HAVING A FORM OF GODLINESS

(2 Timothy 3:5 *KJV*)

The *almost Christian* does nothing which the gospel forbids. He does not take the name of God in vain; he blesses, and does not curse; he does not swear, but his yes is yes and his no is no. He does not profane or abuse the day of the Lord, and neither does he allow profanity within his gates, not even from strangers. He not only avoids all adultery, fornication, and uncleanness, but also, every word or look that directly or indirectly leads thereto; he abstains from idle words, detraction of others, backbiting, telling tales, evil speaking, and foolish talk and jesting; even from the use of conversation that is not edifying. He abstains from drinking an excess of wine, and avoids, as much as it is within his responsibility to do so, all strife and contention, so as to live peaceably. He does not seek vengeance of he is wronged, and he does not return evil for evil. He is no brawler, or scoffer, and he does not willingly hurt or grieve anyone. He abides by that plain rule, "Whatsoever thou wouldest not he should do unto thee, that do not thou to another."[1, 2]

Lord, there is no doubt about it; these virtues and qualities are often to be found in people who make no claim to be Christians: good-living people of all faiths, and none. Nevertheless, we all stand in need of a Saviour, and we share that need to acknowledge Christ as Lord. Bless us each – one and all – with that realization.

1 See Matthew 7:12, *KJV*.
2 From *Fifty Three Sermons*.

April 1st

I will be with you; I will never leave you

(Joshua 1:5 *NIV*)

Lo, God is here! let us adore,
And own how dreadful is this place!
Let all within us feel his power,
And silent bow before his face.

Lo, God is here! Whom day and night
United choirs of angels sing;
To him, enthroned above all height,
The hosts of Heaven their praises bring.

Gladly the toys of earth we leave,
Wealth, pleasure, fame, for thee alone;
To thee our will, soul, flesh, we give,
O take, O seal them for thine own!

Disdain, not, Lord, our meaner song,
Who praise thee with a faltering tongue.
To thee may all our thoughts arise
A true and ceaseless sacrifice.

Being of beings, may our praise
Thy courts with grateful fragrance fill!
Still may we stand before thy face,
Still hear and do thy sovereign will.

In thee we move all things of thee
Are full, thou Source and Life of all;
Thou vast unfathomable sea!
Fall prostrate, lost in wonder fall.

As flowers their opening leaves display,
And glad drink in the solar fire,
So may we catch thine every ray,
And thus thy influence inspire.[1]

Lord, you are with me. That is all; all I need; all I can ask.

1 Gerhard Tersteegen. Translated from the German by Wesley in *Hymns and Sacred Poems*, 1739.

APRIL 2ND

REDEEMING THE TIME

(Ephesians 5:16 *KJV*)

As the weeks and months went by, John was tempering his life and mind to a firm discipline. He began to rise at six, then five, then four – for he caught himself lying awake in bed and believed that lazing between warm sheets was bad for both spiritual and physical health. Equally, there was discipline in his time of going to bed at night. Dr Johnson[1] said in later years, "John Wesley's conversation is good, but he is never at leisure. He is always obliged to go at a certain hour. This is very disagreeable to a man who loves to fold out his legs and have out his talk, as I do."

"I am full of business, but I have found a way to write without taking any time from that," he noted at this time. "It is but rising an hour sooner in the morning and going into company an hour later in the evening." "Idleness slays" is his constant cry and by idleness he means any lesser use of time. Here was the genesis of his later advice to his preachers: "Never be unemployed for a minute. Never be triflingly employed. Never wile away time."[2]

Lord of my hours, minutes, days,
Teach me some useful, holy ways
While duties press and needs are known,
To spend my life before your throne.

1 Samuel Johnson (1709–84), English writer, essayist, moralist, literary critic, biographer, editor, and lexicographer. He was a devout Anglican who admired Wesley's intellect, but lamented the fact that time spent in Wesley's company was invariably brought to an abrupt end.
2 From *John Wesley, Anglican.*

April 3rd

Commit to the Lord whatever you do,
and he will establish your plans
(Proverbs 16:3 *NIV*)

Fri. March 4 [1737] – I sent the trustees for Georgia an account of our year's expenses, from 1 March 1736 to 1 March 1737; which, deducting extraordinary expenses, such as repairing the parsonage house, and journeys to Frederica, amounted, for Mr Delamotte and me, to £44 4s. 4d.[1]

Mon. April 4 – I began learning Spanish, in order to converse with my Jewish parishioners; some of whom seem nearer the mind that was in Christ than many of those who call him Lord.[2]

Tues. 12 – Being determined, if possible, to put a stop to the proceedings of one in Carolina, who had married several of my parishioners without either banns or licence, and declared that he would do so still, I set out in a sloop[3] for Charlestown. I landed there on Thursday, and related the case to Mr Garden, the Bishop of London's Commissary,[4] who assured me, he would take care no such irregularity should be committed in future.[5]

Assist me, God of order, in arranging my affairs and any business matters along straight lines; doing whatever is necessary today to be clear and straightforward in my dealings. Help me to learn from Wesley's example of organization, so that there may be no misunderstandings or ambiguity.

1 English currency was based on the pound Sterling (£) being valued at 20 shillings (s) or 240 pennies (d). One British pound in 1737 would equate to approximately £200 today.
2 A colony of British Jews arrived in Georgia in 1733.
3 Sailing boat.
4 Alexander Garden (c. 1685–1756), Scottish Episcopalian priest.
5 From *John Wesley's Journal (Abridged)*.

ONE WHO HAS UNRELIABLE FRIENDS SOON COMES TO RUIN

(Proverbs 18:24 *NIV*)

Sun. July 3 [1737] – Immediately after the Holy Communion, I mentioned to Mrs Williamson[1] (Mr Causton's niece)[2] some things which I thought reprovable in her behaviour.

At this she appeared extremely angry; said she did not expect such usage from me; and at the turn of the street, through which we were walking home, went abruptly away.

The next day Mrs Causton endeavoured to excuse her; told me she was exceedingly grieved for what had passed the day before, and desired me to tell her in writing what I disliked, which I accordingly did the following day.[3]

Father, my prayers today are for those whose relationships are in trouble – boyfriend, girlfriend, husband, wife – and who discover that bitterness has replaced love. Help those, Lord, who are struggling with such matters; provide them with grace to cope, and wisdom to decide their course of action.

1 Nee Sophia Hopkey. En route to Georgia, John Wesley was employed to teach Sophia Hopkey French. A romance developed, and Miss Hopkey believed Wesley was interested in marriage. Wesley, however, having taken advice from Bishop Spangenburg of the Moravians, ended the relationship, resulting in a great deal of ill-feeling towards him from Sophia Hopkey's family. Soon afterwards, Sophia married William Williamson, a clerk in her uncle's store.

2 Political boss and magistrate for Savannah. His business dealings were corrupt and he was defrauding the Moravians in respect of the arrangements he made for them to use land.

3 From *John Wesley's Journal (Abridged)*.

April 5th

The tongue of the wise brings healing

(Proverbs 12:18 *NIV*)

I sent Mr Causton the following note:

Sir, To this hour you have shown yourself my friend; I ever have and ever shall acknowledge it. And it is my earnest desire that He who hath hitherto given me this blessing, would continue it still.

But this cannot be, unless you will allow me one request, which is not so easy an one as it appears: do not condemn me for doing, in the execution of my office, what I think it my duty to do.

If you can prevail upon yourself to allow me this, even when I act without respect of persons, I am persuaded there never will be, at least not long, any misunderstanding between us. For even those who seek it shall, I trust, find no occasion against me, "except it be concerning the law of my God".[1, 2]

Lord, grant me courage and clarity of mind to deal with difficult situations and difficult people, I pray, and to do so with grace and humility, seeking the best way forward, with your help.

1 See Daniel 6:5.
2 From *John Wesley's Journal (Abridged)*.

April 6th

This is what the Lord Almighty says: "In those days ten people from all languages and nations will take firm hold of one Jew by the hem of his robe and say, 'Let us go with you, because we have heard that God is with you'"

(Zechariah 8:23 *NIV*)

Wesley began to keep a diary, according to a practice which at one time was very general among people of a religious disposition. To this practice the world owes some valuable materials for history as well as individual biography; but perhaps no person has, in this manner, conveyed so lively a picture of himself as Wesley.

During a most restless life of incessant occupation, he found time not only to register his proceedings, but his thoughts, his studies, and his occasional remarks upon miscellaneous subjects, with a vivacity which characterized him to the last.

Eight months after his election to a fellowship, he was appointed Greek lecturer and moderator of the classes. At that time disputations[1] were held six times a week at Lincoln College; and however the students may have profited by them, they were of singular use to the moderator. "I could not avoid," he says, "acquiring hereby some degree of expertness in arguing; and especially in discerning and pointing out well-covered and plausible fallacies. I have since found abundant reason to praise God for giving me this honest art. By this, when men have hedged me in by what they call demonstrations, I have been many times able to dash them in pieces; in spite of all its covers, to touch the very point where the fallacy lay, and it flew open in a moment."[2]

Lord, I think the moral here is that nothing in life is wasted, and that our experiences along the way can often serve us well in later years. Help me, I pray, to see today's lessons in the light of tomorrow's needs, knowing that you watch over all.

1 Formal debates between students and tutors, especially in the disciplines of science and theology.
2 From *John Wesley*.

April 7th

I APPLIED MY MIND TO STUDY AND TO EXPLORE BY WISDOM ALL THAT IS DONE UNDER THE HEAVENS

(Ecclesiastes 1:13 *NIV*)

Wesley formed for himself a scheme of studies, resolving not to vary from it for some years at least. Mondays and Tuesdays were allotted for the classics; Wednesdays to logic and ethics; Thursdays to Hebrew and Arabic; Fridays to metaphysics and natural philosophy; Saturdays to oratory and poetry, but chiefly to composition in those arts; and the Sabbath to divinity. It appears by his diary, also, that he gave great attention to mathematics. But he had come to that conclusion, at which, sooner or later, every studious man must arrive, that life is not long enough for the attainment of general knowledge, and that there are many things of which the most learned must content themselves to be ignorant.[1]

Father, this list is exhausting! I pray today for students – bless their studies and grant them success, and guide them in the knowledge that you are the finest tutor and that all knowledge is from you. Bless Christian Unions as they witness for you, and university chaplains in their ministry.

1 From *John Wesley*.

April 8th

You have made your way around this hill country long enough; now turn north

(Deuteronomy 2:3 *NIV*)

As Wesley's religious feelings grew, that state of mind came on which led the enthusiasts of early ages into the wilderness.

He began to think that such society as that wherein he was placed hindered his progress in spiritual things. He thought it "the settled temper of his soul," that he should, for some time at least, prefer such a retirement as might seclude him from all the world, where he might confirm in himself those habits which he thought best, before the flexibility of youth should be over.

A school was proposed to him, with a good salary annexed to it, in one of the Yorkshire Dales.[1] Some who knew the place gave him what they thought was a frightful description of it, according to the fashion of an age in which the sense of picturesque beauty seems hardly to have existed. They told him that it was a little vale, so pent up between two hills that it was scarcely accessible on any side; little company was to be expected. "I should therefore," says he, "be entirely at liberty to converse with company of my own choosing, whom, for that reason, I would bring with me."[2]

Lord, whatever the situation, grant me the courage of my convictions, even if others disagree with me. Bless me with clarity of mind.

1 An area of outstanding natural beauty in the north of England, renowned for being open, windswept and often inhospitable.

2 From *John Wesley*.

April 9th

In those days came John the Baptist, preaching in the wilderness of Judaea, and saying, Repent ye: for the Kingdom of Heaven is at hand

(Matthew 3:1, 2 *KJV*)

Verse 1. *In those days* – That is, while Jesus dwelt there.

In the wilderness of Judea – This was a wilderness, properly so called; a wild, barren, desolate place; as that was where our Lord was tempted. But, generally speaking, a wilderness, in the New Testament, means only a common, or less cultivated place, as opposed to pasture and arable land.

Verse 2. *The Kingdom of Heaven*, and the Kingdom of God, are two phrases for the same thing. They mean, not merely a future happy state in Heaven, but a state to be enjoyed on earth.[1]

Lord of life, my prayer today is that you would dwell in the hearts of those who find themselves experiencing a wilderness. In your mercy, reach out to those who are walking in barren places, spiritually. Bring them back to a fuller, richer Kingdom experience. Particularly have mercy on those who have wandered into the wilderness of their own accord.

1 From *Notes on the New Testament.*

April 10th

For this is he that was spoken of by the prophet Esaias, saying, The voice of one crying in the wilderness, Prepare ye the way of the Lord, make his paths straight. And the same John had his raiment of camel's hair, and a leathern girdle about his loins; and his meat was locusts and wild honey. Then went out to him Jerusalem, and all Judaea, and all the region round about Jordan, and were baptized of him in Jordan, confessing their sins

(Matthew 3:3–6 *KJV*)

Verse 3. *The way of the Lord* – Of Christ. *Make his paths straight* – By removing everything which might hinder his gracious appearance.

Verse 4. *John had his raiment of camel's hair* – Coarse and rough, suiting his character and doctrine. *A leathern girdle* – Like Elijah, in whose "spirit and power" he came. *His food was locusts and wild honey* – Locusts are ranked among clean eats, Leviathan 11:22. But these were not always available, so he also fed on wild honey.

Verse 6. *Confessing their sins* – Of their own accord; freely and openly. Such prodigious numbers could hardly be baptized by whole-body immersion: nor can we think they were provided with a change of clothing, which would have been impractical for such vast multitudes. Yet, they could not be immersed naked. It seems, therefore, that they stood in ranks on the edge of the river and that John, passing before them, cast water on their heads or faces, baptizing many thousands in a day. This was most naturally signified Christ's baptizing them "with the Holy Ghost and fire"[1] ... when the Holy Ghost sat upon the disciples in the appearance or tongues, or flames, of fire.[2, 3]

In my life, Lord, come today and remove anything that might hinder your grace at work. Help me to hear your word as it comes to me, and then to demonstrate, publicly, my faith in Christ. Touch my heart with holy fire.

1 Matthew 3:11, *KJV*.
2 See Acts 2:3.
3 From *Notes on the New Testament.*

April 11th

I lay prostrate before the Lord

(Deuteronomy 9:25 *NIV*)

My soul before thee prostrate lies;
To thee, her Source, my spirit flies;
My wants I mourn, my chains I see;
O let thy presence set me free.

Jesus, vouchsafe my heart and will
With thy meek lowliness to fill;
No more her power let nature boast,
But in thy will may mine be lost.

Already springing hope I feel,
God will destroy the power of Hell,
And, from a land of wars and pain,
Lead me where peace and safety reign.

One only care my soul shall know,
Father, all thy commands to do;
And feel, what endless years shall prove,
That thou, my Lord, my God, art love.[1]

Lord, there are those times in life when my best option is to simply lie prostrate before you, and to show you my life, my all. Dissolve any reluctance to do so, I pray, lest I deprive myself of mercy.

1 Christian F. Richter. Translated from German by John Wesley, for a *Collection of Psalms and Hymns,* 1737.

April 12th

The heavens declare the glory of God; and the firmament sheweth his handiwork

(Psalm 19:1 *KJV*)

Should not a minister be acquainted … with at least the general grounds of natural philosophy? Is not this a great help to the accurate understanding of several passages of Scripture? Assisted by this, he may comprehend, and explain to others, how the invisible things of God are seen from the creation of the world; how "the heavens declare the glory of God, and the firmament showeth his handiwork"; till they cry out, "O Lord, how manifold are thy works! In wisdom hast thou made them all."[1]

But how far can he go in this, without some knowledge of geometry which is likewise useful, not only on this account, but to give clearness of apprehension, and the habit of thinking closely and connectedly?

It must be understood that some of these branches of knowledge are not as necessary as the rest; and therefore no thinking man will condemn the Fathers of the Church, for having, in all ages and nations, appointed some to the ministry who had not the opportunity of attaining them. But what excuse is this for one who has the opportunity, and makes no use of it! Supposing him to have any capacity, to have common understanding, he is inexcusable before God and man.[2]

Lord, I come to you just as I am, with whatever skills and abilities you have gifted. Help me to use them all, in some way or other, for your sake. Thank you, Lord, that everyone is different; some have levels of intelligence that others do not possess. All that matters is that you take my time and talents and employ them as you see fit.

1 Psalm 104:24, *KJV*.
2 From *Wesley's Works*.

APRIL 13TH

A PEACEFUL HEART LEADS TO A HEALTHY BODY

(Proverbs 14:30 *NLT*)

Water is the wholemost of all drinks; quickens the appetite, and strengthens the digestion most.

Strong, and more especially spirituous liquors, are a certain, though slow, poison.

Coffee and tea are extremely hurtful to persons who have weak nerves.

Tender persons should eat very light suppers; and that two or three hours before going to bed. They ought to go to bed about nine, and rise at four or five.

A due degree of exercise is indispensably necessary to health and long life.

Walking is the best exercise for those who are able to bear it; riding for those who are not. The open air, when the weather is fair, contributes much to the benefit of exercise.[1]

Lord, I thank you today for the measure of health and strength that is mine. I pray for those who are ill, for those who are in pain, and for those whose illnesses are terminal. In good health or weakness, may we all know your abiding presence as a God who loves, cares, and understands. If it is your will, bring healing, whether that appears in this world or the next.

1 From *Primitive Physic.*

April 14th

I call God as my witness

(2 Corinthians 1:23 *NIV*)

Tyerman[1] says, "He [Wesley] was looked upon as a Roman Catholic –

(1) Because he rigidly excluded all Dissenters[2] from Holy Communion, until they first gave up their faith and principles, and, like Richard Turner and his sons,[3] submitted to be re-baptized by him.

(2) Because Roman Catholics were received by him as saints.

(3) Because he endeavoured to establish and enforce confession, penance, and mortification; mixed wine with water at the sacrament; and appointed deaconesses in accordance with what he called the Apostolic Constitutions."[4]

Lord, the inevitability of being misunderstood is sometimes a cross that just has to be carried! Save me, I pray, from the sin of "assumicide" – leaping to conclusions about people or situations when I barely know the facts. I pray for those whose witness is misunderstood or maligned, as Wesley's frequently was; give them strength as you gave him strength.

1 Luke Tyerman (1820–89) English Wesleyan Methodist historian and preacher.
2 Non-conformists.
3 Richard Turner (died 1565?), English Protestant reformer.
4 From *Rev. John Wesley.*

April 15th

Delilah lulled Samson to sleep with his head in her lap, and then she called in a man to shave off the seven locks of his hair. In this way she began to bring him down, and his strength left him

(Judges 16:19 *NLT*)

The opposition he [John Wesley] met with was sometimes very great. Oglethorpe grew weary of the complaints which were made to him of both the Wesleys [John and Charles].[1]

One wicked woman, whom John had offended, knocked him down one day – presumably when he was off his guard – and cut off from one side of his head the whole of those long locks of auburn hair which he had been accustomed to keep in the most perfect order.

Perhaps he made more of this indignity than he need have done, for he preached to the people afterwards with his hair long on one side and short on the other, those sitting on the side which had been cut observing, "What a cropped head of hair the young parson has!"[2]

Lord, I can but marvel at John Wesley's resilience! Not many would still enter the pulpit after a physical assault, having suffered this humiliation! Grant me such a spirit, I pray, in your service; not to be easily discouraged by opposition.

1 Complaints made when the Wesleys were in America.
2 From *Rev. John Wesley.*

APRIL 16TH

BE STRONG AND COURAGEOUS ... FOR THE LORD YOUR GOD GOES WITH YOU; HE WILL NEVER LEAVE YOU NOR FORSAKE YOU

(Deuteronomy 31:6 *NIV*)

General Oglethorpe's troubles began; the trustees accused him of misapplying funds, and of abusing his entrusted powers,[1] but Wesley wrote to him –

"Perhaps in some things you have shown you are but a man: perhaps I myself may have a little to complain of; but oh! What a train of benefits have I received to lay in the balance against it!

I bless God that you were ever born. I acknowledge His exceeding mercy in casting me into your hands. I own your generous kindness all the time we were at sea.

I am indebted to you for a thousand favours here. Though all men should revile you, yet will not I."[2]

Thank you, Lord, that you are a loyal God, great in faithfulness. You do not abandon us. You do not turn your back on us even though we sin. We are indebted to you. Help me to reflect such grace and loyalty in my friendships.

1 Numerous problems arose for the beleaguered General Oglethorpe, as he sought to establish the Georgian colony. As is the lot of many pioneer leaders, he was caught in the middle of disagreements between groups of people each insisting their particular methods would work best. These disagreements led to accusations and a level of mistrust.

2 From *Rev. John Wesley.*

April 17th

LET US CONSIDER HOW WE MAY SPUR ONE ANOTHER ON TOWARD LOVE AND GOOD DEEDS

(Hebrews 10:24 *NIV*)

In doing good, the *almost Christian* does not confine himself to cheap and easy kindnesses – those which cost him nothing – but labours and even suffers for the profit of all, helping others altruistically. In spite of toil or pain, "whatsoever his hand findeth to do, he doeth it with his might";[1] whether it be for his friends, or for his enemies.

He reproves the wicked, instructs the ignorant, confirms the wavering, encourages the good, and comforts the afflicted. He works to awaken those who sleep; and even to lead those whom God has already awakened, spiritually, to the "Fountain open for sin and for uncleanness,"[2] that they may wash therein and be clean; and to stir up those who are saved through faith, to adorn the gospel of Christ in all things.[3]

Heavenly Father, if the "almost Christian" can do so much good for the sake of others, and encourage others in their beliefs, then how much more should we, your people, not only imitate such practices but be exemplary in our behaviour. Lord, help us to rise to the challenge, for Jesus' sake.

1 See Ecclesiastes 9:10, *KJV*.
2 See Zachariah 13:1, *KJV*.
3 From *Fifty Three Sermons*.

April 18th

Let your adorning be the hidden person of the heart

(1 Peter 3:4 *ESV*)

He that has the form of godliness also uses the means of grace; all of them, at all opportunities. He frequents the house of God, and not even in the manner of some who come into the presence of the Most High, loaded with gold and costly apparel, with gaudy vanity of dress … Would to God there were none even among ourselves who fall under the same condemnation! Those, for example, who come to church only to gaze about, with listless, careless indifference, who sometimes seem to pray for God's blessing but are either asleep during the service, or reclined in the most convenient posture for sleep; as though they supposed God too was asleep; talking with one another and looking around. These accusations cannot be made regarding those who portray a form of godliness; he behaves with seriousness and solemn attention during the service, especially when he approaches the table of the Lord; it is with a deportment which speaks nothing but "God be merciful to me a sinner!"[1], [2]

Lord of the Church, help me never to ignore or take for granted those means of grace that are freely available for worship and communion. Grant me an awareness of the privileges I enjoy; freedom to enter a church undisturbed, and as many opportunities as I like to gather for Christian fellowship in your presence. Thank you for them, Lord. Thank you for my church and its life.

1 Luke 18:13, *KJV*.
2 From *Fifty Three Sermons*.

April 19th

There is no fear in love. But perfect love drives out fear, because fear has to do with punishment. The one who fears is not made perfect in love

(1 John 4:18 *NIV*)

To this, if we add the constant use of family prayer … and the setting times apart for private addresses to God, with a seriousness of behaviour; he who practises this outward religion has the form of godliness. There needs but one thing more in order to his being *almost a Christian*, and that is sincerity. By sincerity I mean a real, inward flow of religion, whence outward actions flow:

Oderunt peccare boni, virtutis amore; oderunt peccare mali, formidine poenae.

Good men avoid sin from the love of virtue; wicked men avoid sin from a fear of punishment.

If the almost Christian has no better principle in his heart, he is only a hypocrite. This design runs through the whole tenor of his life. This is the moving principle in his doing good, in his avoiding evil, and in his use of the ordinances of God.

Is it possible that any man should go so far as this and still be only almost a Christian? It is possible to go this far, and yet be but almost a Christian. I learn this not only from the oracles of God, but also from the sure testimony of experience.[1]

Lord, Wesley's distinction here is both helpful and important. Love must rule me; love must shape my service and devotion. If it is fear, or duty, which is my pattern and motivation, then teach me to relax in love, so that I may do the things I do because I am a Christian, not in order to become one.

1 From *Fifty Three Sermons.*

You are a chosen people, a royal priesthood

(1 Peter 2:9 *NIV*)

The option of taking up employment at a school in the Yorkshire Dales, to which he [Wesley] seems at the time to have been so well inclined, was not given him, and his mother was not sorry about that: "That way of life," she said, "would not agree with your constitution, and I hope God has better work for you to do!" words which, perhaps, in after years, carried with them an element of the prophetic and an impulse to his ministry.

The elder Wesley (Reverend Samuel) was now, due to age and infirmity, unequal to the duties of both his livings,[1,2] especially as the road between them was bad, and sometimes dangerous in winter. John, therefore, at his desire, went to reside at Wroote,[3] and officiated there as his father's curate. It was while he held this curacy that he obtained priest's orders from the same prelate who had ordained him curate three years before.[4, 5]

Thank you, Lord, for divine guidance. I pray today for those considering a vocation to the priesthood. Guide them well, I ask, and help them to come to the right decision, under your Spirit's gentle influence.

1 Priests would usually receive their living directly from the church or churches within their charge, either in the form of monetary tithes or other entitlements such as a share of the harvest, etc., or from rents paid on church lands by tenants (farmers, in the main).

2 St Pancras Church, Wroote, Lincolnshire, England and, possibly, St Andrew's, Epworth, approximately five miles away.

3 Or Wroot.

4 Bishop John Potter.

5 From *John Wesley*.

April 21st

The godly give good advice to their friends

(Proverbs 12:26 *NLT*)

In consequence of this summons [to curacy] he once more took up his abode at Lincoln, became a tutor there, and presided as moderator at the disputations which were held six times a week in the hall; an office which sharpened his habits of logical discrimination.

Some time before his return to the university, he had travelled many miles to see what is called "a serious man". This person said to him, "Sir, you wish to serve God and go to Heaven. Remember, you cannot serve him alone: you must therefore find companions or make them: the Bible knows nothing of solitary religion." Wesley never forgot these words; and it happened that while he was residing upon his curacy, such a society was prepared for him at Oxford as he and his serious adviser would have wished.[1, 2]

Lord, I thank you for good friends, and I pray for them today.
What a gift they are to me! Thank you for experiences shared,
counsel offered, and sheer good company.

1 What was to become The Holy Club; groups of like-minded friends meeting for study, discussion, and mutual encouragement.

2 From *John Wesley*.

April 22nd

Above all, love each other deeply, because love covers over a multitude of sins

(1 Peter 4:8 *NIV*)

In America, [Wesley's] stern task was made gentle by the magic of romance. He lost his heart to Sophia Hopkey, the beautiful niece of the colonial magistrate.[1] He gave her daily instruction in French and religion, and longed to enlarge the curriculum with a course on love.

One evening, he escorted her on a journey to her uncle's home, he sat down beside her in the shadows and timidly dared to plan their future – in the silence of fancy. He could not as yet bring himself to translate his daring into words.

But John Wesley knew more about the fixedness of the heavens than he did about the fickleness of the earth. While he was slowly gathering his courage to propose, the young lady gave her hand to another. He had sung psalms to her when she had craved for love songs. In a fit of grief at her "inconstancy", he expelled Sophia from his church services. And Sophia's husband, in retaliation, aroused the anger of the parishioners against their pastor.[2]

Oh Lord! Love and marriage are truly wonderful gifts from your hand, but the path towards those delights can often be rocky and full of twists and turns. Bless and guide those, I pray, who are actively seeking life-partners; grant them wisdom, patience, and insight … and excitement!

1 Mr Causton.
2 From *Living Biographies of Religious Leaders.*

April 23rd

Do not be surprised, my brothers and sisters, if the world hates you

(1 John 3:13 *NIV*)

It was an easy matter to enlist the disgruntled Georgians against Wesley. For the fruits of his evangelical mission "among God's people" were proving bitter to the taste.

His first official act had been to smash a barrel of whisky which they had brought from England. He enforced rigid church services and punished all infractions of the moral code with an iron hand.

The communicants were beginning to grumble that their old incarceration in the debtor's prison was more desirable than their new "life-term in the prison of salvation". This young preacher, they complained, was trying to meddle not only with their souls, but with their purses. The chief access to profit in the southern colonies was through the channel of slavery. And the ardent young prophet inveighed against the slave holders. A dangerous disturber of the peace.[1]

Almighty God, unpopular decisions will lead to unpopularity, yet there are those times when we are called to stand for Christ and Christ alone. Impart grace and wisdom to those who take such a stand today; give them courage in the face of opposition, but also, love for their enemies.

1 From *Living Biographies of Religious Leaders.*

APRIL 24TH

For we do not have a high priest who is unable to empathize with our weaknesses

(Hebrews 4:15 *NIV*)

"Enough of this interference with our business!"

The flock was determined to turn out its "troublesome" pastor. Wesley was indicted before a grand jury which consisted of "A Frenchman who did not understand English, a Roman Catholic who did not understand Anglicanism, a professed infidel, three Baptists and sixteen Dissenters."

Shortly before the trial, however, John Wesley escaped in the night and took ship for England. His zeal for his mission was quite over. It was almost two and a half years since he had set out enthusiastically to preach among his fellowmen. And now he could no longer understand any of them – least of all, the girl he had loved.

The net result of his evangelism was a twist of irony that became interwoven into the texture of his soul. Embittered and disillusioned by the blows he had received from God's people, he now began to doubt the goodness – or at least the wisdom – of a God who had created such people. "I went to America to convert the Indian," he observed sardonically. "And now who shall convert me?"[1]

Christ of the human road, you know our feelings of despair. You have walked this way. I pray today for those who feel they might have failed, and especially for those whose feelings of disappointment have turned into doubt. Draw alongside them with divine reassurance.

1 From *Living Biographies of Religious Leaders.*

April 25th

Man who is born of a woman is few of days and full of trouble

(Job 14:1 *ESV*)

Wed. 6 [July, 1737] – Mr Causton came to my house with Bailiff Parker and Mr Recorder, and warmly asked, "How could you possibly think I should condemn you for executing any part of your office?" I replied curtly, "Sir, what if I should think it the duty of my office to repel one of your family from the Holy Communion?" He replied, if you repel me or my wife, I shall require a legal reason. But I shall trouble myself about none else. Let them look to themselves."

Sun. Aug. 7 – I repelled Mrs Williamson[1] from the Holy Communion.[2]

Lord, whatever the rights and wrongs of this particular case, I bring before you today ministers who are in dispute with members of their congregations. Whatever the issues, Lord, come and untie the knots, please, so that peace and harmony may prevail. I pray for my own minister, and any problems s/he may have to confront, that no one else may know about.

1 Sophia Williamson, nee Hopkey, Mr Causton's niece.
2 From *John Wesley's Journal (Abridged)*.

APRIL 26TH

ON MY ACCOUNT YOU WILL BE BROUGHT BEFORE GOVERNORS

(Matthew 10:18 *NIV*)

Monday 8 [August, 1737] – Mr Recorder, of Savannah, issued out the warrant following:

To all Constables, Tithingmen,[1] and others, whom these may concern: You, and each of you, are hereby required to take the body of John Wesley, Clerk:

And bring him before one of the Bailiffs of said town to answer the complaint of William Williamson and Sophia, his wife, for defaming the said Sophia, and refusing to administer to her the sacrament of the Lord's supper in a public congregation without cause; by which the said William Williamson is damaged one thousand pound sterling; and for doing so, this is your warrant, certifying what you are to do in the premises. Given under my hand and seal the 8th day of August, Anno. Dom. 1737. Tho. Christie.[2,3]

Lord, I think of those who even now are hauled before courts and magistrates on account of their witness, on all manner of trumped-up charges and allegations made against them by people with axes to grind. Bless them, Lord; may they know your presence alongside them.

1 A parish officer or "underconstable" with responsibility to preserve order in churches and enforce Sabbath observance.

2 Thomas Christie, aged 32, is listed as a Merchant, Bailiff & Recorder, but was suspended from being a Recorder when he defaulted on his account with the stores. He was accused of "adultry" (sic) and left Georgia in 1740, proposing to settle in England, but he later returned.

3 From *John Wesley's Journal (Abridged).*

He will be called Wonderful Counsellor

(Isaiah 9:6 *NIV*)

Tues. 9 – Mr Jones, the constable, served the warrant, and carried me before Mr Bailiff Parker and Mr Recorder. My answer to them was, that the giving or refusing the Lord's supper being a matter purely ecclesiastical, I could not acknowledge their power to interrogate me upon it.

Mr Parker told me: "However, you must appear at the next court, holden for Savannah." Mr Williamson, who stood by, said: "Gentlemen, I desire Mr Wesley may give bail for his appearance." But Mr Parker immediately replied: "Sir, Mr Wesley's word is sufficient."

Thur. 11 – Mr Causton came to my house, and, among many other sharp words, said: "Make an end of this matter; thou hadst best … I have drawn the sword, and I will never sheath it till I have satisfaction!" Soon after, he added: "Give the reason of your repelling her before the whole congregation." I answered: "Sir, if you insist upon it, I will; and so you may be pleased to tell her." He said, "Write to her, and tell her so yourself." I said, "I will."[1]

Lord, how awfully embarrassing this ordeal must have been for John Wesley; to be faced with the prospect of detailing his love affair in front of his congregation, many of whom would no doubt have delighted in gossip. Thank you, Lord, that what we confide in you remains confidential, even our most intimate thoughts; you are a trustworthy confidant.

1 From *John Wesley's Journal (Abridged).*

April 28th

When he saw many of the Pharisees and Sadducees coming to where he was baptizing, he said to them: "You brood of vipers! Who warned you to flee from the coming wrath?"

(Matthew 3:7 *NIV*)

Verse 7. *The Pharisees* were a very ancient sect among the Jews. They took their name from an Hebrew word, which signifies *to separate,*[1] because they separated themselves from all other men. They were outwardly strict observers of the law, fasted often, made long prayers, rigorously kept the Sabbath, and paid all tithe, even of mint, anise, and cumin.[2] Hence they were in high esteem among the people. But, inwardly, they were full of pride and hypocrisy.

The Sadducees were another sect among the Jews, only not so considerable as the Pharisees. They denied the existence of angels, and the immortality of the soul, and, by consequence, the resurrection of the dead.

Ye brood of vipers – In like manner, the crafty Herod is styled "a fox";[3] and persons of insidious, ravenous, profane, or sensual dispositions are named respectively by Him who saw their hearts, "serpents, dogs, wolves, and swine": terms which are not the random language of passion, but a judicious designation of the persons meant by them. For it was fitting such men should be marked out, either for a caution, to others, or a warning to themselves.[4]

Lord, preserve us from cults and sects focusing on minor points of detail while overlooking much more important points of grace and devotion. Likewise, preserve my heart from doctrinal errors if they lead me away from truths that Jesus taught. Grant me discernment in all such matters, I pray.

1 In Aramaic, "peras" ("to divide and separate").
2 Mosaic law required Jews to tithe of their agricultural produce if it was to be sold for commercial profit.
3 Luke 13:32.
4 From *Notes on the New Testament.*

APRIL 29TH

BRING FORTH THEREFORE FRUITS MEET FOR REPENTANCE: AND THINK NOT TO SAY WITHIN YOURSELVES, WE HAVE ABRAHAM TO OUR FATHER: FOR I SAY UNTO YOU, THAT GOD IS ABLE OF THESE STONES TO RAISE UP CHILDREN UNTO ABRAHAM

(Matthew 3:8, 9 *KJV*)

Verse 8. *Repentance* is of two sorts; that which is termed *legal*, and that which is styled *evangelical* repentance. The former, which is the same that is spoken of here, is a thorough conviction of sin. The latter is a change of heart (and consequently of life) from all sin to all holiness.

Verse 9. *And say not confidently* – The word in the original, vulgarly rendered "think not", seems here, and in many places, not to diminish, but rather add to, the force of the word with which it is joined. *We have Abraham to our father* – It is almost incredible how great the presumption of the Jews was, on this their relation to Abraham. One of their famous sayings was, "Abraham sits near the gates of hell, and suffers no Israelite to go down into it."[1, 2]

"From all sin to holiness" – thank you, Lord.

1 This was taught in the Jewish book *Akedath Jizehak* ("Binding of Isaac") by Isaac ben Moses Arama (1420–94), a Spanish rabbi and author.

2 From *Notes on the New Testament.*

APRIL 30TH

HE HAS RECONCILED YOU BY CHRIST'S PHYSICAL BODY THROUGH DEATH TO PRESENT YOU HOLY IN HIS SIGHT, WITHOUT BLEMISH AND FREE FROM ACCUSATION

(Colossians 1:22 *NIV*)

O thou to whose all searching sight
The darkness shineth as the light,
Search, prove my heart; it pants for thee;
O burst these bonds, and set it free!

Wash out its stains, refine its dross,
Nail my affections to the cross;
Hallow each thought; let all within
Be clean, as thou, my Lord, art clean!

If in this darksome wild I stray,
Be thou my light, be thou my way;
No foes, no violence I fear,
No fraud, while thou, my God, art near.

When rising floods my soul o'erflow,
When sinks my heart in waves of woe,
Jesu, thy timely aid impart,
And raise my head, and cheer my heart.

Saviour, where'er thy steps I see,
Dauntless, untired, I follow thee!
O let thy hand support me still,
And lead me to thy holy hill!

If rough and thorny be the way,
My strength proportion to my day;
Till toil, and grief, and pain shall cease,
Where all is calm, and joy, and peace.[1]

Thank you, Lord Jesus, for that wonderful transaction, when my affections were nailed to the cross. Thank you for being my Saviour. This is my prayer today.

1 Nikolaus L. von Zinzendorf. Translated from German by Wesley in *Psalms and Hymns, 1738.*

May 1st

Everyone ought to examine themselves before they eat of the bread and drink from the cup

(1 Corinthians 11:28 *NIV*)

To Mrs Sophia Williamson.

At Mr Causton's request, I write once more. The rules whereby I proceed are these:

Those who intend to partake of the Holy Communion, shall signify their names to the curate, at least some time the day before. This you did not do.

If any of these people have done any wrong to his neighbours, by word or deed, so that the congregation be offended, the curate shall advise him that he may not come to the Lord's table until he has openly declared his repentance.

If you offer yourself at the Lord's table on Sunday, I will advertise your attendance (as I have done more than once) and why you have done wrong. When you have openly declared yourself to have truly repented, I will administer to you the mysteries of God.

John Wesley. August 11, 1737.[1]

Gracious Father, whatever the rights and wrongs of Wesley's dispute with Mrs Williamson, grant me the grace to examine my spiritual condition before I come to church for worship, and to welcome your searchlight into my heart. Grant me that Christ like spirit of humility whereby I might be willing to make amends.

1 From *John Wesley's Journal (Abridged)*.

May 2nd

God's business is putting things right; he loves getting the lines straight, setting us straight. Once we're standing tall, we can look him straight in the eye

(Psalm 11:7 *MSG*)

Mr Causton said, among many other warm[1] sayings:

"I am the person that am injured. This affront is offered to me; and I will espouse the cause of my niece. I am ill-used, and I will have my satisfaction."

Mr Causton declared to many persons that:

"Mr Wesley had repelled Sophy (sic) from the Holy Communion purely out of revenge, because he made proposals of marriage to her which she rejected, and married Mr Williamson."[2]

Father, there is something awfully sad about this squabble between Christians, whoever is right and whoever is wrong. Lord, the truth of the matter is, we, your people, get things horribly wrong at times. In your mercy, forgive us and straighten us out.

1 Warm as in heated, not as in friendly.
2 From *John Wesley's Journal (Abridged)*.

May 3rd

Listen now to me and I will give you some advice, and may God be with you

(Exodus 18:19 *NIV*)

We may strengthen any weak part of the body by constant exercise. The lungs may be strengthened by loud speaking … the digestion and the nerves, by riding; the arms and thighs, by strongly rubbing them daily. The studious ought to have stated times for exercise, at least two or three hours a day; one half of this before dinner, the other before going to bed. They should frequently shave, and frequently wash their feet. Those who read or write much, should learn to do it standing; otherwise it will impair their health. The fewer clothes anyone uses, by day or night, the hardier he will be. Exercise, first, should always be on an empty stomach; secondly, should never be continued to weariness; thirdly, after it, we should take care to cool by degrees; otherwise we shall catch cold. The flesh brush is a most useful exercise, especially to strengthen any part that is weak. Cold bathing is of great advantage to health: it prevents abundance of diseases. It promotes perspiration, helps the circulation of the blood, and prevents the danger of catching cold. Tender people should pour water upon the head before they go in … To jump in with the head foremost, it is too great a shock to nature.[1]

Help me, Lord, to be someone who is willing to take good advice!

1 From *Primitive Physic.*

May 4th

Let us not pass judgment on one another any longer, but rather decide never to put a stumbling block or hindrance in the way of a brother

(Romans 13:14 *NIV*)

The one place where John relaxed his regime a little – and could even be said to have wiled away the time – was in those gracious Cotswold vicarages, just a day's ride from Oxford. He took that ride often, sometimes with Charles, sometimes with Robert Kirkham,[1] sometimes alone. There he spent the days walking and riding, singing, reading, dancing, and conversing with the charming young ladies of those households.

As the fashion of his day demanded, each of the group took a nickname. John was Cyrus and his brother Araspes: the Kirkham girls were Varanese and Sappho; and the Granville sisters, Aspasia and Selina.[2] When they were parted, frequent letters passed between them.

John – and later Charles – took to this society easily and delightfully, as young men who were good company and had been used to a crowd of clever sisters. As might be expected, John's affections speedily became engaged – as did several of the young ladies. On almost his first visit, he fell more than a little in love with Varanese [Sally Kirkham] … She was already engaged to the local schoolmaster, and, in fact, married him in December 1725, having five children and growing increasingly in love with her husband. Yet for several years John's sweet serious dalliance with her continued.[3]

Lord, this seems like an unusual and inappropriate friendship, but I realize the culture of Wesley's day might have viewed things differently. Help me to be sensitive to what is right and what is wrong, appropriate and inappropriate. Likewise, grant me sensitivity to whichever cultural norms are expected of me, lest my witness be impaired.

1 An intimate friend of the Wesleys, and one of the first Oxford Methodists.
2 Characters from ancient history and Greek legends.
3 From *John Wesley, Anglican.*

May 5th

Treat older women as you would your mother, and treat younger women with all purity as you would your own sisters

(1 Timothy 5:2 *NIV*)

[John Wesley and Sally Kirkham] freely spoke of their "love" for each other, and one evening John leant his head against her breast, clasping both her hands in his, while her sister tenderly looked on. "You know you make me a little uncomfortable and I think it is almost sinful to use the expressions of tenderness which I use in relation to you in relation to other people," he told Sally in October 1726. "It is not expedient or right to break off our friendship," he added, as much as it would seem to convince himself as her. "It is one of my main incentives to virtue." Her sisters, Betty and Damaris, also seem to have entertained hopes of John, and he told them he wished to have exactly the same freedom with them as with their sister. Later he was to carry on for a year or more a correspondence as intimate, if less amorous, with Mrs Pendarves, the elegant young widow among them who was already becoming a light of London society.[1, 2]

Lord, friendships and relationships can be complex! Take us, I pray, with all our complexities and weaknesses, and hold tight to our lives. I pray especially today for any struggling with feelings and emotions that can sometimes be overpowering. Minister your gentle peace to any inner turmoil.

1 Godmother to the Duke of Wellington and a close friend of King George III. In later years, she said of the Wesleys, "The vanity of being singular and growing enthusiasts made them endeavour to gain proselytes and adopt a system of religious doctrine which many reasonable people thought pernicious."

2 From *John Wesley, Anglican*.

May 6th

He prayed for his friends

(Job 42:10 *NASB*)

Charles [Wesley], then pursuing contentedly his scholastic course, had been elected from Westminster to Christ Church, just after his brother John obtained his fellowship. He was diligent in study, and regular in his conduct; but when John sought to press upon him the importance of austere habits, and a more active devotion, he protested against becoming a saint all at once, and turned a deaf ear to his admonitions.

While John, however, resided at Wroote, the process which he had vainly sought to accelerate in his brother, was going on. His disposition, his early education, the example of his parents and of both his brethren, were in unison; not knowing how or when he woke out of his lethargy, he imputed the change to the efficacy of another's prayers – most likely, he said, his mother's.[1]

Lord, for the prayers of others, I give you thanks. Thank you for people who take the time to pray for me, for their concern and effort. And thank you, most of all, for answered prayer, and the difference that can make to my life.

1 From *John Wesley.*

May 7th

Be not conformed to this world

(Romans 12:2 *KJV*)

Meeting with two or three undergraduates, whose inclinations and principles resembled his own, they [John & Charles Wesley] associated together for the purposes of religious improvement, lived by rule, and received the sacrament weekly.

Such conduct would at any time have attracted observation in an English university; it was particularly noticeable at that time, when a laxity of opinions as well as morals obtained, and infidelity, a plague which had lately found its way into the country, was becoming so prevalent, that the vice-chancellor had, in a *programma*,[1] exhorted the tutors to discharge their duty by double diligence, and had forbidden the undergraduates to read such books as might tend to the weakening of their faith.[2]

Father, it isn't easy to take a stand against popular opinion. I pray your blessing upon those who do, whether that be at university, at work, or in their neighbourhood. Help and strengthen those whom you call to swim against the tide.

1 A public notice or announcement.
2 From *John Wesley*.

THE DISCIPLES WERE CALLED CHRISTIANS FIRST AT ANTIOCH

(Acts 11:26 *NIV*)

They [the Wesleys and their undergraduate friends] were called in derision the Sacramantalists, Bible-bigots, Bible-moths, the Holy, or the Godly Club. One person, with less irreverence and more learning, observed, in reference to their methodical manner of life, that a new sect of Methodists was sprung up, alluding to the ancient school of physicians known by that name. Appellations, even of opprobrious origin, have often been adopted by the parties to which they were applied, as well as by the public, convenience legitimating the inventions of malice. In this instance there was neither maliciousness nor wit, but there was some fitness in the name; it obtained vogue … it has become the appropriate designation of the sect of which Wesley is the founder. It was to Charles Wesley and his few associates that the name was first given. When John returned to Oxford, they gladly placed themselves under his direction; their meetings acquired more form and regularity.[1]

Lord, may I always be proud to carry the name of Christian, even if it is sometimes used as a term of derision or ridicule. I pray for those who experience persecution today, because of their refusal to deny the name of Jesus. Bless them.

1 From *John Wesley.*

May 9th

He is far above any ruler or authority or power or leader or anything else – not only in this world but also in the world to come

(Ephesians 1:21 *NLT*)

After a brief spell of cynicism [following the debacle of his American experience], John Wesley saw once again the simple path of his duty.

He began to associate with a sect of German revivalists called Moravians. They told him to cease looking for external signs of failure or of success in the performance of God's mission. They declared that the proof of the power of God lay within the faith of man.

As he pondered over these utterances, the last words of his father, Sam Wesley, came back to him with commanding force. What was the true test of Christianity? "The inward witness, my son, *that* is the proof, the strongest proof, of Christianity."

The people of Georgia, John Wesley decided, were merely the product of an age that had become more intolerant in its easy going scepticism. In this age of George II[1] and of Voltaire,[2] the "believing" priests of the Church of England, no less than the churchless priests of unbelief, proved through their action that the living faith in Him was gone. The Lord had become the incarnation of "sweet reasonableness".[3]

Lord, in the face of increasingly secular propaganda, give your people courage to uphold the eternal gospel. Equip us for a modern witness. Preserve your Church from irrelevance.

1 King George II, nominally head of the Church, kept the company of several mistresses, and was renowned for an uncouth and crude manner.

2 Author and philosopher, famous for his written attacks on the Catholic Church and his strong advocacy of the separation of Church and State.

3 From *Living Biographies of Religious Leaders.*

May 10th

If you are insulted because of the name of Christ, you are blessed, for the Spirit of glory and of God rests on you

(1 Peter 4:14 *NIV*)

The prophets who had spoken for God were centuries dead. The mathematicians and anatomists and the generals and the free lovers were the pipers of the new order. The world, to be sure, had long since learned to love the ancient gentlemen of prophecy. But everybody would be terribly embarrassed to see them come to life again – vigorous and intense and exacting as of old. The world would be hard put to find them a night's lodging – let alone a throne.

John Wesley knew from experience how the world could deride a man who took his religion seriously. In his days at Oxford he had formed, together with his brother Charles, a "Holy Club" of young communicants who met together to discuss their spiritual problems and to lay plans for the reawakening of a religious enthusiasm among their fellow collegians. The club became the laughing stock of the whole university – professors and students alike. The members of the club were dubbed as the "Bible-bigots" and the "Bible-moths".[1]

Lord, I think today of "the persecuted church" – believers in some countries who are at the mercy of state-sponsored persecution ranging from harassment to torture and death. I pray for them today. I pray too for those responsible for their persecution. In your mercy, hear and answer prayer.

1 From *Living Biographies of Religious Leaders.*

May 11th

The Spirit himself testifies with our spirit
that we are God's children

(Romans 8:16 *NIV*)

[In regard to being an *almost Christian*], I did go thus far for many years, as many can testify; using all diligence to reject all evil, and to make sure my conscience was void of offence; using my time well and wisely; buying up every opportunity of doing all good to everyone; constantly and carefully using all the public and all the private means of grace; adopting a seriousness in my behaviour, at all times and in all places; and, as God is my record, before whom I stand, doing all of this sincerely, having a real desire to serve God; a hearty desire to do his will in all things, to please him who had called me to "fight the good fight",[1] and to "lay hold of eternal life".[2] Yet my own conscience bears witness to me in the Holy Ghost, that all this time I was but *almost a Christian*.[3]

Thank you, Holy Spirit, for your abiding presence in the life of the believer, bestowing reassurance and offering guidance and loving correction. Thank you, Holy Spirit, for your gentle and ever-gracious fellowship in our hearts. Travel with me today.

1 1 Timothy 6:12.
2 See 1 Timothy 6:12, *KJV*.
3 From *Fifty Three Sermons*.

May 12TH

I love those who love me

(Proverbs 8:17 *ESV*)

It might be enquired: What more than this, then, is necessary to be *altogether* a Christian? I answer,

First, the love of God. His word says, "Thou shalt love the Lord thy God with all thy heart, and with all thy soul, and with all thy mind, and with all thy strength."[1] Such a love as this engrosses the whole heart and takes up all the affections. It fills the entire capacity of the soul, employing the fullest extent of its faculties. He that loves the Lord his God, his spirit continually "rejoiceth in God his Saviour".[2] His delight is in the Lord. His Lord is his all, to whom "in everything he giveth thanks. All his desire is unto God, and to the remembrance of his name." His heart is always crying out, "Whom have I in Heaven but thee? And there is none upon earth that I desire beside thee."[3] Indeed, what can he desire beside God? Not the world, or the things of the world: for he is "crucified to the world, and the world crucified to him". [4], [5]

Claim my heart today, Saviour, and refresh my love for you and all that is of you.

1 Matthew 22:37, *KJV*.
2 See Luke 1:47.
3 Psalm 73:25, *KJV*.
4 See Galatians 6:14.
5 From *Fifty Three Sermons*.

May 13th

Greater is he that is in you, than he that is in the world

(1 John 4:4 *KJV*)

Causton and his friends tried to make the people of Savannah believe that Wesley had acted from spite in treating his niece so harshly, because she had married someone else; and, indeed, Wesley seemed to have known that such a motive might be attributed to him in acting as he did; but, on the other hand, was he to lay himself open to the charge that, because of their previous relations, he overlooked, in her, conduct which he should have felt bound to notice in another?

Mr Causton industriously read aloud to all who would hear selected portions of Wesley's letters to him and his niece. In the midst of all this Wesley writes: "I still sat at home, and I thank God, easy, having committed my cause to him, and remembering his word, 'Blessed is the man that endureth temptation; for when he is tried he shall receive the crown of life, which the Lord hath promised to them that love him.'"[1,2]

Father God, I pray for those experiencing temptation today, that you would strengthen them. Whatever the nation of their temptation, I ask you to provide them with the power to overcome.

1 See James 1:12, *KJV*.
2 From *Rev. John Wesley.*

May 14th

My God, whom I praise, do not remain silent, for people who are wicked and deceitful have opened their mouths against me; they have spoken against me with lying tongues. With words of hatred they surround me; they attack me without cause

(Psalm 109:1 – 3 *NIV*)

Mrs Williamson's affidavit was read, and then Causton delivered to the grand jury a paper entitled "A List of Grievances", which, with some immaterial alterations, was "returned as a true bill", charging John Wesley with having "broken the laws of the realm, contrary to the peace of our Sovereign Lord the King, his crown and dignity". The indictment contained ten counts, of which the first was for speaking and writing to Mrs Williamson against her husband's consent; the others related to his repelling her from the Communion, the division of the service, and his conduct respecting baptisms and burials. He appeared before the court, and declared that as nine of these counts related to his ecclesiastical matters, they were not within the cognisance of that tribunal; but that which concerned speaking and writing to Mrs Williamson was of a secular nature, he said, and therefore he desired that it might be tried upon the spot where the facts complained of had occurred. But it was in vain that he repeatedly demanded a hearing on this charge; and in this manner more than three months elapsed.[1]

Lord, for Christians brought before "kangaroo courts" for your name's sake, I pray your divine help and intervention. When they face accusations and charges, give them the right words to say. When they are scared, give them courage. When they are tempted to deny you, give them strong faith.

1 From *Rev. John Wesley.*

May 15th

Be kind to one another

(Ephesians 4:31 *ESV*)

John Wesley became so interested in the Moravians that he even went to Herrnhut[1] "to see the place where the Christians live"...

Soon after Wesley's visit to Herrnhut, trouble began to develop in the Fetter Lane society.[2] James Hutton[3] had always insisted that in his society everyone should be free to speak his mind on any topic that came up for discussion. Now freedom of speech is a grand thing but it does not always follow, however, that what everybody says is true or helpful to others. Some of the members of the society (like the Wesleys) were highly trained theologians; others had little or no education. One young man, for instance, began to assert that since God did everything, those who desired to become Christians should not pray or read the Bible or do anything; they should simply sit back and let God do his work.[4]

Gracious Father, you love your Church through all kinds of disagreements and troubles, some more valid than others – thank you for doing so. Grant us grace, Lord, to air our differences kindly, and with respect. Even if we don't all agree on everything, help us to maintain cordiality, charity and goodwill.

1 The Moravian Church has its central settlement at Herrnhut, Germany.

2 The Moravian Church in the UK was first established in Fetter Lane, Chelsea, London.

3 James Hutton (1715–95), the founder of a small prayer society in London and a leading light in the Moravian Church.

4 From *Through Five Hundred Years.*

May 16th

I APPEAL TO YOU ... THAT ALL OF YOU AGREE, AND THAT THERE BE NO DIVISIONS AMONG YOU

(1 Corinthians 1:10 *ESV*)

One day a man named John Bray[1] got up and announced, "It is impossible for anyone to be a true Christian outside of the Moravian Church." Since a careful search of early records indicates that this man never joined the Moravian Church himself, this was, to say the least, a strange statement!

John Wesley was alarmed at this kind of thing. He had been brought up to believe that Christian doctrines were to be accepted, not argued about. When he could not put a stop to all the talking, he lost patience completely and "plainly told our poor, confused, shattered society" that Satan was taking over ... he stood up in the meeting, read a statement, and walked out. Eighteen members of the society followed him.

When Zinzendorf[2] was in London ... he arranged to meet Wesley, thinking that he might be able to pour oil on the troubled waters. Wesley was not very fond of Zinzendorf, whom he accused of being a dictator. What he did not realize, however, was that it was his own desire to dictate which had led to his break with the society in Fetter Lane. Needless to say, the conference was unsuccessful. Two dictators are not apt to make much progress at a peace conference.[3]

Lord, where there is discord, help me to do my best to bring about harmony. Help me to be a bringer of peace.

1 John and Charles Wesley lodged at John Bray's house, which also served as an unofficial centre for early Methodist and Moravian activities.

2 Nikolaus Ludwig Reichsgraf von Zinzendorf (died 1760), German religious reformer, bishop of the Moravian Church.

3 From *Through Five Hundred Years*.

May 17th

Songs from the Spirit

(Ephesians 5:19 *NIV*)

John Wesley ... has rendered immense service to English theology by calling conspicuous attention to important elements, previously overlooked, in Christ's message...

The real embodiment of Methodist theology is the Methodist hymn-book and especially Charles Wesley's hymns. Thus the active labour of one brother found a needful supplement in the other's quiet thought. This last has permanent embodiment in the most useful form possible, in the hymns which appeal to the intelligence and the heart of all who read the English language.

One may question whether the active Revival period of the 1740s,[1] in which Charles Wesley wrote some of his greatest hymns, often impromptu expressions of high emotion, left much time for quiet meditation. But it is certainly true that his, and not John's, was the most effective and comprehensive statement of Methodist doctrine. He expressed in attractive and forceful verse what sometimes John wrote in laboured syllogisms.[2, 3]

**Thank you, Lord, for those you have gifted to write heart-lifting hymns;
thank you for the tremendous contribution they make to worship.
Great truths are embodied in their works. Help me to savour and
enjoy their collections. Bless their efforts.**

1 A noted period of spiritual awakening and religious revival marked by an unusual receptivity to the gospel.

2 The Wesley brothers were, and are, sometimes referred to as "The Preacher and the Poet", John being the former and Charles the latter.

3 From *The Evangelical Doctrines of Charles Wesley's Hymns.*

May 18th

Addressing one another in psalms and hymns

(Ephesians 5:19 *ESV*)

John was well aware of the theological range and value of his brother's verse. In the Preface to his "pocket hymn-book" of 1785 he wrote that in the large hymn-book of 1780, 93 per cent of which was the work of Charles, "the judicious and candid reader may find clear expressions of every branch of speculative and practical divinity".

This claim has been widely endorsed, particularly by Dr Martineau,[1] who regarded the Methodist hymn-book as the best compendium of popular divinity in the English language. Thus he echoes John Wesley's famous Preface to "the large" hymn-book; which he summed up as "a little body of practical and experimental divinity", and claimed that, though small – 525 hymns – was large enough to contain "all the important truths of our holy religion, whether speculative or practical," and "to illustrate them all and prove them by Scripture and reason". Why he wrote "reason" is hardly clear; Charles reasoned little. Perhaps John meant that the Scripture phrases out of which the hymns were woven were, in themselves, reasons.[2]

Lord, you have placed a new song in my heart. Thank you.
In your mercy, keep that melody alive. Help me, Lord, today,
to carry the songs of the Kingdom in my heart.

1 Professor James Martineau (1805–1900), English religious philosopher.
2 From *The Evangelical Doctrines of Charles Wesley's Hymns.*

MAY 19TH

TRULY, TRULY, I SAY TO YOU, WHOEVER HEARS MY WORD AND BELIEVES HIM WHO SENT ME HAS ETERNAL LIFE

(John 5:24 *ESV*)

For many years I have been asked to publish a hymn-book as might be generally used in all our congregations throughout Great Britain and Ireland.

I have withstood requests, as I believed such a publication was needless, considering the various hymn-books which my brother and I have published…

But my refusals have been answered, "Such a publication is highly needful because the greater part of the people are poor, and not able to purchase many books … A proper collection of hymns for general use, carefully made from the contents of other books, is therefore necessary, and wanted; one that is easy to carry and not expensive."[1]

Your gospel, Lord, is for all, and I praise you today for the inclusive message of salvation. Your love includes rich and poor alike, and I thank you for such grace.

1 From the Preface to *Wesley's Hymns and New Supplement.*

May 20th

Paul and Silas were praying and singing hymns to God

(Acts 16:25 *NIV*)

Such a hymn-book you have now before you. It is not so large as to be either cumbersome or expensive; and it is large enough to contain such a variety of hymns as will not soon be worn threadbare. It is large enough to contain all the important truths of our most holy religion, whether speculative or practical; yes, to illustrate them all and to prove them both by Scripture and reason; and this is done in a regular order.

The hymns are not carelessly jumbled together, but carefully ranged under proper headings, according to the experience of real Christians. This book is, in effect, a little body of experimental and practical divinity.

As only a small part of these hymns are of my own composing, I do not regard it as immodest to declare that no such hymn-book as this has yet been published in the English language. In what other publication of the kind have you so distinct and full an account of Scriptural Christianity? Such a declaration of the heights and depths of religion? Cautions against plausible errors? Clear directions for making your calling and election sure, and for perfecting holiness in the fear of God?[1]

Lord, I thank you for my Bible, but I also thank you for hymn-books, in which the truths of the Bible are set to music, and sometimes made easier to understand or remember. Help me to treasure both for the blessings they contain.

1 From the Preface to *Wesley's Hymns and New Supplement.*

May 21st

The governor ... kept guards at the city gates to catch me

(2 Corinthians 16:32 *NIV*)

Savannah: The trial.

Wesley had ... zealous friends. Even among the Jurors twelve persons were found who, in a paper addressed to the trustees, protested against the indictment as a scheme for gratifying personal malice by blackening Wesley's character. This, indeed, the whole affair seems to have been; again and again a further trial was delayed, until, after the seventh postponement, the defendant, finding he could neither obtain justice nor be of any use as a clergyman under such conditions, gave up in despair and announced his determination to return to England. Upon this the magistrates asked him to give bail for his appearance when wanted, but this Wesley would not do; so, in return, they gave orders that he should not be permitted to leave the colony, and forbade any person to assist him in so doing.[1]

Lord, this ordeal must have been humiliating for such a learned man as John Wesley; finding himself in such a dreadful situation. I pray for those whose circumstances have not turned out well, and who experience failure and even degradation. Draw alongside them, I pray.

1 From *Rev. John Wesley.*

May 22nd

A GOOD NAME IS MORE DESIRABLE THAN GREAT RICHES; TO BE ESTEEMED IS BETTER THAN SILVER OR GOLD

(Proverbs 22:1 *NIV*)

That same evening Wesley, with four other fugitives who had reasons for leaving the colony, started out in an open boat for Port Royal, in South Carolina, which place they reached, after hard toiling and rowing by sea and many hardships by land, on 6 December 1737.

On the 8th Wesley was joined at Port Royal by Delamotte, when they took a small craft and started for the port of Charleston, which they reached on the 13th.

On the 22nd John Wesley quitted (sic) America, having experienced the failure of many hopes, and learned many useful though painful lessons.

It seems that when he had actually left them, some of his late parishioners began to think more kindly and justly about him, for when his friend and successor, Whitefield,[1] arrived, they found some good things to say about him. In a letter from Georgia, Whitefield says – "The good Mr John Wesley has done is inexpressible. His name is a very precious thing among the people, and he has laid a foundation that I hope neither man nor devils will ever be able to shake."[2]

Lord, how fickle life can be! Help me to speak kindly of others this day, and if I have nothing kind to say, then to say nothing at all. By the same token, help me to remember that today's critics can be tomorrow's fans, and not to take either criticism or flattery overly seriously.

1 Reverend George Whitefield (or Whitfield), 1714–70, Anglican cleric and one of the founders of Methodism. He was introduced to the Wesleys at the Oxford "Holy Club" and sailed for Georgia a day after John Wesley arrived in England.

2 From *Rev. John Wesley.*

May 23rd

Since the children have flesh and blood, he too shared in their humanity so that by his death he might break the power of him who holds the power of death – that is, the Devil – and free those who all their lives were held in slavery by their fear of death

(Hebrews 2:14, 15 *NIV*)

It was natural that Wesley should feel depressed and be the subject of many heart-searchings during his return voyage to England, for he had had many disappointments and some bitter trials in America. Resolute had been his purpose, high his hopes, and ardent his zeal when he went out on his missionary expedition, yet he had accomplished little, and of that little recent events had tended to undo much. And now he was obliged to confess to himself that what he had thought his Heaven-sent mission had been a failure, and he recognized the fault might be, nay, probably was, in himself.

It was during a storm, as he was returning to England, that he discovered a great fear in his heart of death, and the discovery of that fear much disturbed him, for he knew a Christian should not be afraid to die.[1]

Lord, your death and resurrection has released me from the power of sin and death. Let that truth sink ever deeper into my heart, I pray, so that I may come to welcome death as a friend – my gateway to Paradise, in Christ, my Saviour. Thank you, Lord Jesus, for dying in my place.

1 From *Rev. John Wesley.*

May 24th

So Jesus said to the Jews who had believed in him, "If you abide in my word, you are truly my disciples, and you will know the truth, and the truth will set you free"

(John 8: 31, 32 *ESV*)

In the 1700s, John Wesley had numerous encounters with and experiences of the Moravian Church. Wesley had important conversations with Augustus Spangenberg[1] and Peter Böhler,[2] two significant members of the Moravian Church. The Moravian Church had a deep influence upon Wesley, helping him to find an assurance of faith which he felt he lacked. On the evening of Wednesday, 24 May 1738, Wesley attended a meeting off Aldersgate Street, in London. The meeting is often said to have been a meeting of a largely Moravian society. At this meeting, while a passage was being red from Martin Luther's preface to the Epistle to the Romans, Wesley felt his "heart strangely warmed", and felt a deep assurance of faith.[3]

One night John Wesley walked home from a religious meeting in Aldersgate Street. It was the springtime of the year, only five months after his escape from Georgia. And on this spring night he dedicated himself to the life of a prophet.[4]

What I like about this story, Lord, is the speed of your grace. You can change a heart in an instant. Thank you for doing this for John Wesley. I pray today for anyone known to me, that you will provide an assurance of faith wherever there is doubt and warm uncertain hearts with a certainty of your love.

1 August Gottlieb Spangenberg (1704–92), German theologian and Moravian bishop.

2 Peter (Petrus) Böhler (1712–75), German-English Moravian bishop and missionary influential in Moravianism.

3 From the notes of Brother Philip Cooper, Fairfield Moravian Church, Manchester, England.

4 From *John Wesley's Journal (Abridged)*.

May 25th

The promise comes by faith

(Romans 4:16 *NIV*)

In the evening I went very unwillingly to a society in Aldersgate Street, where one was reading Luther's preface to the Epistle to the Romans. About a quarter before nine, while he was describing the change which God works in the heart through faith in Christ, I felt my heart strangely warmed. I felt I did trust in Christ, Christ alone, for salvation; and an assurance was given me that He had taken away my sins, even mine, and saved me from the law of sin and death. I began to pray withal my might for those who had in a more especial manner despitefully used me and persecuted me. I then testified openly to all there what I now first felt in my heart. But it was not long before the enemy suggested, "This cannot be faith; for where is thy joy?" Then I was taught that peace and victory over sin are essential to faith in the captain of our salvation; but that, as to the transports of joy that usually attend the beginning of it, especially in those who have mourned deeply, God sometimes giveth, sometimes withholdeth them, according to the counsels of his own will. After my return home, I was much buffeted with temptations; but cried out, and they fled away. They returned again and again. I as often lifted up my eyes, and he "sent me help from his holy place".[1] And herein I found the difference between this and my former state chiefly consisted. I was striving, yea, fighting with all my might under the law, as well as under grace. But then I was sometimes, if not often, conquered; now, I was always conqueror.[2, 3, 4]

Saving God, in the battle that takes place for the souls of the newly converted and assured, I pray your grace will prevail. Be with those who are fighting doubts and are under attack. Give them victory, as you did John Wesley, and establish them in faith.

1 See Psalm 20:2, *KJV*.
2 See Romans 8:37.
3 From *John Wesley's Journal (Abridged)*.
4 I have left these words unmodernized and unaltered from Wesley's original (unlike other pages). This is because they mark a hugely significant change in Wesley's life, and it seemed particularly appropriate to read his testimony in his own words.

May 26th

Fixing our eyes on Jesus, the pioneer and perfecter of faith

(Hebrews 12:2 *NIV*)

Thur. 25 [June 1738] – The moment I awoke, "Jesus, Master," was in my heart and in my mouth; and I found all my strength lay in keeping my eye fixed upon him, and my soul waiting on him continually.

Being again at St Paul's in the afternoon, I could taste the good word of God in the anthem, which began, "My song shall be always of the loving-kindness of the Lord: with my mouth will I ever be showing forth thy truth from one generation to another."[1]

Yes the enemy injected a fear, "If you really do believe, why is there not more of a change within you?" I answered (yet it wasn't really me who answered), "I know not. But this I do know, I now have peace with God. I sin not today, and Jesus my Master has forbidden me from worrying about tomorrow."[2, 3]

There's the secret, Lord, in the heat of the battle, when the enemy whispers doubt and discouragement – to keep our eyes on Jesus. Remind me to do so, please, Lord, lest I be defeated. I pray too for any in need of such help today, who are feeling the weight of spiritual warfare.

1 From Psalm 89.
2 See Matthew 6:34.
3 From *John Wesley's Journal (Abridged)*.

May 27th

He causeth the grass to grow for the cattle, and herb for the service of man

(Psalm 104:14 *KJV*)

For an Ague.*

Get into the cold bath, just before the cold fits.

Nothing tends to prolong an Ague more than indulging a lazy indolent disposition. The patient ought therefore between the fits to take as much exercise as he can bear; and to use a light diet, and for common drink, lemonade is the most proper.

When all other means fail, give blue Vitriol,[1] from one grain to two grains, in the absence of the fit, and repeat it three or four times in twenty-four hours.

Or, take a handful of Groundsel,[2] shred it small, put it in a paper bag, four inches square, pricking that side which is to be next to the skin full of holes. Cover this with a thin linen, and wear it on the pit of the stomach, renewing it two hours before the fit. (Tried.)

Or, apply to the stomach, a large onion, slit.[3]

*An Ague is an intermitting fever, each fit of which is preceded by a cold shivering, and goes off in a sweat.

Lord, I can't vouch for this advice, but what I do know is, you have filled this planet with good things, many of which are natural remedies for ailments. Thank you for doing so. Thank you for those whose skill and knowledge means that many will today find relief from pain. I lift to you in prayer, those known to me who are experiencing illness. Bless them, I pray, and may they find suitable treatments.

1 Crystalline copper sulphate.
2 A leafy plant whose leaves were sometimes boiled for medicinal purposes.
3 From *Primitive Physic*.

My tongue will sing of your righteousness

(Psalm 51:14 *NIV*)

John's theological purpose in the publication of hymns is clearly shown … The Methodist hymns were from the first treated by him as doctrinal documents. Not only in his prefaces to hymn-books, but in his treatises and sermons, he refers to them as authoritative expressions of Methodist theology.

For instance, in his sermon of 1765 "on the Lord our righteousness", after quoting from an earlier discourse of 1738, in order to show that his opinions on Justification by Faith had not changed, he turned to the hymns and wrote: those "published a year or two after this and since republished several timers (a clear testimony that my judgment was still the same) speak full to the same purpose. To cite all the passages to this effect would be to inscribe a great volume."[1]

Charles Joseph Mahaney, Senior Pastor of Sovereign Grace Church, Louisville, USA, calls church singing "Take-Home Theology" because the best songs we sing together end up serving as an easily memorizable, deeply biblical summary of important truths from Scripture.

Lord, perhaps I could spend some time with my hymn-book today, poring over those truths that speak of your love. Whisper to me as I do so, I pray.

1 From *The Evangelical Doctrines of Charles Wesley's Hymns.*

May 29th

Let the Spirit renew your thoughts and attitudes

(Ephesians 4:23 *NLT*)

The best evidence that John regarded the hymns as doctrinal manifestoes is not to be found so much in his frequent illustrative use of them in his Standard Sermons, though that is striking, not even in the fact that they were often first published as appendices to his writings, but in his treatise on Christian Perfection, in which the citations from his brother's hymns, as statements of Methodist doctrine, are numerous.

He quotes many verses as evidence that the two brothers consistently preached Christian Perfection from the beginning. The Preface on the same subject to the hymn-book of 1740 is especially interesting, since Wesley afterwards softened some of its statements and altered a few phrases in certain verses because he could not suffer what he claimed to be serious doctrinal statements to remain uncorrected when deeper thought and experience made an odd expression, here or there, untenable.[1]

Lord, what a lovely grace it is when we are able to improve or mellow our thinking as the years go by, when we realize we may have been sincerely incorrect. Keep me ever-learning, I pray, and not fixed in ways or thoughts that might be wrong or mistaken. Truth does not change, Lord, but it is possible I may need to!

1 From *The Evangelical Doctrines of Charles Wesley's Hymns.*

JESUS WENT AROUND TEACHING FROM VILLAGE TO VILLAGE

(Mark 6:6 *NIV*)

Wesley returned to Lincolnshire to act as his father's curate at the twin parishes of Epworth and Wroote. There, among parishioners whom sister Hetty[1] described as "asses dull on dungheaps born," he visited, shot plovers on the ploughland, wrote sermons for his father and himself, and went to every fair within reach.

He also wrote long letters to the young ladies in the Cotswolds, fell a little in love with Miss Kitty Hargreaves, laboriously copied out his father's *Dissertations on Job* and read mightily, summarising as he went. Not was the Saturday evening self-examination neglected.

"What a contrast between the daily life of 1726 and that of 1739," writes the indefatigable editor of his journals.[2] "At Wroote we see a better sort of country parson in times degenerate. He is gentlemanly, refined, familiar with the best literature of the day, a congenial companion; to some extent worldly, yet standing absolutely clear of grossness; not exempt from temptation, but 'buffeting' his body and bringing himself under the iron rule of law and resolution."[3]

Today, Lord, I pray for country parsons and ministers in rural parishes. Theirs is a specialized ministry as they involve themselves in the countryside lives of their parishioners. Bless them, I pray, and those to whom they minister.

1 Mehetabel Wesley Wright (or "Hetty" or "Kitty"; 1697–1750), poet. One of John Wesley's eight sisters.
2 Probably Reverend Nehemiah Curnock, a former minister of Rayleigh Wesleyan Church, Essex, England, who deciphered John Wesley's Journals, which were handwritten and scribbled in English, Latin and shorthand.
3 From *John Wesley, Anglican.*

May 31st

Hear, O sons, a father's instruction

(Proverbs 4:1 *ESV*)

In Christ Church [Oxford University], a meeting of officers and seniors was summoned to discuss the "new enthusiasm" (Wesley's "Holy Club") and it was rumoured that the authorities were about to "blow up the Godly Club".

John, meeting persecution … appealed to his father, who on hearing that John was called the Father of Holy Club, had written: "If it be so, I am sure I must be the Grandfather of it, and I need not say that I had rather any of my sons should be so dignified and distinguished to have the title of 'His Holiness.'"

Old Samuel was as brisk as ever. "I can scarcely think so meanly of you as that you would be discouraged with the 'crackling of thorns under a pot,'"[1] he wrote to John. "Preserve an equal temper of mind under whatever treatment you meet with from a not very just or well-natured world. Bear no more sail than is necessary, but steer steady."[2]

What great advice, Lord! Thank you for parents who offer wise and helpful counsel to their children at times of anxiety or distress. Thank you for the perspective that Samuel Wesley's comments provided. Bless parents, I pray!

1 See Ecclesiastes 7:6.
2 From *John Wesley, Anglican.*

June 1st

THE PEOPLE WHICH SAT IN DARKNESS SAW GREAT LIGHT; AND TO THEM WHICH SAT IN THE REGION AND SHADOW OF DEATH LIGHT IS SPRUNG UP. FROM THAT TIME JESUS BEGAN TO PREACH, AND TO SAY, REPENT: FOR THE KINGDOM OF HEAVEN IS AT HAND

(Matthew 4:16, 17 *KJV*)

Verse 16. Here is a beautiful gradation: first, they "walked," then they "sat in darkness," and lastly, "in the region of the shadow of death".

Verse 17. *From that time Jesus began to preach* – He had preached before, both to Jews and Samaritans. John 4: 41, 45. But from this time began his solemn, stated preaching. Repent, for the Kingdom of Heaven is at hand – Although it is the peculiar business of Christ to establish the Kingdom of Heaven in the hearts of men, yet it is observable, he begins his preaching in the same words with John the Baptist; because the repentance which John taught, still was, and ever will be, the necessary preparation for the inward Kingdom. But that phrase is not only used with regard to individuals, in whom it is to be established, but also with regard to the Christian church, the whole body of believers.[1]

Lord, I love that little phrase in Wesley's commentary: "the inward Kingdom". I pray today that your Kingdom may be established in my inward life. Remind me to hang on to that gem today, and to keep it as a personal motto.

1 From *Notes on the New Testament.*

June 2nd

Blessed are the poor in spirit: for theirs is the Kingdom of Heaven. Blessed are they that mourn: for they shall be comforted. Blessed are the meek: for they shall inherit the earth

(Matthew 5: 3–5 *NIV*)

Verse 3. *Happy are the poor in spirit* – They who are unfeignedly penitent; they who are truly convinced of sin; who see and feel the state they are in by nature, being deeply aware of their sinfulness, guiltiness, helplessness.

For theirs is the Kingdom of Heaven – The present, inward Kingdom; righteousness, peace, and joy in the Holy Ghost,[1] as well as the eternal Kingdom, if they endure to the end.

Verse 4. *They that mourn* – Either for their own sins, or for other men's, and are steadily and habitually serious. *They shall be comforted* – More solidly and deeply even in this world; and eternally, in Heaven.

Verse 5. *Happy are the meek* – They that hold all their passions and affections evenly balanced. *They shall inherit the earth* – They shall have all things really necessary for life and godliness. They shall enjoy whatever portion God hath given for them here, and shall hereafter possess the new earth, wherein dwelleth righteousness.[2]

Thank you, Lord, for Wesley's insights and clarifications. Help me, Lord, when I read my Bible, to rely upon you for correct understanding; enable me, by your Spirit, to know what your word is saying to me today.

1 Romans 14:17, *KJV*.
2 From *Notes on the New Testament*.

June 3rd

Examine yourselves to see whether you are in the faith; test yourselves

(2 Corinthians 13:5 *NIV*)

Wesley reviewed the progress of his religious life. "For many years," he said, "I have been tossed about by various winds of doctrine. I asked long ago, 'What must I do to be saved?'"[1] The Scripture answered, Keep the commandments, believe, hope, love. I was early warned against laying, as the Papists do, too much stress on outward works, or on a faith without works, which, as it does not include either, will never lead to true hope or charity. Nor am I aware that to this hour I have placed too much stress on either. But I spent time with some Lutherans and Calvinists who stressed faith to such an amazing extent that it hid all the rest of the commandments. I did not see then that this was the natural effect of their overgrown fear of Popery, being so terrified with the claims of merit and good works, that they plunged into the other extreme.

In this labyrinth I was utterly lost, not being able to find out what the error was, and unable to reconcile the hypothesis with either Scripture or common sense. The English writers, Bishop Beveridge,[2] Bishop Taylor,[3] and Mr Nelson,[4] relieved me from these well-meaning, wrong-headed Germans, except that when they interpreted Scripture in different ways, I was at a loss. And there was one thing much insisted upon in Scripture – the unity of the Church, which none of them, I thought, clearly explained.[5]

Lord, should the winds of doubt blow my way, please draw alongside me with reassurance. Speak to me through Scripture until matters are once again settled in my heart and mind.

1 See Acts 16:30.
2 William Beveridge (1637–1708), English writer and clergyman.
3 Jeremy Taylor (1613–67).
4 John Nelson (1707–74), Official Preacher to Methodist Circuits.
5 From *Rev. John Wesley.*

June 4th

Lead me in your truth and teach me, for you are the God of my salvation

(Psalm 25:5 *ESV*)

It was not long before Providence brought me to those who showed me a sure rule of interpreting Scripture, *consensus veterum: quod ab omnibus, quod ubique, quod semper creditum*;[1] at the same time they insisted upon a due regard to the one church at all times and in all places…

I grew acquainted with the mystic writers, whose noble descriptions of union with God and internal religion made everything else appear mean, flat, and insipid … They gave me an entire new view of religion, nothing like I had before.[2] But, alas! it was nothing like that religion which Christ and his Apostles loved and taught … I fluctuated between obedience and disobedience; I had no heart, no vigour, no zeal in obeying, continually doubting whether I was right or wrong, and never out of perplexities and entanglements. Nor can I … give a distinct account how or when I came back toward the right way.[3]

Thank you, Lord, that when we seek your will, you guide us into truth.
I pray for any who are seeking truth today, especially if they are confused.
Lead them in their search and protect them from being misled.
Protect them too from discouragement.

1 Vincentian Canon (from Vincent of Lerins): *quod ubique, quod semper, quod ab omnibus creditum est* ("what has been believed everywhere, always, and by all".)

2 Wesley was initially intrigued by Christian mysticism, then became something of a reluctant mystic, before coming to despise many elements of mysticism. He came to think it wasn't sufficiently grounded in spiritual reality.

3 From *Rev. John Wesley.*

Praise the Lord your God, who is from everlasting to everlasting

(Nehemiah 9:5 *NIV*)

As the Spirit of the living Head has never deserted the Church, it follows that those in all ages who by the Holy Ghost have called Jesus Lord should have been occupied with attempts to set forth his praise. As in the old times, they "prophesy and do not cease"[1] so that our age is richer in good hymns than any that have gone before it.

The Committee [working on *A Collection of Hymns for the use of the People called Methodists*][2] have been glad to make use of the labours of the works of both contemporary hymn-writers and their predecessors; accordingly, the present volume is enriched by a selection from the works of modern hymnologists as well as from the accumulated treasures of the past ... illustrating the substantial unity existing between all believers in Christ, notwithstanding the many causes which at present hinder a full demonstration of this to the world.[3]

Lord of the ages, your truth stands through century after century, and in every era your people find ways of praising you. You are eternal God and I join my voice with the millions lifting your name on high.

1 See Numbers 11:25.
2 Published 1780.
3 From the Preface to *Wesley's Hymns and New Supplement.*

June 6th

When I preach the gospel, I cannot boast, since I am compelled to preach. Woe to me if I do not preach the gospel!

(1 Corinthians 9:16 *NIV*)

Sun. September 17 [1738] (London) – I began again to declare in my own country the glad tidings of salvation, preaching three times, and afterwards expounding the Holy Scripture, to a large company in the Minories.[1] On Monday I rejoiced to meet with our own little society,[2] which now consisted of thirty-two persons.

The next day I went to see the condemned felons, in Newgate,[3] and offered them free salvation. In the evening I went to a society in Bear Yard, and preached repentance and remission of sins. The next evening I spoke the truth in love at a society in Aldersgate Street:[4] some contradicted at first, but not long; so that nothing but love was present at our parting.[5]

Lord, here we see John Wesley preaching again, back in England, after the failure of his American mission. Thank you for grace that enables us to rebound from our disappointments and to continue in your service. Thank you too, Lord, for the growth of Wesley's Societies. I pray today for anyone who feels they have let you down. Restore them to ministry, I pray.

1 A former civil parish (Minories Holy Trinity), and a street nearby the Tower of London. The parish church was Holy Trinity, Minories.
2 John Wesley was beginning to establish Methodist Accountability Discipleship Groups, or Methodist Societies, Class Meetings, or Band Societies. As these were not formally under the control of the Church of England, though Wesley was an Anglican minister, they met with a mixed response.
3 A London prison, opened 1769, demolished 1902.
4 East London, the site of Wesley's conversion experience.
5 From *John Wesley's Journal (Abridged)*.

Loving one another as brothers

(Hebrews 13:1 *NIV*)

Since only that section of Charles Wesley's hymns which can be proved to have been authorized by John can legitimately be claimed to be the expression of Methodist doctrine, it is necessary to ask how many of the 7,300 which he wrote met with his brother's approval.[1]

From a theological point of view, I would hazard the guess, 7,000, yet he cannot be said explicitly to have authorized 1,200. To some of them he is known to have made objection, and even to have warned his people against their teaching. He expressed disagreement with hymns published in the book of 1749,[2] the first which Charles brought out independently, because he detected traces of Mysticism in some of their verses[3] ... Views different from John's in relation to Mysticism and Christian Perfection[4] can be found now and then in all the later compositions of Charles.[5]

Thank you, Lord, for that unique gift of brothers and sisters – even when we disagree! My prayers today are for brothers and sisters who are at loggerheads, for whatever reason. Help us to savour family unity.

1 Charles Wesley was a prolific hymn-writer, but estimates vary regarding the actual number of hymns he wrote. Some sources say approximately 6,000 and others approximately 9,000.
2 *Hymns and Sacred Poems.*
3 John Wesley disapproved of many of the teachings in Christian Mysticism.
4 John Wesley maintained the theological stance that sinless perfection is possible in this life as well as the next.
5 From *The Evangelical Doctrines of Charles Wesley's Hymns.*

June 8th

Gifts that differ according to the grace given to us

(Romans 12:6 *ESV*)

Tues. Nov. 25 [1746] – I laboured much to convince someone who had known me for several years, that she had left her first love,[1] and was in the utmost danger of also losing all the benefits she had experienced; but she was resistant to argument as well as persuasion, and she very politely renounced all fellowship with me, "Because (she said) I wasn't a supporter of the government!"[2] Is there anything those who are resolved to a desperate cause will not assert!

Sun. 30. John Jones (a zealous Calvinist)[3] preached for the first time at the Foundery.[4] I trust he will never rest, until He who "died for all"[5] has "cleansed him from all unrighteousness".[6]

Thur. Dec. 4. I mentioned to the Society[7] my idea of giving physic [medicine] to the poor. About thirty came the next day, and in three weeks about three hundred; this we continued for several years, till the number of patients was still increasing and the expense became greater than we could bear: meantime, through the blessing of God, many who had been ill for months or years, were restored to perfect health.[8]

Lord, what a wide range of people are mentioned here! In these brief extracts from Wesley's journal, we see a glimpse of the different people he met in his ministry. Thank you, Lord, that we aren't all boringly the same! Help me today to enjoy and appreciate diversity in those I meet. Thank you for variety!

1 See Revelation 2:4.
2 Wesley's social and moral ethic was based largely in the transformation (conversion) of individuals. He had only a little faith in the ability of political legislation to effect the changes he believed could only come from God.
3 John Jones, Talysarn (1796–1857), Welsh Calvinistic Methodist minister. Any number of people in Wales were called John Jones, and the inclusion of the name of one's home village (in this case Talysarn) after one's name was by no means unusual. John Jones was sympathetic towards Methodism but never relinquished Calvinism, which annoyed Wesley.
4 The Foundery (or Foundry), the first London foundry for casting brass cannon. (Subsequently, the first Wesleyan Methodist chapel.)
5 2 Corinthians 5:15.
6 See 1 John 1:9.
7 Wesley formed his early Methodist converts into Societies, modelled upon the Religious Societies (Groups) of his Oxford days.
8 From *The Journal of the Rev. John Wesley, Volume 2.*

MAKE THE MOST OF EVERY OPPORTUNITY

(Ephesians 5:16 *NLT*)

Fri. Nov. 3 [1738] – I preached at St Antholin's:[1] Sunday, 5, in the morning, at St Botolph's, Bishopsgate; in the afternoon, at Islington; and in the evening, to such a congregation as I have never seen before, at St Clement's, in the Strand. As this was the first time of my preaching here, I suppose it is to be the last.

Sun. Dec. 3 (Oxford) – I began reading prayers at Bocardo (the city prison),[2] which had been long discontinued. In the afternoon I received a letter, earnestly desiring me to publish my account of Georgia; and another, equally earnestly dissuading me from it, "because it would bring much trouble upon me".

I consulted God in His word, and received two answers: the first, Ezek. 33:2–6: the other, "Thou therefore endure hardship, as a good soldier of Jesus Christ."[3, 4]

Lord, Wesley sets an example here of hard work and a tireless commitment to sharing the gospel wherever he was and in whichever company he found himself – in churches in London or in a prison in Oxford, with all the travelling involved. Bless me, I pray, with all the energy I will need this day, for all that you ask me to do.

1 Budge Row, Watling Street, London.
2 Closed 1771.
3 2 Timothy 2:3–5.
4 From *John Wesley's Journal (Abridged)*.

June 10th

The stone the builders rejected has become the cornerstone

(Psalm 118:22 *NIV*)

Wed. 9 [May 1739] – We took possession of a piece of ground near St James's Churchyard, in the Horse Fair, Bristol,[1] where it was planned to build a room large enough to contain both the societies of Nicholas and Baldwin Street,[2] and anyone of their acquaintance who desired to be with them when the Scripture was expounded. And on Saturday, 12, the first stone was laid with the voice of praise and thanksgiving.[3, 4]

Lord, the laying of this stone marks tremendous progress in Wesley's progress, after his early setbacks. Thank you that when we make you the cornerstone of our lives, hopes and dreams, you see us through hard times in order to fulfil your will in our lives. Help those who are struggling, Lord, not to lose heart, but to trust you for brighter days.

1 Horse Fairs were popular social gatherings at which horses and sheep were bought and sold. Farm workers looking to be hired, and farm managers looking to hire workers, would meet at Horse Fairs and arrange employment. They were also useful meeting places for single people looking to be married!

2 In June 1739, these two fledgling societies joined to become the first United Society.

3 From *John Wesley's Journal (Abridged)*.

4 Whereas the Foundry in London became the first Wesleyan Methodist Chapel when its use was redesignated, it was already established as a building. The construction of an entirely new premises at the Bristol Horse Fair marked a significant point in the development of what was to eventually become a separate denomination. The Bristol building was to serve as a centre for preaching and teaching, but would also be used as a medical dispensary.

Fear of man will prove to be a snare

(Proverbs 29:25 *NIV*)

I had not the least intention of being personally engaged in the expense of this work [of building on the Horse Fair land], or in the direction of it, having appointed eleven feoffees,[1] on whom I assumed such burdens would fall. Of course, I quickly realized I was mistaken.

With regard to the expense, I soon realized the whole project would have come to a standstill had I not immediately taken it upon myself to pay the workmen; so that before I knew where I was, I had plunged into a debt of more than one hundred and fifty pounds. I didn't know how this would be reimbursed to me, as the subscriptions of both societies did not amount to one quarter of that sum.

As to the direction of the work, I received letters from my friends in London, Mr Whitefield[2] in particular, that neither he nor they would have anything to do with the building unless I instantly discharged all the feoffees and did everything in my own name. Many reasons they gave for this, but one was enough: "that such feoffees would always have it within their power to control me, and if my preaching was not to their liking, they could turn me out of the room I had built." I accordingly yielded to their advice.[3]

May it never be, Lord, that preachers of your word feel beholden to their paymasters. Such restrictions and impositions can be stifling and detrimental to the cause of the gospel. Thank you, Lord, for the advice offered to Wesley on this occasion. Deliver preachers from such fears, I pray.

1 Managing Trustees, normally in connection to charitable trusts.
2 George Whitefield.
3 From *John Wesley's Journal (Abridged).*

June 12th

He grants a treasure of common sense to the honest

(Proverbs 2:7 *NLT*)

After his conversion [Wesley considered 24 May 1738 the date of his conversion] John Wesley continued about a fortnight "in heaviness, because of manifold temptations, in peace, but not in joy". A certain letter which reached him perplexed him, because it maintained that "no doubting could co-exist with … faith; that whoever at any time felt any doubt or fear was not weak in faith, but had no faith at all".

Praying to God to direct him, he opened his Bible,[1] and his eye fell on that passage where St Paul speaks of babes in Christ, who were not able to bear strong meat,[2] yet to whom he said, "Ye are God's building; ye are the temple of God."[3]

Surely then, thought Wesley, these men had some degree of faith, though it is plain their faith was but weak.[4]

Lord, I like Wesley's application of common sense and reasoned logic to a situation where he might have had cause to doubt. Help me, I pray, to add a healthy mixture of God-given common sense to my faith, perhaps especially when doubts and queries arise. Grant me clarity of thought at such times.

1 A habit with the Wesleys, and with early Methodists. In times of difficulty or uncertainty, they would pray, and then read the first verse that appeared to them when they opened their Bible. They trusted God to guide them in this way.

2 See 1 Corinthians 3:1, 2.

3 See 1 Corinthians 3:16, *KJV*.

4 From *Rev. John Wesley*.

June 13th

If any of you lacks wisdom, you should ask God,
who gives generously to all without finding fault,
and it will be given to you

(James 1:5 *NIV*)

With his own spiritual stare [Wesley] was … dissatisfied:

St Paul tells us that the fruit of the Spirit is love, peace, joy, long-suffering, gentleness, meekness, temperance.[1] Now although, by the grace of God in Christ, I find a measure of some of these in myself – peace, long-suffering, gentleness, meekness, temperance; yet others I find not: I cannot find in myself the love of God, or of Christ; hence my deadness and wanderings in private prayer.… even in the Holy Communion I have rarely any more than a cold attention; hence, when I hear of the slightest instance of God's love, my heart is still senseless and unaffected.… at this moment I feel no more love to him than to one I had never heard of. Again, I have not that joy in the Holy Ghost, no settled, lasting joy; nor have I such a peace as excludes the possibility either of fear or doubt. When holy men have told me I had no faith, I have often doubted … and these doubts have made me very uneasy, until I was relieved by prayer and the Holy Scriptures.[2]

Lord Jesus, you have walked the human road. You understand our feelings, including our doubts. I hold before you in prayer today, those who are passing through seasons of doubt, and for whom the light of faith and spiritual experience burns low. Draw alongside them, I pray, according to your word.

1 See Galatians 5:22.
2 From *Rev. John Wesley.*

June 14th

When you pray, go into your room, close the door and pray to your Father, who is unseen. Then your Father, who sees what is done in secret, will reward you

(Matthew 6:6 *NIV*)

The people called Methodists were supposed by their Founder to have many uses for good hymns besides singing them in public assemblies; and he selected for them accordingly.

Here will also be found some adapted to personal and private, rather than to collective worship, or to praising the Lord "secretly among the faithful", rather than "in the congregation"; but none, it is hoped, which will not minister "to exhortation, edification or comfort": and for these objects they humbly invoke the blessing of God upon their work.[1]

Lord, the privilege of daily time alone with you is one of the greatest gifts you offer. Thank you for meeting me there in a special way, and for your grace in calling me to commune with you day by day. Help me, Lord, to make the most of my "quiet times" and private communion.

1 From the Preface to *Wesley's Hymns and new Supplement.*

June 15th

For if ye love them which love you, what reward have ye? Do not even the publicans the same? And if ye salute your brethren only, what do ye more than others? Do not even the publicans so? Be ye therefore perfect, even as your Father which is in Heaven is perfect

(Matthew 5:46–48 *KJV*)

Verse 46. *The publicans* – were officers of the revenue, farmers, or receivers of the public money; men employed by the Romans to gather the taxes and customs which they exacted of the nations they had conquered. These were generally odious for their extortion and oppression, and were reckoned by the Jews as the very scum of the earth.[1]

Verse 47. *And if you salute your friends only* – Our Lord probably glances at those prejudices which different sects had against each other; and intimates that he would not have his followers imbibe that narrow spirit. Would to God this intimation had been heeded by the Church, which has crumbled beneath the weight of subdivisions and unhappy divisions; would that we would cordially embrace our brothers and sisters in Christ, of whatever denomination they are.

Verse 48. *Therefore ye shall be perfect, as your Father who is in Heaven is perfect* – referring to all that holiness … which our Lord in the beginning of the chapter recommends as happiness, and in the close of it as perfection. How wise and gracious this is, to sum up and seal all his commandments with a promise.[2]

Division, discrimination and discipleship. Father God, help me to pick through those first two minefields in order to successfully pursue the third!

1 Suspicions of collaboration were rife, and were often well founded.
2 From *Notes on the New Testament*.

June 16th

YOUR FATHER KNOWETH WHAT THINGS YE HAVE NEED OF, BEFORE YE ASK HIM. AFTER THIS MANNER THEREFORE PRAY YE: OUR FATHER WHICH ART IN HEAVEN, HALLOWED BE THY NAME

(Matthew 6:8 9 *KJV*)

Verse 8. *Your Father knoweth what things you need of* – We do not pray to inform God of our wants. Omniscient as he is, he cannot be informed of anything which he knew not before: and he is always willing to relieve them. What is lacking, chiefly, is a fit disposition on our part to receive his grace and blessing. Consequently, one great element of pray is to produce such a disposition within us; to exercise our dependence upon God in order to increase our desire of the things we ask for; to make us so aware of our wants that we may never cease wrestling till we have prevailed for the blessing.

Verse 9 *Thus therefore pray ye*[1] – He who best knew what we ought to pray for, and how we ought to pray; what manner of desire, what manner of address, would most please himself and would best become us, is here dictated as a perfect and universal form of prayer, comprehending all our real wants, expressing all our lawful desires; a full exercise of all our devotions.[2]

What a lovely truth it is, Lord, that you know all our needs before we utter one word in prayer. Likewise, the way in which prayer changes us – that too is a great blessing. Thank you, Father, for your awareness of my needs. Thank you for your grace at work in my life.

1 Wesley's notes introducing the Lord's Prayer (Matthew 6:9–13).
2 From *Notes on the New Testament.*

JUNE 17TH

[SOLOMON] STOOD AND BLESSED THE WHOLE ASSEMBLY ...
IN A LOUD VOICE

(1 Kings 8:55 *NIV*)

Wesley's fellow enthusiast, George Whitefield, had electrified the country folk of England when he had mounted a horse to preach in the open air. It was so utterly unconventional to speak the word to five thousand villagers from miles around – men and women who sat on the hillside or leaned against the trees – humble folk with untutored minds and hungry hearts.

Wesley decided to emulate Whitefield. "I will seek for God's inspiration in the free winds rather than in the stuffy air of the chapel."

He had an ideal background for an itinerant preacher. In Georgia he had loved to swing the axe and do his thinking in the garden while the flowers fed his eye. A small but keenly built man. A picturesque figure in a multitude of worshipers gathered under heaven. Five feet four of dynamic energy. "In the company of larger men, he compared as a rapier with a sword."[1]

Thank you, Lord, for those whose passion is to share your love with those who might never set foot inside a church. Bless them and their initiatives. Help your Church to look outwards as well as inwards.

1 From *Living Biographies of Religious Leaders.*

June 18th

Charity suffereth long, and is kind; charity envieth not; charity vaunteth not itself, is not puffed up, Doth not behave itself unseemly, seeketh not her own, is not easily provoked, thinketh no evil; Rejoiceth not in iniquity, but rejoiceth in the truth; Beareth all things, believeth all things, hopeth all things, endureth all things

(1 Corinthians 13:4–7 *KJV*)

Implied in being *altogether a Christian* is the love of our neighbour. Our Lord said, "Thou shalt love thy neighbour as thyself."[1] If anyone asks, "Who is my neighbour?"[2] we reply, everyone in the world; every child of the Father of all.

Nor may we in any way exclude our enemies from this demand, nor the enemies of God. Christians love these also "as Christ loved us".[3] In order to understand what manner of love this is, we may consider St Paul's description of it. It is "long-suffering and kind". It "envieth not". It is not rash or hasty in judging. It "is not puffed up"; it makes the person who loves, the servant of all. Love "doth not behave itself unseemly"; but becomes "all things to all men". Love "seeketh not her own"; but only the good of others, that they may be saved. "Love is not provoked." It casts out fear. "It thinketh no evil. It rejoiceth not in iniquity, but rejoiceth in the truth. It covereth all things, believeth all things, hopeth all things, endureth all things."[4]

Lord of love, teach me how to love you, and teach me how to love others; even – or, perhaps, especially – those who might be regarded as my enemies. Thank you, Lord, for that love of Christ which serves as my great example.

1 Matthew 22:39, *KJV*.
2 Luke 10:29.
3 John 13:34.
4 From *Fifty Three Sermons*.

Encourage others by sound doctrine

(Titus 1:9 *NIV*)

As a measure of doubt exists as to John's agreement with Charles's hymns of 1749 and later, caution obviously must be exercised before they are accepted as Methodist doctrine … Quite naturally, he did not publish in his Collections verses to which he objected. Literary taste accounted for most of his omissions and emendations, although he did sometimes alter lines to make good hymns conform with his own views. When, for instance, he varied certain words of the hymn 'Come, then, my God, the promise seal', written by Charles at the time when he was protesting vehemently against professors of John's doctrine of Instantaneous Perfection, so as to make it teach that very doctrine, he must have smiled rather grimly. Charles wrote:

'Tis done: Thou dost this moment save,
Thou dost with pardon bless;
but he did not write, as John published it:
With full salvation bless.

Charles continued:

Redemption through thy blood I have,
And heaven in thy peace;
but he did not write what John published:
And spotless love and peace.[1]

Lord, if this spat between Charles and John teaches me nothing else, it reminds me of the importance of studying that which I read, hear, preach or sing, and not simply to be content with a "parrot fashion" faith. Help me, Lord, to examine and test that which I consider, to make sure it is true and trustworthy.

1 From *The Evangelical Doctrines of Charles Wesley's Hymns.*

June 20th

The Lord brought his people out ... and not one among the tribes of Israel even stumbled

(Psalm 105:37 *NIV*)

Mon. 29 [November, 1746] – I resumed my vegetable diet (which I had now discontinued for several years), and found it of use both to my soul and body; but after two years, a violent flux, which seized me in Ireland, obliged me to return to the use of animal food.

Wed. 31. I heard an amazing instance of the providence of God. About six years ago, Mr Jeber (as he related it himself) and all his family, being eight persons, were in bed, between ten and eleven at night. All of a sudden he heard a great crack, and the house instantly fell, all at once, from the top to the bottom. They were all buried in the ruins: an abundance of people gathered together, and in two or three hours dug them out. The beds in which they had lain, were smashed in pieces, as was all the furniture of the house; but neither man, nor woman, nor child, was killed or hurt, only he had a little scratch on his hand.[1]

What I like here, Lord, is John Wesley's mention of everyday detail about his eating habits, quickly followed by a remarkable story of your protection. Help me to live in such a way that both the mundane and the miraculous are noted; appreciating the rich tapestry of life you have provided. Thank you for today, whether it proves to be uneventful or exciting; teach me to appreciate both.

1 From *The Journal of the Rev. John Wesley, Volume 2.*

We rejoice in our sufferings, knowing that suffering produces endurance, and endurance produces character, and character produces hope

(Romans 3:3, 4 *ESV*)

Sat. Jan. 3 [1747] – I called upon poor Mr C, who once "largely tasted on the good word, and the powers of the world to come".[1] I found him very loving, and very drunk, as he commonly is, day and night; but I could fix nothing upon him: "He may fall foully, but not finally!"

Sun. 11. In the evening I rode to Brentford; the next day to Newbury, and Tuesday, the 13th, to Devizes. The town was in uproar from end to end, as if the French were just entering;[2] and we heard an abundance of swelling noise; oaths, curses, and threats. The most active man in stirring up the people, we were informed, was Mr J. the C.; he had been indefatigable in the work, going all the day from house to house. He had also gone to the trouble of setting up an advertisement in the most public places of the town, "Of an obnubilative[3] pantomime entertainment, to be exhibited at Mr Clark's" (where I was to preach). The latter part of it contained a double entendre, which a modest person cannot well repeat. I began preaching at seven on "The grace of our Lord Jesus Christ". Many of the mob came in, listened a little, and stood still. No one opened his mouth, but attention was on the face of every hearer.[4]

Thank you, Lord, for Wesley's perseverance – firstly, with a drunk man, and then in the face of a noisy mob and a pantomime! Grant your people everywhere holy belligerence; that spiritual gift of digging one's heels in for the gospel's sake.

1 See Hebrews 6:5.
2 Devizes, Wiltshire, England, bore the scars (literally) of French invasion.
3 Sleep or coma inducing.
4 From *The Journal of the Rev. John Wesley, Volume 2.*

June 22ND

Go into all the world and proclaim the gospel

(Mark 16:15 *ESV*)

I could scarce reconcile myself to this strange way of preaching in the fields, of which [Whitefield] set me an example … having been all my life (till very lately) so tenacious of every point relating to decency and order, that I should have thought the saving of souls almost a sin, if it had not been done in a church…

I submitted to be more vile, and proclaimed in the highways the glad tidings of salvation…

Thence I went to Baldwin Street[1] and expounded … the fourth chapter of the Acts. We then called upon God to confirm His word. Immediately one that stood by (to our no small surprise) cried out aloud, with the utmost vehemence, even as in the agonies of death.

But we continued in prayer till "a new song was put in her mouth, a thanksgiving unto our God".[2] Soon after, two other persons … were seized with strong pain, and constrained to "roar for the disquietness of their heart".[3] But it was not long before they likewise burst forth into praise to God their Saviour.[4]

Your word, Lord, has its own power to touch the hearts of people in a way that nothing else can. I pray for preachers everywhere – in fields and in churches – that you would back home their message with the gracious power of your Spirit. I pray too for those listening, that you would bless then with conviction of sin that turns into cries of praise.

1 Bristol.
2 See Psalm 40:3.
3 See Psalm 38:8.
4 From *Methodism.*

June 23RD

For the word of God is alive and active. Sharper than any double-edged sword, it penetrates even to dividing soul and spirit, joints and marrow; it judges the thoughts and attitudes of the heart

(Hebrews 4:12 *NIV*)

Wesley preached to the women in Newgate Gaol in Bristol:

I was insensibly led to declare strongly and explicitly that God "willeth all men to be saved";[1] and to pray that "if this were not the truth of God, he would not suffer the blind to go out of the way; but if it were, he would bear witness to his word".

Immediately one, and another, and another sunk to the earth; they dropped on every side as thunderstruck. One of them cried aloud. We besought God on her behalf, and he turned her heaviness into joy.

A second being in the same agony, we called upon God for her also; and he spoke peace unto her soul.[2]

Lord, your word is powerful. Thank you for this testimony. Thank you for your grace, reaching into unlikely places with light and truth. I pray today for those who are called to preach and minister in difficult locations, taking the gospel outside the four walls of the church; bless their efforts, and bring your love and peace to many.

1 See 1 Timothy 2:4, *KJV*.
2 From *Methodism.*

June 24th

Miraculous signs will accompany those who believe

(Mark 16:17 *NLT*)

Strange events were often repeated during the first few years of Wesley's mission; there is even a case of a man who was ... relieved by reading one of Wesley's sermons. The pattern seems to have been much the same in most cases. The hearer became distressed ("cut to the heart", as Wesley puts it) by the realization of what sort of person he was (not specifically by the fear of Hell, for Wesley's preaching laid no special emphasis on that, though he has often been charged with threatening hell-fire in and out of season); distress turned to despair, which expressed itself physically in trembling and shrieking, and then in sinking unconscious to the ground. Meanwhile, Wesley and his friends prayed urgently for the afflicted one's release from torment, and usually peace and sober joy supervened as suddenly as the disturbance had arisen.[1]

Thank you, Lord, for blessing John Wesley's preaching ministry in these dramatic ways! Today I pray for preachers known to me, and I ask that you would confirm and encourage them in their work. Grant them signs confirming your word. Likewise, I pray for those who hear the word – touch their hearts with gracious conviction.

1 From *Methodism.*

June 25th

When the day of Pentecost came, they were all together in one place. Suddenly a sound like the blowing of a violent wind came from heaven and filled the whole house

(Acts 2:1, 2 *NIV*)

"On the first night of the new year," says Wesley, "Mr Hall, Kinchin, Ingham, Whitefield, Hutchins, and my brother Charles were present at our love-feast, with about sixty of our brethren.[1]

"About three in the morning, as we continued in prayer, the power of god came mightily upon us, so much so that many cried out for exceeding joy, and many fell to the ground. As soon as we recovered a little from that awe and amazement at the presence of His Majesty, we broke out with one voice, *We praise thee, O God: we acknowledge thee to be the Lord*."[2]

"It was a Pentecost season, indeed," says Whitefield: "sometimes whole nights were spent in prayer. Often have we been filled as with new wine;[3] and often I have seen them overwhelmed with the divine presence, and cry out, 'Will God indeed dwell with men upon earth? How dreadful[4] is this place! This is no other than the house of God and the gate of heaven!'"[5, 6]

Almighty God, grant me those moments of awe when I worship you. Enable me to gaze upon at least a glimpse of your majesty.

1 Members and friends of the Fetter Lane Society, London.
2 Te Deum Laudamus, an early Christian hymn of praise.
3 Matthew 9:17.
4 Awesome, not terrible.
5 See Genesis 28:17, *KJV*.
6 From *John Wesley*.

JUNE 26TH

THE SPIRIT OF THE SOVEREIGN LORD IS ON ME, BECAUSE THE LORD HAS ANOINTED ME TO PROCLAIM GOOD NEWS TO THE POOR. HE HAS SENT ME TO BIND UP THE BROKENHEARTED, TO PROCLAIM FREEDOM FOR THE CAPTIVES AND RELEASE FROM DARKNESS FOR THE PRISONERS

(Isaiah 61:1 *NIV*)

The first violent case which occurred, was that of a middle-aged woman … who for three years had been "under strong convictions of sin, and in such a terror of mind, that she had no comfort in anything, nor any rest day or night". The minister of her parish, whom she had consulted, assured her husband that she was stark mad, and advised him to send immediately for a physician; and the physicians being of the same opinion she was bled, blistered, and drenched accordingly. One evening in a meeting where Wesley was expounding to five or six hundred persons, she suddenly cried out as if in the agonies of death, and appeared to some of those about her to be in that state; others, however, who began to have some experience in such cases, understood that it was the crisis of her spiritual struggles. "We prayed," says Wesley in a letter to Whitefield, "that God who had brought her to the birth would give her the strength to bring forth, and that he would work speedily that all might see it, and fear, and put their trust in the Lord … Five days she travailed and groaned being in bondage; then," he continues, "our Lord got himself the victory," and from that time the woman was full of joy and love, and thanksgivings were rendered on her account.[1]

Victorious God, I bring to your throne of grace today, those who are trapped by sin of any kind. I think of addicts, and those who are beset by sin. In your mercy, break their chains and replace their misery with joy, as only you can.

1 From *John Wesley*.

June 27th

Keep your servant also from wilful sins; may they not rule over me. Then I will be blameless, innocent of great transgression

(Psalm 19:13 *NIV*)

Methodism in London had reached its highest point of extravagance ... and these things gave offence at first, and caused disputes in the Society. Charles Wesley thought them "no sign of grace"...

Another woman was affected under more remarkable circumstances: Wesley visited her because she was "above measure enraged at the *new way*, and zealous in opposing it". He argued with her till he perceived that argument had its usual effect of inflaming more and more a mind that was already feverish. He then broke off the dispute and asked that she would join him in prayer, and she so far consented as to kneel down: this was, in fact, submitting herself.

"In a few minutes she fell into an extreme agony both of body and soul, and soon after cried out with the utmost earnestness, 'Now I know I am forgiven for Christ's sake!' ... From that hour God set her face as a flint to declare the faith,[1] which before she persecuted." This Wesley calls one of the most surprising instances of divine power that he ever remembered to have seen.[2]

Almighty God, your power is great, but your love is greater. Thank you for this testimony. Assist me, Lord, always to bend my will to yours, and to place my life in submission, lest I deprive myself of a blessing.

1 See Isaiah 50:7.
2 From *John Wesley*.

June 28th

Luke, the beloved doctor

(Colossians 4:14 *NLT*)

The Apoplexy.*

To prevent, use the cold bath, and drink only water.

In the fit, put a handful of salt into a pint of cold water, and if possible, pour it down the throat of the patient. He will quickly come to himself. So will someone who seems dead by a fall. But send for a good physician immediately.

If the fit is soon after a meal, do not bleed the patient, but induce vomiting.

Rub the head, feet and hands strongly, and let two strong men carry the patient upright, backward and forward about the room.

A Seton[1] in the neck, with a low diet, has often prevented a relapse.

*An Apoplexy is a total loss of all sense, and voluntary motion, accompanied with a strong pulse, hard breathing, and snorting.[2]

Today, Lord, my thoughts and prayers turn towards surgeons, doctors and nurses working in chaotic, war-torn situations around the world, who seek to administer help and healing in chaotic, violent circumstances, often without the medicines they need or decent facilities. Bless them, I pray.

1 A surgical stitch.
2 From *Primitive Physic.*

June 29th

In his hand are the depths of the earth

(Psalm 95:4 *NIV*)

[Wesley] mounted his horse and took his first assignment among the miners of Kingswood, near Bristol. These dwellers of the coal-smeared regions had hardly ever been inside a church. No one had seen fit to build a house of God among them. They were so long used to working in the caverns of the earth, they had forgotten Heaven.

Wesley preached to them as they emerged from their mines in the sunset. He selected what he pleased out of the liturgy, and led them in the singing of simple hymns. And the men who had seen nothing but darkness wept a few tears.

Then he left for other village folk who needed him, galloping throughout the countryside of England. And wherever he spoke, he comforted the people. And infuriated the priests. For he invaded their parishes and emptied their churches. What right had this traditionally ordained minister to break the rules of the Church of England and to preach wherever he willed? "I look upon the whole world as my parish!" Surely these were the words of a lunatic. A man with a messianic complex who would destroy the Church itself given the chance.[1]

Thank you, Lord, for those who are concerned to share the gospel with those "outside" the established church – those who take the good news of Christ into the workplace. I pray today for industrial chaplains and all those whose particular ministry is to reach people who might otherwise not hear about Jesus.

1 From *Living Biographies of Religious Leaders.*

June 30th

You gave abundant showers, O God; you refreshed your weary inheritance

(Psalm 68:9 *NIV*)

The very manner of his preaching, declared the priests, was a proof of his madness. People wept and shouted aloud and rolled wailing on the floor in response to his impassioned words. At one of his "conversions", it was reported, "people swooned, sank down on the ground as if dead ... shrieked and trembled in every limb ... A domestic servant remained in a trance-like condition, as if possessed ... and she did not recover properly for fourteen hours." Such was the technique of the revivalist who had cast aside all the outward decorum of the Church ceremony and who called for the soul to testify aloud to the joyousness of its conversion to the revealed truth. All this was very un-English! "Pretending to extraordinary revelations is a horrid thing, a very horrid thing." But Wesley was not ashamed of his work – even if a few of his converts were oversensitive to suggestion and lost themselves in a hysteria of emotion. The vast majority received his message sensibly where it belonged – in their hearts – like a drink of fresh rain after the musty theological disputations of the Sunday sermons in the parish churches.[1]

Oh, Lord, deliver us, please, from musty theological disputations! Yours is not a musty gospel, and there is nothing musty about salvation. Pour fresh rain over your Church, and plenty of it.

1 From *Living Biographies of Religious Leaders.*

July 1st

One of the criminals who hung there hurled insults at him: "Aren't you the messiah? Save yourself and us!" But the other criminal rebuked him. "Don't you fear God," he said, "since you are under the same sentence? We are punished justly, for we are getting what our deeds deserve. But this man has done nothing wrong." Then he said, "Jesus, remember me when you come into your Kingdom." Jesus answered him, "Truly I tell you, today you will be with me in paradise"

(Luke 23:39–43 *NIV*)

Driven out of many churches, the Wesleys went to the prisons and hospitals, and wherever they went and preached and expounded the word of God, souls seem to have been awakened, and many turned to the Lord . . .

Wesley records in his journal: … My brother and I went, at their earnest desire, to do the last good office to the condemned malefactors.[1] It was the most glorious instance I ever saw of faith triumphing over sin and death. One, observing the tears run fast down the cheeks of one of them in particular, while his eyes were steadily fixed upwards, a few moments before he died, asked, "How do you feel your heart now?"

He calmly replied, "I feel a peace which I could not believe to be possible; and I know it is the peace of God which passeth all understanding."[2], [3]

Heavenly Father, your mercy extends to the prisoner on death row and the prisoner on the cross – you are truly the God of "last minute grace"! Thank you, Lord, that the gracious offer of salvation extends until our dying breath.

1 Prisoners on "Death Row", awaiting execution.
2 Philippians 4:7, *KJV*.
3 From *Rev. John Wesley*.

July 2ND

A bishop is a supervisor appointed by God

(Titus 1:7 GWT)

Wesley left for Oxford, and spent Saturday evening with "a little company" … He was grieved to find that prudence had made them leave off singing psalms, and was afraid it would not stop there. "God deliver me," he wrote, "and all that seek him in sincerity, from what the world calls Christian prudence."

The Wesleys were both of them still tenacious of "Church order"; they had done nothing, nor did they intend to do anything, which was contrary to that order. But it became necessary that they should give explanations to Dr Gibson, the Bishop of London.[1] The latter, we are told, was "of a mild and conciliatory temper, a distinguished antiquary, a sound scholar, equally frugal and beneficent, perfectly tolerant as becomes a Christian, and conscientiously attached as becomes a bishop to the doctrines and disciplines of the Church."[2]

When John and Charles Wesley waited upon him "to justify their conduct", he said to them, in reference to that tenet which now notoriously characterized their preaching, "If by assurance you mean an inward persuasion, whereby a man is conscious in himself, after examining his life by the law of God and weighing his own sincerity, that he is in a state of salvation and acceptable to God, I do not see how any good Christian can be without such an assurance."[3]

Being a bishop, Lord, is a tremendous privilege, yet a heavy responsibility – having to handle church disputes and make judgments on situations when, at best, only half the people know only half the story at any one time. Bless bishops, I pray, and all those in positions of senior leadership within the Church, across the denominations. I pray for the leaders of my own denomination.

1 Edmund Gibson (1669–1748).

2 Noted by Abel Stevens, American clergyman, writer and editor who wrote about Methodism and studied its history.

3 From *Rev. John Wesley*.

As thy days, so shall thy strength be

(Deuteronomy 33:25 *KJV*)

Sun. 13 [May 1739] – My ordinary employment, in public, was now as follows:

Every morning I read prayers and preached at Newgate.[1] Every evening I expounded a portion of Scripture at one or more of the societies.

On Monday, in the afternoon, I preached abroad, near Bristol; on Tuesday, at Bath and Two Mile Hill alternately; on Wednesday, at Baptist mills; every other Thursday, near Pensford; every other Friday, in another part of Kingswood; on Saturday in the afternoon, and Sunday morning, in the Bowling-green (which lies near the middle of the city); on Sunday, at eleven, near Hannam-mount; at two, at Clifton; and at five on Rose-green.[2]

And hitherto, as my days, so my strength has been.[3]

What a schedule! Lord, strengthen and uphold busy ministers. I pray for my own minister today. Please give him/her the energy he/she needs.

1 Newgate Prison, London.
2 Areas in or around Bristol and Bath, south-west England.
3 From *John Wesley's Journal (Abridged)*.

He thunders with his majestic voice

(Job 37:4 *NIV*)

Sun. 20 [May 1739] – Seeing many of the rich at Clifton church,[1] my heart was much pained for them, and I was earnestly desirous that some even of them might "enter into the Kingdom of Heaven"[2] … I did not know where to begin in warning them to flee from the wrath to come[3] until my Testament opened with these words: "I came not to call the righteous, but sinners to repentance"[4] … I could have cried out … "Give me where to stand, and I will shake the earth."[5]

God sent lightning with the rain, but that did not hinder about fifteen hundred from staying at Rose-green. Our Scripture was, "It is the glorious God that maketh the thunder. The voice of the Lord is mighty in operation; the voice of the Lord is a glorious voice."[6] In the evening [the Lord] spoke to three whose souls were all storm and tempest, and immediately there was a great calm.[7, 8]

You, Lord, are Almighty God.

1 Clifton is one of the oldest and most affluent areas of Bristol.
2 Possibly a reference to Matthew 19:24.
3 See Luke 3:7, *KJV*.
4 Luke 5:32–34, *KJV*.
5 From Archimedes, when he was demonstrating his scientific principle of the lever; "Give me a lever and a place to stand and I will move the earth".
6 See Psalm 29, *KJV*.
7 Possibly, a reference to Mark 4:35–41.
8 From *John Wesley's Journal (Abridged)*.

When one of you says, "I am a follower of Paul," and another says, "I follow Apollos," aren't you acting just like people of the world?

(1 Corinthians 3:4 *NLT*)

It is very important to be sure which of Charles [Wesley's] hymns were authorized by John, because the known divergencies of view of the brothers have caused people to say of the sentiments of Charles which they disliked, "Oh, that is Charles, not John, but I am a John, not a Charles, Wesleyan."

In point of fact, no Methodist hymn-book was more endorsed by John Wesley [than *Hymns on the Lord's Supper*].[1] His name, along with that of Charles', was printed on the title page of every edition; the book had the widest circulation,[2] with the exception of General Collections, of all their hymn-books.

Internal evidence and structure suggest that Charles was the author of nearly all these hymns, but there are a few which … may well be John's, who was probably responsible for the emended verses of George Herbert[3] which are the "highest church" of them all. No book more characteristic of the beliefs of the Wesleys was ever published by them.[4]

Lord, help it not to matter too much to me who wrote the hymns, so long as they point me to Jesus.

1 Published 1745.
2 This ran to ten editions, the tenth being published in 1792.
3 1593–1633, poet, orator and Anglican priest.
4 From *The Evangelical Doctrines of Charles Wesley's Hymns.*

July 6th

You say you have faith, for you believe that there is one God. Good for you! Even the demons believe this, and they tremble in terror

(James 2:19 *NLT*)

There is yet one more thing that may be … considered … which is implied in being *altogether a Christian*; and that is the ground of everything – faith. Very excellent things are spoken of faith throughout the oracles of God. "Everyone," says the beloved disciple, "that believeth is born of God."[1] "To as many as received him, gave he power to become the Sons of God, even to them that believe on his name."[2] And "this is the victory that overcometh the world, even our faith."[3] Our Lord himself declares, "He that believeth in the Son hath everlasting life: and cometh not into condemnation, but is passed from death unto life."[4]

But let no one deceive their own soul. It should be noted that faith which fails to bring forth repentance, and love, and all good works, is not a right faith, but a dead and devilish one. Even the devils believe that Christ was born of a virgin; that he wrought all kinds of miracles, declaring himself very God; that for our sakes he suffered a most painful death, to redeem us from death everlasting; that he rose again the third day; that he ascended into heaven, and sits at the right hand of the Father, and at the end of the world shall come again as judge. The devils believe all that is written in the Old and New Testament. Yet, for all this faith, they are but devils. They remain still in their damnable state, lacking the true Christian faith.[5]

Thank you, Lord, for this clear definition of true faith.

1 See 1 John 5:1, *KJV*.
2 See John 1:, 13, *KJV*.
3 1 John 5:4, *KJV*.
4 See John 5:24, *KJV*.
5 From *Fifty Three Sermons*.

July 7th

Our Father which art in Heaven, hallowed be thy name

(Matthew 6:9 *KJV*)

Verse 9. *Our Father* – Who is good and gracious to all, our Creator, our Preserver; the Father of our Lord, and of us in him, children by adoption and grace; not *my* Father only … but the Father of the universe, of angels and people.

Who art in Heaven – Beholding all things, both in Heaven and earth; knowing every creature, and all the works of every creature, and every possible event from everlasting to everlasting; the almighty Lord and Ruler of all, superintending all things.

In Heaven – supreme there, but not there alone, filling Heaven and earth.

Hallowed be thy name – Truly known by all intelligent beings, with affection corresponding to that knowledge; honoured, loved, feared, by all in Heaven and earth, by angels and by people![1]

So many marvellous points, Heavenly Father, in just one verse! Yet, they represent but a glimpse of your greatness. You are God, my Father. Impress that thought upon my heart and soul today, I pray.

1 From *Notes on the New Testament.*

July 8th

Thy kingdom come, thy will be done in earth, as it is in Heaven. Give us this day our daily bread

(Matthew 6:10, 11 *KJV*)

Verse 10. *Thy kingdom come* – May your kingdom of grace come quickly, and swallow up all the kingdoms of the earth! May all humankind, receiving Christ as king, truly believing in your name, be filled with righteousness, and peace, and joy; with holiness and happiness, until they are removed into your kingdom of joy, to reign with you for ever and ever.

Thy will be done on earth as it is in Heaven – May all the inhabitants of the earth do your will as willingly as the holy angels! May these do it continually even as they, without any interruption of their willing service; yes, and as perfectly as the angels! Spirit of grace, through the blood of the everlasting covenant, make them perfect in every good work to do your will, and work in them all that is pleasing in your sight!

Verse 11. *Give us* – O Father (from whom we claim nothing of right or merit, but only of your free mercy) *this day* (for we take no thought for tomorrow)[1] *our daily bread* – all that is needful for our souls and bodies; not only "the meat that perisheth",[2] but the sacramental bread too, your grace, the food "which endureth to everlasting life".[3, 4]

Lord, thank you for these helpful insights. Lord, in your mercy, hear my prayer.

1 See Matthew 6:34, *KJV*.
2 John 6:27, *KJV*.
3 John 6:27, *KJV*.
4 From *Notes on the New Testament*.

July 9th

SHE SAID TO HERSELF, "IF I ONLY TOUCH HIS CLOAK, I WILL BE HEALED"

(Matthew 9:21 *NIV*)

Unclean, of life and heart unclean,
How shall I in his sight appear?
Conscious of my inveterate sin
I blush and tremble to draw near;
Yet, through the garment of his word,
I humbly seek to touch my Lord.[1]

Lord, the language of this hymn may be outdated, but the glorious truth it contains is as relevant as ever; we are indeed unclean, and unworthy, yet your word promises grace, and in Christ we see more than enough mercy to cover every sin. This is humbling. This is true. This is God.

1 Written by John Wesley (as opposed to translated). From the Wesley manuscripts: www.hymntime.com

July 10th

Jesus turned and saw her

(Matthew 9:22 *NIV*)

Turn then, thou good physician, turn,
Thou source of unexhausted love;
Sole comforter of souls forlorn,
Who only canst my plague remove,
O cast a pitying look on me
Who dare not lift mine eyes to thee![1]

Lord, you see those who reach out to you. You are not a distant deity; not remote, not unfeeling. You notice, and nothing in our lives escapes your attention. This is true. This is God.

1 As July 9th.

July 11th

"Take heart, daughter," he said, "your faith has healed you." And the woman was healed at that moment

(Matthew 9:22 *NIV*)

Yet will I in my God confide,
Who comes to meet my seeking soul;
I wait to feel thy blood applied,
Thy blood applied shall make me whole;
And lo! I trust thy gracious power
To touch, and heal me, in this hour.[1]

Lord Jesus, I pray for those in need of your healing touch today; bless them with your comforting presence. I pray too, for those caring for those who are ill; friends, neighbours, relatives, patients. Bless them all according to their needs.

1 As July 10th.

July 12th

We cannot but speak of what we have seen and heard

(Acts 4:20 *ESV*)

I was almost continually asked, either by those who purposely came to Bristol to enquire concerning this strange work, or by my old and new correspondents, "How can these things be?" [Signs and wonders following the preaching of the word.]

Innumerable cautions were given me (generally grounded on gross misinterpretations of things), to disregard visions or dreams, and I was cautioned not to think people had received remission of their sins just because of their cries, or tears, or outward professions. To someone who had written to me many times on this subject, my answer was as follows:

"The chief question is that you deny God now works in these ways. I have heard these things with my own ears, and have seen with my eyes. I have seen (so far as this kind of thing can be seen) many people changed in a moment from a spirit of fear, horror, despair, to the spirit of love, joy, and peace: and from sinful desire, until then reigning over them, to a pure desire for doing the will of God. These are matters of fact, and I am an eye and ear witness."[1]

Lord, I may not always understand your works. Nevertheless, keep me ready to share words of testimony to what I have seen and heard of you, even if I risk being misunderstood.

1 From *John Wesley's Journal (Abridged)*.

July 13th

The Spirit lifted me up and brought me to the exiles …
in the vision given by the Spirit of God

(Ezekiel 11:24 *NIV*)

"What I have to say concerning visions or dreams, is this:

"I know several people in whom this great change was brought about through a dream, or during a strong representation to the eye of their mind, of Christ either on the cross or in glory.

"This is the fact; let anyone judge of it as they please. The fact that such a change was then wrought appears from the whole tenor of their life thereafter, not from their shedding tears only, or falling into a fit, or crying out – these are not the fruits whereby I judge. They were wicked in many ways, but from that time on, just, holy, and good. I could show you the man who was a lion, but then a lamb; a drunkard, but now sober. These are living arguments for what I now assert.

"If these things be not so, then I am a false witness before God. But to these things I will, by his grace, testify."[1]

Almighty God, grant me discernment in such matters; not to dismiss the supernatural simply because it is unusual, but to check all things to see if they are from you. Thank you, Lord, for changed lives touched by your power.

1 From *John Wesley's Journal (Abridged).*

July 14th

I am compelled to preach. Woe to me if
I do not preach the gospel!

(1 Corinthians 9:16 *NIV*)

When Wesley was questioned regarding holding out-of-door services without the consent of the local clergymen, he replied:

"You ask, 'How is it that I assemble Christians who are not under my charge, to sing psalms, and pray, and hear the Scriptures expounded … in other men's parishes?'

"Permit me to speak plainly … Any means other than Scriptural means carry no weight with me. I allow no other rule, whether of faith or practice, than the Holy Scriptures; and on Scriptural principles I do not think it hard to justify what I do. God in Scripture commands me, according to my power, to instruct the ignorant, reform the wicked, confirm the virtuous. Man forbids me to do this in another's parish; effectively, to do it at all, seeing as I have no parish of my own. Whom then shall I hear – God or man? … Woe is me if I preach not the Gospel. But where shall I preach it if I apply the principles you mention? In Europe, Asia, or America? For all these are, after a sort, divided into parishes. How could I return to Georgia and preach, according to your principles, for all the heathens there now belong to the parish either of Savannah or Frederica."[1]

Lord, the fact of the matter is, horses neigh, fish swim, canaries sing, and preachers preach! Bless those who are facing opposition today. Strengthen them so that they are not discouraged.

1 From *Rev. John Wesley.*

July 15th

[Jesus] made himself nothing by taking the very nature of a servant

(Philippians 2:7 *NIV*)

It must have required some amount of moral courage in a gentleman, well born and well educated as Wesley was, the distinguished Fellow of an Oxford College, to mount upon a table, or on the stump of a tree, or climb into a cart, and then, attired in his [clerical] gown and bands, preach to a multitude of unwashed, uncombed, uncultivated people, down whose swarthy faces tears marked little white channels, as they hung upon his words.

Anyhow, the sight seemed so wonderful that it attracted the notice of the "higher classes", and frequently among the crowd were to be seen their carriages.

Wesley ... spoke just as fearlessly to these nobility and gentry as to the poorer people, on which account he came to be considered by some as a rude, ill-mannered person.[1]

Your gospel, Lord, is for the whosoever – rich and poor, washed and unwashed. Thank you, Lord, that our salvation depends upon your grace, not upon our worthiness. This is good news for everyone!

1 From *Rev. John Wesley.*

July 16th

Do not worry about what to say or how to say it. At that time you will be given what to say, for it will not be you speaking, but the Spirit of your Father speaking through you

(Matthew 10:19, 20 *NIV*)

During a visit to ... Bath, which was at that time a centre of fashionable life, a notoriously bad character, called "Beau" Nash ... attempted to stop Wesley's meetings. Shortly after the preacher had begun his sermon, the dandy appeared in gorgeous array, impudently demanding "By what authority dare you do what you are doing now?" "By the authority of Jesus Christ, conveyed to me by him who is now Archbishop of Canterbury, when he laid his hands upon my head and said, 'Take thou authority to preach the Gospel,'" answered Mr Wesley deliberately. "But this is a conventicle,"[1] said Nash, "and contrary to Act of Parliament." "No," answered Wesley, "conventicles are seditious meetings, but here is no sedition; therefore it is not contrary to Act of Parliament." "I say it is," stormed the fellow; "and, besides, your preaching frightens people out of their wits." "Sir," said Wesley, "did you ever hear me preach?" "No." "How can you judge of what you have never heard?" "I judge by common report." "Is not your name Nash?" asked Wesley. "It is," said the "Beau." "Well, sir, I dare not judge *you* by common report," was Mr Wesley's stinging reply. The pretentious fop was confounded.[2]

Lord, you gave Wesley the right words at the right moment. I pray today for any of your people who are called to account for their witness, in lands hostile to Christianity. Give them courage, Lord, and speed of mind as they speak.

1 An unlawful religious gathering.
2 From *Rev. John Wesley.*

See to it that no one takes you captive through hollow and deceptive philosophy, which depends on human tradition and the elemental spiritual forces of this world rather than on Christ

(Colossians 2:8 *NIV*)

[Wesley's] opponents were trying to involve him in controversies ... Did he believe in salvation by faith, by grace through good works, or by the predetermined election of the Holy Few?

They sent letters to the press seeking to draw him out and to indict him on the ground of his intellectual conviction. What *was* his conviction? They kept asking him again and again.

And finally he replied to the Calvinists[1] and the Anabaptists[2] and the Atinomians[3] and all the other doctors of the various schools who wrote learned treatises on the articles of faith. "You would have philosophical religion, but there can be no such thing. Religion is the plainest and simplest thing in the world. It is only this – *We love him, because he first loved us*."[4, 5]

Thank you, God, for John Wesley!

1 A branch of Protestant Christianity following the theological traditions of John Calvin (1509–64). Calvinists stress the doctrine of predestination.

2 Protestant Christians who stressed the importance of "baptizing again" – that is, if a person was converted to Christianity as an adult, having been baptized as a baby, then re-baptism was regarded as necessary to salvation.

3 Antinomians believe that Christians are released by grace from following the moral law. "Antinomianism" comes from the Greek for "lawless". Their views on Old Testament laws are controversial.

4 1 John 4:19, *KJV*.

5 From *Living Biographies of Religious Leaders*.

July 18th

By His breath the heavens are cleared

(Job 26:13 *NASB*)

The Asthma.*

Take a pint of cold water every morning washing the head therein immediately after, and using the cold bath once a fortnight.

Or, cut an ounce of stick liquorice into slices. Steep this is a quart of water, four and twenty hours, and use it, when you are worse than usual, as common drink. I have known this give much ease.

Or, half a pint of tar-water,[1] twice a day.

Or, live a fortnight on boiled carrots only. It seldom fails.

Or, take an ounce of quicksilver[2] every morning, and a spoonful of Aqua Sulphurataor,[3] or fifteen drops of Elixir of Vitriol,[4] in a large glass of springwater at five in the evening. This has cured an inveterate asthma.

Or, take from ten to sixty drops of Elixir of Vitriol, in a glass of water, three or four times a day.

*An asthma is a difficulty of breathing from a disorder in the lungs. In the common (or moist) asthma, the patient spits much.[5]

Lord, to be honest, I don't really know what to make of Wesley's advice today! Would it be enough to pray for those who are sick, and for those who try to help them? Please bless them.

1 Pine tar and water.
2 Mercury.
3 Medicinal water.
4 Aromatic sulphuric acid.
5 From *Primitive Physic.*

July 19th

They remained for a long time, speaking boldly for the Lord, who bore witness to the word of his grace, granting signs and wonders to be done by their hands

(Acts 14:3 *ESV*)

One day, after Wesley had expounded the fourth chapter of Acts, the persons present "called upon God to confirm his word"[1] ... The last who called upon God as out of the belly of Hell, was a stranger in Bristol; and in a short time he also was overwhelmed with joy and love, knowing that God had healed his backslidings...

At another place, "a young man was suddenly seized with a violent trembling all over, and in a few minutes, the sorrows of his heart being enlarged,[2] sunk down to the ground; but we ceased not calling upon God, till he raised him up full of peace and joy in the Holy Ghost."[3, 4]

More of the same, please, Lord!

1 See Mark 16:20.
2 See Psalm 25:17.
3 See Romans 14:17.
4 From *John Wesley.*

July 20th

The weapons we fight with are not the weapons of the world. On the contrary, they have divine power to demolish strongholds

(2 Corinthians 10:4 *NIV*)

Wesley certainly thought at first that these happenings were the work of God, sent, as he says, to "confirm his word".

They became steadily rarer after the first extravagances, rarer, that is, when the Revival was rapidly gaining ground and was arousing expectation and excitement wherever Wesley went. He could not fail to notice this; he also observed that it was possible to counterfeit the emotions thus expressed. A man of his century could hardly be expected to reach a purely naturalistic explanation, especially when the after-effects of the convulsions were for the most part entirely good – immediate peace of mind, and afterwards an evident change of character. He therefore conceived the theory that the tremblings and agony were the work of Satan, making his last efforts to retain his victim, and that the ensuing peace indicated God's victory over the Adversary. After pondering the matter for many years he definitely rejected the view that they were necessary accompaniments of the work of grace; he admitted that the Devil sometimes had a hand in them; but claimed that "God suddenly and strongly convinced many.... the natural consequences whereof were sudden outcries and strong bodily convulsions."[1]

Lord, you want people to be free. Having said that, a battle takes place whenever anyone decides to move from the captivity of sin to the freedom of your love. I pray today for anyone caught in the thick of that spiritual battle; demonstrate your power and protection in their lives, I pray.

1 From *Methodism.*

July 21st

Put off your old self

(Ephesians 4:22 *ESV*)

Modern psychological man is bound to look at such things in a different light. He will at once think of exhibitionism, mass hysteria, and other states with even more sinister names than these.

Their presence, in a highly infectious form, cannot be denied. But it has to be noted that Wesley's words were working on highly suggestible but not necessarily neurotic people; he was saying things of tremendous import that they had never heard before, for their authorized pastors had neglected to teach them, and they were bound to be struck violently, both with dismay and with joy, as they thought first of their sins and then of God's incredible grace and mercy; and many, perhaps very many, of those who went through these shattering experiences continued for the rest of their lives in quiet and practical goodness. It may be that for them a sudden shock was the only, or the best, or at least a harmless way of appropriating divine truth. And it should be remembered that the vast majority of Wesley's converts over the years, and perhaps even in Bristol in the early years, never went through such experiences at all.[1]

Lord, I don't suppose it matters too much, really, how lives are changed, so long as they are changed. How you work is a sovereign matter. Life-changing God, I pray today for those known to me personally whose lives need your touch. Bless them as I think of them just now.

1 From *Methodism.*

July 22nd

Give us this day our daily bread. And forgive us our debts, as we forgive our debtors. And lead us not into temptation, but deliver us from evil

(Matthew 6:11–13 *KJV*)

Verse 12. *And forgive us our debts, as we also forgive our debtors* – Give us, O Lord, redemption in thy blood, the forgiveness of sins, as thou enablest us freely and fully to forgive every man, so do thou forgive all our trespasses.

Verse 13. And lead us not into temptation, but deliver us from evil – Whenever we are tempted, O thou that helpest our infirmities, suffer us not to "enter into temptation"; or to be overcome, or to suffer loss. Make a way for us to escape, so that we may be more than conquerors,[1] through thy love, over sin and all the consequences of it.

Now, the principal desire of a Christian's heart being the "daily bread" of soul and body (the support of life, animal and spiritual), pardon of sin, and deliverance from the power of it and of the Devil; there is nothing more than a Christian can wish for; this prayer comprehends all his desires. Eternal life is the consequence, or rather completion, of holiness.[2]

Lord, I give you my day. I want to start this day with a clean slate in your sight, so I pray for your forgiveness for any outstanding sins. Please, as I navigate all that today will bring, guard me and guide me at every step.

1 Romans 8:37.
2 From *Notes on the New Testament.*

When the Son of Man comes, will he find faith on the earth?

(Luke 18:8 *NIV*)

The right and true Christian faith is ... not only to believe that Holy Scripture and the Articles of our Faith are true,[1] but also to have a sure trust and confidence to be saved from eternal damnation by Christ.

It is a sure trust and confidence which a man has in God that, by the merits of Christ, his sins are forgiven, and he is reconciled to the favour of God; whereof follows a loving heart to obey his commandments.

Whoever has such faith, which "purifies the heart"[2] (by the indwelling power of God) from pride, anger, desire, "from all unrighteousness",[3] from "all filthiness of flesh and spirit";[4] filling it with love stronger than death,[5] both towards God and all mankind; love that does the works of God and is spent for all men, and that endures with joy not only the reproach of Christ, being mocked, despised and hated (including whatever the wisdom of God permits men and devils to inflict) – whoever has this faith, outworking it with love, is not almost only, but altogether, a Christian.[6]

Lord, I like Wesley's description of the fruits of authentic faith. I invite you today to impart faith to my heart, so that the fruit of my life this day may please you.

1 *The Thirty Nine Articles of Religion (1562) – Church of England.*
2 See Acts 15:9.
3 1 John 1:9, *KJV*.
4 See 2 Corinthians 7:1.
5 See Song of Solomon 8:6.
6 From *Fifty Three Sermons.*

July 24th

You shall love the Lord your God

(Deuteronomy 6:5 *ESV*)

Are not many of you conscious that you never came thus far; that you have not even been *almost a Christian*; that you have not come up to the standard of heathen honesty ... much less hath God seen sincerity in you, any real intent of pleasing him in all things. You never so much as intended to devote all your words and works, your business, your studies, your pastimes, to his glory. You never even desired or intended that whatever you did should be done "in the name of the Lord Jesus"[1] and as such should be "a spiritual sacrifice, acceptable to God through Christ".[2]

But supposing you had – do good intentions and desires make a Christian? By no means, unless they are turned into actions. "Hell is paved," the saying goes, "with good intentions."[3] The great question of all, then, still remains. Is the love of God shed abroad in your heart? Can you cry out, "My God, and my All"? Do you desire nothing but him? Are you happy in God? Is He your glory, your delight, your crown of rejoicing?[4] And is this commandment written in your heart, "That he who loveth God his brother also"?[5] Do you then love your neighbour as yourself[6] ... even your enemies?[7, 8]

Lord, sit with me as I ponder these questions, I pray.

1 Colossians 3:17.
2 1 Peter 2:5.
3 "The way of sinners is made plaine with stones, but at the ende thereof is the pit of hell," *KJV* Apocrypha.
4 See 1 Thessalonians 2:19, 20.
5 See 1 John 4:21, *KJV*.
6 Mark 12:31.
7 Matthew 5:44.
8 From *Fifty Three Sermons*.

July 25th

Do your best to get here before winter

(2 Timothy 4:21 *NIV*)

Our servant[1] came up and said, "Sir, there is no travelling today; such a quantity of snow has fallen in the night, that the roads are quite filled up." I told him, "At least we can walk twenty miles a day, with our horses in our hands." So in the name of God we set out. The north-east wind was piercing as a sword, and had driven the snow into such uneven heaps, that the main road was not passable: however, we kept on, on foot or on horseback, till we came to the White Lion, at Grantham.[2]

Some from Grimsby[3] had appointed to meet us here; but not hearing anything of them (for they were at another house, by mistake) after an hour's rest, we set out straight for Epworth. On the road we overtook a clergyman and his servant, but the toothache[4] quite shut my mouth: we reached Newark[5] about five. Soon after we were set down, another clergyman came and inquired for our fellow-traveller: it was not long before we engaged in close conversation.[6]

Thank you, Lord, my fellow-travellers on life's journey; those who are there when mistakes happen, when the elements are hostile, or when life can be painful. I thank you today, Lord, for such friends, and for experiences shared over the years. They have been your gift to me.

1 It was the norm for clergy to employ "servants" – often young men (teenagers) responsible for a variety of menial tasks.
2 Lincolnshire, England.
3 Lincolnshire, England.
4 John Wesley subsequently tried electrifying himself through the teeth as a cure for his toothache!
5 Nottinghamshire, England.
6 From *The Journal of the Rev. John Wesley, Volume 2.*

July 26th

HE DID NOT WAVER THROUGH UNBELIEF REGARDING THE PROMISE OF GOD, BUT WAS STRENGTHENED IN HIS FAITH

(Romans 4:20 *NIV*)

... Another clergyman came and inquired for our fellow-traveller: it was not long before we engaged in close conversation. He told me some of our preachers had frequently preached in his parish; and his judgment was that their preaching ... had done some good, but more harm, because those who attended it had only turned from one wickedness to another; they had only exchanged Sabbath-breaking, swearing, or drunkenness, for slandering, backbiting, and evil-speaking; and those who did attend it were provoked to return evil for evil so that the former were, in effect, no better; the latter worse than before. The same objection ... has been made in most other parts of England; it therefore deserves a serious answer...

I concede that our preaching has done some good; common swearers, Sabbath-breakers, drunkards, thieves, fornicators, have been reclaimed from those outward sins ... "Those who have left their outward sins," it is affirmed, "have only changed drunkenness or Sabbath-breaking for backbiting and evil-speaking." I answer, if you affirm this of them all, it is notoriously false. We came name many who left cursing, swearing and backbiting, drunkenness and evil-speaking altogether, and who are to this day just as fearful of slandering as they are of cursing or swearing, and if some of them are not yet aware enough of the Devil, we hope they will be soon. Meantime, see that you bless God for what he has done.[1]

Loving Father, I hold before you in prayer, those who are just stepping out in their Christian experience. Of course there will be stumbles and relapses along the way, but please help them to grown in faith and experience. In your love, never let them go.

1 From *The Journal of the Rev. John Wesley, Volume 2.*

JULY 27TH

WHEN THEY HAD SUNG A HYMN, THEY WENT OUT

(Matthew 26:30 *NIV*)

John Wesley's prefaces to hymn-books were among his most notable writings. Those of 1739 and 1740, for instance, give a key to the deep doctrinal purpose which underlies all his selections, and that of 1780 is among the best known of his compositions:

"In what other publication of the kind have you so distinct and full an account of Scriptural Christianity? Such a declaration of the heights and depths of religion, speculative and practical? So strong cautions against the most plausible errors: particularly those that are now prevalent? And so clear directions for making your calling and election sure;[1] for perfecting holiness in the fear of God?"

In other words, where is a better description of Methodism, which he himself calls Scriptural Christianity, to be found?[2]

Thank you, Lord, once again, for good hymns. Help me never to skip over the truths held within their lines, even if the tunes to which they are sung are familiar.

1 See 2 Peter 1:10.

2 From *The Evangelical Doctrines of Charles Wesley's Hymns.*

July 28th

In Christ we, though many, form one body

(Romans 12:5 *NIV*)

[The Large Hymn-Book] is a theological manifesto ... [disclosing] the mind of John Wesley.

It is "A collection of hymns for the use of the people called Methodists". The collection generally used until 1780 was published in 1752 and entitled: "Hymns and spiritual songs intended for the use of real Christians *of all denominations*". Wesley carefully formulated the 1752 title ... as a protest against bigotry: "It is hoped that the ensuing collection of hymns may in some measure contribute, through the blessing of God, to advance the glorious end, to promote the spirit of freedom, not confined to any one opinion or party."

In 1780, however, he collected and arranged hymns, not for all denominations, but particularly for his own people. It was meant to be definitely a Methodist hymn-book. Later he fell back on variants of the 1752 title in his pocket hymn-books of 1785 and 1787, but in the large hymn-book he desired to define his object of publishing a volume of hymns exclusively for Methodists.[1]

Lord of the Church, I thank you for Christian friends across different denominations. I give you thanks for my own denomination and church family, but I gladly pray for them too, and for your blessing upon their churches.

1 From *The Evangelical Doctrines of Charles Wesley's Hymns.*

July 29th

Personal vows

(2 Kings 12:4 *NIV*)

Whitefield's preaching had led to the foundation, before Wesley's arrival, of Religious Societies in Kingswood and Bristol. These were speedily enlarged and increased in number by Wesley. At the very start they received – partly from Whitefield, but much more from Wesley – the character which came to be known as distinctively Methodist.

The adjective most used for describing this is "experimental" ... it was the practice of Wesley to expound a passage of Scripture whenever he visited a Society, and he did so in personal terms, that is, he applied the message to those whom he saw before him; prayer was offered in the same personal manner, that those who were present might receive the benefits of salvation, be cured of their illnesses, and be helped in time of temptation.

Hymns were sung ... in other words, the whole emphasis was on a religion which was to be personally accepted, and on an experience of God's forgiveness and power and presence which was to be consciously enjoyed. And the only condition of membership of the Societies was "the desire to flee from the wrath to come".[1, 2]

Lord, your gospel is both universal and personal; you loved the world so much that you gave your only Son, yet that gift has to be received personally. Thank you, Lord, for saving my soul. Thank you that Jesus died for me personally.

1 Luke 3:7.
2 From *Methodism*.

JULY 30TH

AND HE LOOKED UP AND SAW THE RICH PUTTING THEIR GIFTS INTO THE TREASURY, AND HE SAW ALSO A CERTAIN POOR WIDOW PUTTING IN TWO MITES. SO HE SAID, "TRULY I SAY TO YOU THAT THIS POOR WIDOW HAS PUT IN MORE THAN ALL; FOR ALL THESE OUT OF THEIR ABUNDANCE HAVE PUT IN OFFERINGS FOR GOD, BUT SHE OUT OF HER POVERTY PUT IN ALL THE LIVELIHOOD THAT SHE HAD"

(Luke 21:1–4 NKJV)

I preached at Laseby[1] ... to a quiet and serious congregation. We reached Grimsby at five, and spoke to as many of the Society as could conveniently come at that time. At seven I would have preached to a very large audience; but a young gentleman with his companions quite drowned my voice, till a poor woman took up the cause, and, by remind him of a few incidents of his life, wittily turned the laughter of all his companions full upon him. He could not stand it, but hastened away. When he was gone, I went on with little interruption. I wrote to Mr C., giving him an account of the man's behaviour. He came straight to me and begged my pardon. Since that time we have had no disturbance at Grimsby...

I examined the little Society at Tetney.[2] I have never seen one like it in England ... I noticed that one member gave eight pence, often ten pence a week (the contribution for the poor), another, thirteen, fifteen, or even eighteen pence; another, sometimes one, two shillings. I asked Micah Elmoor (an Israelite indeed), "How is this? Are you the richest Society in England?" He answered, "I suppose not; but all of us, who are single people, have agreed together to give both ourselves and all we have to God: and we do it gladly, whereby we are able from time to time to entertain all the strangers that come to Tetney, who have no food to eat, nor any friend to give them a lodging."[3]

Lord Jesus, you gave your all for me. Help me to give my all for you.

1 Or Laseby, north-east Lincolnshire, England.
2 Lincolnshire, England.
3 From *The Journal of the Rev. John Wesley, Volume 2.*

JULY 31ST

AWAKE, THOU THAT SLEEPEST, AND ARISE FROM THE DEAD, AND CHRIST SHALL GIVE THEE LIGHT

(Ephesians 5:14 *KJV*)

I shall, with the help of God, describe the sleepers here spoken to. By sleep is signified the natural state of mankind; that deep sleep of the soul, into which the sin of Adam has cast all his descendants; that supineness, indolence, and stupidity, an insensibility to his real condition wherein everyone comes into the world until the voice of God awakes them … The natural state of mankind is a state of utter darkness; a state wherein "darkness covers the earth, and gross darkness the people".[1] The poor unawakened sinner, regardless of how much he may know about other things, has no knowledge of himself: in this respect "he knoweth nothing yet as he ought to know".[2] He knows not that he is a fallen spirit, whose only business in the present world is to recover from his fall, to regain that image of God in which he was created. He sees no necessity for the one thing needful, not even that inward change, that "birth from above"[3] … which is the beginning of that total renovation and sanctification of spirit, soul, and body, "without which no man shall see the Lord".[4, 5]

Gracious Father, I pray today for those known to me who are fast asleep, spiritually speaking. In your mercy, wake them up by shining the light of your love into their eyes and hearts. As friends and loved ones come to mind just now, I pray for them.

1 See Isaiah 60:2, *KJV*.
2 1 Corinthians 8:2, *KJV*.
3 See John 3.
4 Hebrews 12:14, *KJV*.
5 From *Fifty Three Sermons.*

August 1st

ENLARGE THE PLACE OF YOUR TENT, STRETCH YOUR TENT CURTAINS WIDE, DO NOT HOLD BACK; LENGTHEN YOUR CORDS, STRENGTHEN YOUR STAKES

(Isaiah 54:2 *NIV*)

That part of the Methodist discipline was introduced which [Wesley] had adopted from the Moravians, and male and female bands were formed … that the embers might meet together weekly, to confess their faults one to another, and pray one for another. "How dare any man," says Wesley, "deny this to be … a means of grace ordained by God?"

A more important measure was the foundation of the first Methodist preaching-house; and this, like the other steps which led inevitably to a separation from the Church [of England], was taken without any such intention, or any perception of its consequences. The rooms in which the societies at Bristol had hitherto met in Nicholas Street, Baldwin Street, and the Back Lane, were small, incommodious, and not entirely safe. They determined, therefore, to build a room large enough for all the members, and for as many of their acquaintances as might be expected to attend.[1]

Thank you, Lord, for churches that experience numerical and spiritual growth under your good hand. Bless them richly as they expand; give them new converts and premises to match. Meet their needs, I pray.

1 From *John Wesley.*

August 2nd

To God belong wisdom and power; counsel and understanding are his

(Job 12:13 *NIV*)

Thine, Lord, is wisdom, thine alone;
Justice and truth before thee stand:
Yet, nearer to thy sacred throne,
Mercy withholds thy lifted hand.

Each evening shows thy tender love,
Each rising morn thy plenteous grace;
Thy wakened wrath doth slowly move,
Thy willing mercy flies apace.

To thy benign, indulgent care,
Father, this light, this breath, we owe;
And all we have, and all we are,
From thee, great Source of being, flow.

Thrice Holy! thine the kingdom is,
The power omnipotent is thine;
And when created nature dies,
Thy never ceasing glories shine.[1]

You are God: uniquely wise, just and true. You are God: Tender, gracious, merciful. You are God: Holy Father, eternal and glorious. You are my God.

1 Ernst Lange. Translated from the German by John Wesley, in *Collection of Psalm and Hymns, 1737.*

August 3rd

If anyone is in Christ, the new creation has come:
The old has gone, the new is here!

(2 Corinthians 5:17 *NIV*)

[Wesley] proceeded to organize his thousands of followers into clubs of communicants after the Holy Club which he and his brother had formed in their Oxford days. All over England and Ireland and Wales these societies sprang up. Simple people they were who composed them – friendless bits of human wreckage, derelicts for whom nobody who *was* much cared much.

They gathered together twice a week and reported to one another how it was with their spirit and gave mutual advice and shared their all-but-empty purses with the sickliest and the most destitute among them. Many who had frequently come home reeling with drink now took an oath never to drink again, and chronic ruffians suddenly straightened up with a new light and set themselves to steady work. Soon it became apparent to all who could see that there was a new "lift" to the underdogs of the community. And the scoffers who had dubbed the new sect as *Methodists* because of the seriousness with which they laid down their systematic programme for spiritual conversion, began to wonder whether there wasn't a method to their madness after all.[1]

Life-changing God, your power to lift lives from the gutter is the same as it ever was. Today I pray for ministers, churches and organizations whose ministry specifically reaches "the least of these" – the destitute, the unwanted, the unwashed, and the marginalized. Bless them as they serve you in that particular way.

1 From *Living Biographies of Religious Leaders.*

I pray that they will all be one, just as you and I are one – as you are in me, Father, and I am in you. And may they be in us so that the world will believe you sent me

(John 17:21 *NLT*)

It [Methodism] was a religion of democracy that Wesley founded.

Anybody who was upright could join one of the Wesleyan clubs of High Conscience. A man's sect[1] didn't matter, provided he only loved Christ.

Wesley never attempted to turn anybody away from his belief. "My own belief," he said, "is no rule for another … If thou lovest God and all mankind, I ask no more: Give me thine hand."[2]

Welcoming God, thank you for the blessings of church unity, when denominations work together in the cause of Christ. I pray for such initiatives and efforts where I live, and ask that such visible unity may be a good witness.

1 Denomination.
2 From *Living Biographies of Religious Leaders.*

August 5th

We preach Christ crucified

(1 Corinthians 1:23 *NIV*)

In regard to [Wesley's] doctrine, we may say his chief and almost only aim was to explain to the people the plan of Scriptural salvation; for … almost all his texts have an immediate bearing on this the greatest of all pulpit themes.

Believing that he was himself in a state of salvation, his whole soul was bent upon expounding the truth which above all other truths is the means of saving sinners.[1]

Lord, I pray for those who preach the gospel of salvation, whether that be from a pulpit or in some other location. Inspire them. Touch the hearts of those who listen to their message, as you pursue them in love.

1 From *Rev. John Wesley.*

August 6th

You will know how people ought to conduct themselves in God's household

(1 Timothy 3:15 *NIV*)

Although there was nothing in the doctrine which Wesley preached to justify the clergymen of that time in prohibiting him from their pulpits, we can easily understand that some of the violent demonstrations which took place while he was preaching were exceedingly disliked by all who wished the worship of Almighty God to proceed with decency and in order…

Wesley's congregations were composed of every description of persons, who, without the slightest attempt at order, cried "Hurrah!" with one breath, and with the next burst into tears, while some poked each other's ribs, and others shouted "Hallelujah!" It was a jumble of extremes of good and evil; and so distracted alike were both preacher and hearers, that it was enough to make one cry to God for his interference. Here thieves, prostitutes, fools, people of every class, several men of distinction, a few of the learned, merchants, and numbers of poor people who had never entered a place of worship, assembled in crowds and became godly.[1]

Lord, it isn't always easy to accept noise and chaos in church – to be honest, it can sometimes be challenging! However, if people come to Christ in the midst of the interruptions, then please help me to see through the disturbances to the greater good.

1 From *Rev. John Wesley.*

August 7th

A Pharisee named Gamaliel ... addressed the Sanhedrin: "Men of Israel, consider carefully what you intend to do to these men ... I advise you: Leave these men alone! Let them go! For if their purpose or activity is of human origin, it will fail. But if it is from God, you will not be able to stop these men; you will only find yourselves fighting against God"

(Acts 5:34–39 *NIV*)

A Quaker, who stood by [as Wesley was preaching], was not a little displeased ... and was biting his lips and knitting his brows, when he dropped down as thunderstruck. The agony he was in was terrible to behold. We besought God not to lay folly to his charge; and he soon lifted up his heart, and cried aloud, "Now I know thou art a prophet of the Lord."

Another step in these manifestations was reached when these terrible emotions seized upon people in their own homes ... A zealous Churchman, one, too, who was against Dissenters of every denomination, being informed that people fell into strange fits at the "Societies", came to see and judge for himself. He then felt less satisfied than before, and so "went about to his acquaintance one after another," says Wesley, "and laboured above measure to convince them 'it was a delusion of the devil.' We were going home when one met us in the street and informed us that [he] was fallen raving mad."[1]

Lord of the Church, these experiences must have seemed strange, and even frightening. To be honest, I have some sympathy with those who were startled. However, help me, I pray, to be open-minded to what might be a work of your Spirit.

1 From *Rev. John Wesley*.

August 8th

My sanity was restored

(Daniel 4:36 *NIV*)

He was fallen raving mad…

It seems he had sat down to dinner, but had a mind first to end a sermon he had borrowed on "Salvation by Faith". In reading the last page he changed colour, fell off his chair, and began screaming terrible and beating himself against the ground.

His convulsions were frightful, the neighbours hurried in; and when Wesley too entered he was greeted with the exclamation, "This is he who said I was a deceiver of the people; but God has overtaken me. I said it was all a delusion, but this is no delusion."

Wesley prayed with him, and by-and-by he was quiet, and "both his soul and body were set at liberty".[1]

Thank you, Lord, for liberty in Christ – salvation, freedom – and for the holistic nature of the gospel. Your will for your people is restoration. You do not leave a job half-done.

1 From *Rev. John Wesley.*

AUGUST 9TH

LARGE CROWDS FROM GALILEE, THE DECAPOLIS, JERUSALEM, JUDEA, AND THE REGION ACROSS THE JORDAN FOLLOWED [JESUS]

(Matthew 4:25 *NIV*)

The street was full of people, hurrying to and fro, and speaking great words. But when any of them asked, "Which is he?" and I replied, "I am he," they were immediately silent.

Several ladies followed me into Mr Merchant's house, where there were some people who wanted to speak to me. I went to them, and said, "I believe, ladies, the maid was mistaken: you only wanted to look at me." I added, "I do not expect that the rich and the great should want either to speak with me, or to hear me; for I speak the plain truth – something you hear little of, and do not desire to hear." A few more words passed between us, and I left.[1]

This, Lord, is amusing in that John Wesley was being treated as something of a novelty, but sad, too, in that his message was of no interest. Forgive us, Lord, when personalities take priority over preaching. Help your Church to resist such mistakes. By your grace, may I follow only Jesus.

1 From *John Wesley's Journal (Abridged)*.

THE GOD OF PEACE BE WITH YOU ALL

(Romans 15:13 *NIV*)

A woman, feeling this strange agitation coming upon her, ran out of the meeting so that she could avoid being made a public spectacle, but so powerful was the mysterious influence to which she was a prey that she sank down in the street and had to be carried home, where Wesley found her in violent agony, which was removed while he prayed with her.

It is quite painful to read some of the cases reported by Wesley, but the wildest ravings never failed to give way to peace and calm while he as praying.[1]

Gracious Father, I pray that you will reach out in compassion to those who can find no peace; to those who are worried, or disturbed, or tormented. Bless them, Lord, with a peace that only you can provide. God of peace, be with them.

1 From *Rev. John Wesley.*

August 11th

In my name shall they cast out devils

(Mark 16:17 *NIV*)

Perhaps the worst case was that of an illiterate girl ... apparently taken ill at her own house. "It was a terrible scene," says Wesley. "Anguish, horror, and despair above all description appeared in her pale face; the thousand distortions of her body showed how the dogs of hell were gnawing her heart. The shrieks intermixed were scarce to be endured, but her stony eyes could not weep. She screamed out, as soon as words could find their way, 'I am damned, damned, for ever! Six days ago you might have helped me, but it is past; I am the devil's now, I have given myself to him. I will be his, I will serve him, I will go with him to hell!' She then began praying to the devil. We began singing – "Army of the Lord, awake, awake!" She immediately sunk down as asleep, but as soon as we left off, broke out again with inexhaustible vehemence, 'Stony hearts, break! I am a warning to you. Break, break, poor stony hearts! I am damned that you may be saved; you need not be damned, though I must.' We interrupted her by calling on God, on which she sank down as before, and another young woman began to roar out as she had done. We continued in prayer ... when God in a moment spoke peace unto the soul, first of the first tormented, and then of the other, and they both joined in singing praises to him who had stilled the enemy and the avenger."[1]

Almighty God, bring release to those who need your touch today; bring deliverance and release by your sovereign power. Visit those who are held captive.

1 From *Rev. John Wesley.*

August 12th

THE PRESIDENTS AND THE SATRAPS SOUGHT TO FIND A GROUND FOR COMPLAINT AGAINST DANIEL WITH REGARD TO THE KINGDOM, BUT THEY COULD FIND NO GROUND FOR COMPLAINT OR ANY FAULT, BECAUSE HE WAS FAITHFUL, AND NO ERROR OR FAULT WAS FOUND IN HIM

(Daniel 6:4 *ESV*)

John Wesley continued to "live by preaching". And this meant to live by toil and trouble. For the general public took none too kindly to any procedure which they could not clearly understand. This "Methodist business" baffled them. "The Methodist preachers are plotting some terrible overthrowal, else why do they 'sneak' into a man's home and convert his wife and get up five o'clock mornings and sing hymns all day long?"[1]

These preachers, it was rumoured, had organized into a secret society to overthrow the British monarchy ... "There can be no doubt of it!" A Methodist-inspired French invasion of England, it was whispered, might be expected hourly. "And Wesley is the cause of it all."[2, 3]

Lord, false accusations and "red herrings" are nothing new, but they can be an immense distraction, and the problem is, many people believe them to be true. Lord, give your people the presence of mind just to carry on regardless, trusting you to silence such nonsense and rumour.

1 The basis of this accusation is unclear.
2 This outlandish accusation had little, if any, basis in reality.
3 From *Living Biographies of Religious Leaders*.

AUGUST 13TH

THE JEWS WHO WERE NOT PERSUADED, BECOMING ENVIOUS, TOOK SOME OF THE EVIL MEN FROM THE MARKETPLACE, AND GATHERING A MOB, SET ALL THE CITY IN AN UPROAR

(Acts 17:4 *NIV*)

Wherever [Wesley] preached, he was pelted with mud and threatened with worse. But always in the end the charm of his personality won over "God's children" before they went too far in their ungodly business. The following entry in his journal is characteristic of a hundred cases:

"Finding the uproar increase, I went into the midst, and brought the head of the mob up with me to the desk. I received but one blow in the head: after which we reasoned the case, till he grew milder and milder and at length undertook to quieten his companions."

Once a ruffian raised his hand, brought it down upon Wesley's head, and suddenly checked the blow as he murmured, "What soft hair he has!" Always when he squarely faced a crowd, "the lions became lambs".[1]

I pray for hostile ringleaders and opponents of the gospel today, Lord. In your mercy, still their hands so that your work may continue uninterrupted.

1 From *Living Biographies of Religious Leaders.*

August 14th

Oh, the depth of the riches and wisdom and knowledge of God! How unsearchable are his judgments and how inscrutable his ways!

(Romans 11:33 *ESV*)

O God, of good the unfathomed Sea!
Who would not give his heart to thee?
Who would not love thee with his might?
O Jesus, Lover of mankind,
Who would not his whole soul and mind,
With all his strength, to thee unite?[1]

Lord God, you are indeed "of good the unfathomed sea". I have barely scratched the surface of your love, your might, and your wisdom. I pause to worship you this day, Almighty God.

1 Johann Scheffler. Translated from the German by Wesley for *Hymns and Sacred Poems, 1739.*

August 15th

Be still, and know that I am God; I will be exalted among the nations, I will be exalted in the earth

(Psalm 46:10 *NIV*)

Primeval Beauty! in thy sight
The first-born, fairest sons of light
See all their brightest glories fade:
What then to me thine eyes could turn,
In sin conceived, of woman born,
A worm, a leaf, a blast, a shade?

Hell's armies tremble at thy nod,
And trembling own the almighty God,
Sovereign of earth, hell, air, and sky:
But who is this that comes from far,
Whose garments rolled in blood appear?
'Tis God made man, for man to die![1]

Lord, grant me some time today, simply to silently ponder these words. Let me, I pray, find you in the quiet stillness of my pondering.

1 As August 14th.

August 16th

You are a chosen people, a royal priesthood

(**1 Peter 2:9** *NIV*)

Some of the disciples in London … insisted that a priesthood was an unnecessary and unscriptural institution, and that [they] had as good a right to preach, baptise, and administer the sacraments, as any other man. Such [teaching] found ready believers; the propriety of lay-preaching was contended for at the Society in Fetter Lane, and Charles Wesley strenuously opposed what he called these pestilent errors.

In spite of his opposition, a certain Mr Bowers set the first example. Two or three more ardent innovators declared that they would no longer be members of the Church of England. "Now," says Charles, in his journal, "I am clear of them; by renouncing the Church, they have discharged me." Bowers, who was not obstinate in his purpose, acknowledged that he had erred, and was reconciled to Charles Wesley: but owing to these circumstances, and to some confusion which the French Prophets, as they were called,[1] were exciting among the Methodists, it was judged expedient to summon John with all speed from Bristol.[2]

Thank you, Lord, for the amazing variety of gifts that different people bring to the Church – all sorts of skills and sensitivities, all manner of talents and traits. Thank you, Lord, that everyone has a part to play. I re-offer you myself this day; take my life and use me as you see fit.

1 In 1688, six hundred French Protestants proclaimed themselves to be prophets of the Holy Ghost, and attracted thousands of followers. Their ministry was characterized by fits, tremblings, and faintings, and they testified to visions of Heaven and angelic beings. "The French Prophets" came to England in 1706 and preached a powerful message of repentance.

2 From *John Wesley.*

August 17th

BE KINDLY AFFECTIONED ONE TO ANOTHER WITH BROTHERLY LOVE; IN HONOUR PREFERRING ONE ANOTHER

(Romans 12:10 *KJV*)

Wesley arrived, and on the day after his arrival accompanied [George Whitefield] to Blackheath, expecting to hear him preach: but when they were upon the ground, where about twelve or fourteen thousand persons were assembled, Whitefield desired him to preach instead. Wesley was a little surprised at this, and somewhat reluctant, for his nature recoiled; he did not however refuse, and being greatly moved with compassion for the rich that were present, he addressed his discourse particularly to them: "Some of them seemed attentive, while others drove away with their coaches from so uncouth a preacher." Whitefield noted this circumstance in his journal with great satisfaction: "I had the pleasure," he says, of introducing my honoured and reverend friend Mr John Wesley to preach at Blackheath. The Lord gave him ten thousand times more success than he has given me! I went to bed rejoicing that another fresh inroad was made into Satan's territories by Mr Wesley's following me in field-preaching in London as well as in Bristol."[1]

Thank you, Lord, for George Whitefield's wonderful example of grace here; his generous willingness to acknowledge John Wesley's gifts as a preacher, and to offer him such encouragement.

1 From *John Wesley.*

August 18th

The hour has already come for you to wake up from your slumber

(Romans 13:11 *NIV*)

By one who sleeps we are to understand (and would to God we might all understand it!) a sinner satisfied in his sins; content to remain in his fallen state, to live and die without the image of God; one who is ignorant both of his disease, and of the only remedy for it; fast bound in misery and iron, he dreams that he is at liberty. He says "Peace! Peace!" while the devil is in full possession of his soul.

He sleeps on still, taking his rest, though Hell is moved from beneath to meet him; though the pit from whence there is no return opens its mouth to swallow him up. A fire is kindled around him, yet he knows it not.

He is one who was never warned, or never regarded the warning voice of God, "to flee from the wrath to come"[1] : he never saw that he was in danger of hell-fire, or cried out in the earnestness of his soul, "What must I do to be saved?"[2, 3]

Father, give your Church a fresh concern for the lost. May your Church once again serve as a megaphone of salvation to those who are fast asleep.

1 Matthew 3:7, *KJV*.
2 Acts 16:30.
3 From *Fifty Three Sermons*.

YE BLIND GUIDES, WHICH STRAIN AT A GNAT, AND SWALLOW A CAMEL

(Matthew 23:24 *KJV*)

I snatched a few hours to read "The History of the Puritans".[1]

I stand in amazement, firstly at the execrable spirit of persecution, which drove these venerable men out of the Church,[2] and with which Queen Elizabeth's Clergy[3] were as deeply tinctured as ever Queen Mary's were;[4] secondly, at the weakness of those holy confessors, many of whom spent so much tie and strength in disputing surplices and hoods, or kneeling at the Lord's Supper![5]

Oh, Lord, preserve us from clergy who spend their time arguing about secondary matters, please! Give us clergy who will speak truth, defend the persecuted, and stand up for Jesus. For God's sake, deliver us from straining at gnats while swallowing camels!

1 Five volumes by Daniel Neal, first published in 1732.
2 Puritan believers were expelled from the Church of England because of what was viewed as their repressive morality. Puritans were openly critical of many Church of England practices, which they claimed were merely adaptations of Roman Catholic heresies and superstitions.
3 Queen Elizabeth I was willing to tolerate Puritan activity, but the Puritans were unwilling merely to be tolerated, and continued to challenge the established Church. This made a collision with Queen Elizabeth inevitable, and she offered them little protection. Her clergy collaborated in this.
4 Queen Mary was determined – bloodthirsty and ruthless – to restore Roman Catholicism to England, and waged a zealous campaign against her opponents. Very few clergy dared to stand in her way.
5 From *The Journal of the Rev. John Wesley, Volume 2.*

August 20TH

One day Elisha went on to Shunem, where a wealthy woman lived, who urged him to eat some food. So whenever he passed that way, he would turn in there to eat food. And she said to her husband, "Behold now, I know that this is a holy man of God who is continually passing our way. Let us make a small room on the roof with walls and put there for him a bed, a table, a chair, and a lamp, so that whenever he comes to us, he can go in there"

(2 Kings 4:8–10 *NIV*)

The Bristol Societies met at first in private houses, but the growth of two of them quickly made it necessary to find a building of their own. Under Wesley's guidance they united to acquire a piece of land in the Horsefair and build a "Society Room".

Wesley himself undertook to find the money, and in 1741 "the New Room in the Horsefair" was opened. It was at first meant to be simply a place for the Societies to meet; but it became a preaching place also, where men and women not yet members of the Society gathered to hear the sermons. It was seen to be inadequate for the purposes for which it was being and could be used, and a few years later was rebuilt. Equipped with a room leading off from the chapel below and a Common Room above, and with smaller rooms as bedchambers for itinerant preachers (with one of them especially set apart for Wesley's own use whenever he was in Bristol), it became Wesley's headquarters for the whole of his work in the West of England.[1]

Thank you, Lord, for calling some to be itinerant preachers; evangelists who travel the world sharing the news of salvation. Bless them as they spend time away from home, separated from their families, for the Kingdom's sake. Thank you too, for those who serve you by offering hospitality and a "home from home".

1 From *Methodism.*

AUGUST 21ST

NOT GIVING UP MEETING TOGETHER, AS SOME ARE IN THE HABIT OF DOING, BUT ENCOURAGING ONE ANOTHER

(Hebrews 10:25 *NIV*)

When the rebuilding of the New Room was under discussion, it was clearly necessary for effective means of raising money to be discovered; the Methodists were for the most part poor people. A certain captain Foy earned his right to immortality by the simple suggestion that the members of the Society should be divided into groups of eleven under a leader who should collect a penny a week from each of the eleven. The suggestion was adopted, and it soon became the custom for the "classes", as they were called, to meet weekly, not only for the payment of "class money" – though this was continued after the New Room was built, and became a Methodist institution – but also for prayer, Bible study, and religious conversation. This is the origin of the Methodist Society Class, which became the unit of Society membership, the training ground of lay leaders, and a potent instrument of evangelism.[1]

Thank you, Lord, for the rich blessing of "small groups" – house groups, Bible study groups and the like. Thank you for the unique opportunities of fellowship and friendship that exist in such gatherings, as distinct from more formal Sunday services.

1 From *Methodism.*

August 22nd

When ye fast, be not, as the hypocrites, of a sad countenance: for they disfigure their faces, that they may appear unto men to fast. Verily I say unto you, They have their reward. But thou, when thou fastest, anoint thine head, and wash thy face

(Matthew 6:16, 17 *KJV*)

Verse 16. *When ye fast* – Our Lord does not instruct or promote either fasting, alms-deeds, or prayer; all these being duties which were fully established in the church of God.

Disfigure – By the dust and ashes which they put upon their head, as was usual at the times of solemn humiliation.

Verse 17. *Anoint thy head* – So the Jews frequently did. Dress yourself as usual.[1]

Father God, assist me not to overlook or neglect those spiritual patterns and disciplines which should be the norm, and which should be part and parcel of my walk with you. Help me always to find you in the ordinary, and the routine. Help me to do that today.

1 From *Notes on the New Testament.*

August 23rd

CHRIST HAS RESCUED US FROM THE CURSE PRONOUNCED BY THE LAW. WHEN HE WAS HUNG ON THE CROSS, HE TOOK UPON HIMSELF THE CURSE FOR OUR WRONGDOING. FOR IT IS WRITTEN IN THE SCRIPTURES, "CURSED IS EVERYONE WHO IS HUNG ON A TREE"

(Galatians 3:13 *NLT*)

Extended on a curséd tree,
Besmeared with dust, and sweat, and blood,
See there, the king of glory see!
Sinks and expires the Son of God.

Who, who, my Saviour, this hath done?
Who could thy sacred body wound?
No guilt thy spotless heart hath known,
No guile hath in thy lips been found.

I, I alone, have done the deed!
'Tis I thy sacred flesh have torn;
My sins have caused thee, Lord, to bleed,
Pointed the nail, and fixed the thorn.[1]

My Jesus. My Saviour.

1 Paul Gerhardt. Translated from German by Wesley for *Hymns and Sacred Poems, 1740.*

AUGUST 24TH

I LOVE YOU, LORD

(Psalm 18:1 *NIV*)

A fact which I confess I have found baffling and for a long time could not explain is the omission from the large hymn-book of some of Charles Wesley's best-loved hymns, some of which are known to be among those which John most admired.

The omission of two, "Jesu, Lover of my soul" and "Thou Shepherd of Israel, and mine" has often been remarked and explained because of the endearing mystical language which they contain.

It is true that [John] Wesley's clean mind and known dislike of sentimental language may account for his omission of "Thou Shepherd of Israel", with its use of the amorous metaphor of the Canticles,[1] but this very partially explains the omission of "Jesu, Lover of my soul", which he himself included in 1752 and 1785. Still it may be that his dislike of sentimentality caused him to guard his people in this specifically Methodist book from the dangers of devotional extravagances which in earlier days had menaced his Society.[2]

Lord, whatever the rights and wrongs of this omission,
let it be enough today for me to say I love you.

1 A chant or part of a hymn, but also an alternative name for Song of Songs.
2 From *The Evangelical Doctrines of Charles Wesley's Hymns.*

AUGUST 25TH

YOU ALSO, WHEN YOU HEARD THE WORD OF TRUTH,
THE GOSPEL OF YOUR SALVATION, AND BELIEVED IN HIM,
WERE SEALED WITH THE PROMISED HOLY SPIRIT

(Ephesians 1:13 *ESV*)

The Methodist hymn-book of 1780 was a Methodist manifesto; it was at once a programme of the Society's work and a compendium of its doctrine; it was a body of practical and speculative divinity – chiefly practical, because, to John Wesley, divinity was practical and experimental or nothing. He selected the hymns of Charles which were most calculated to spread, illustrate, and keep his own distinctive teaching alive.

Since John claimed that his Collection contained every branch of speculative and practical divinity, and as 487 of the 525 hymns were from the pen of Charles, it is important to see in what ways he used them as his instruments for disseminating doctrines. The book is not divided under theological titles such as "God", "The Holy Trinity", "The Incarnation", "The Atonement"; it does not follow the Christian year, thought the Wesleys personally followed it. It is a book for penitents and believers and the Societies in which they were organized.[1]

How wonderful it is, Lord, to be clear in one's beliefs, and one's theology – not to pretend to know all the answers, but to be sure of one's salvation and the great truths of Christianity. Thank you, Lord, for these convictions. These things I know.

1 From *The Evangelical Doctrines of Charles Wesley's Hymns.*

August 26th

You will be my witnesses in Jerusalem, and in all Judea and Samaria, and to the ends of the earth

(Acts 1:8 *NIV*)

Wesley could not visualize Methodism as anything but a Society for the evangelization of England and then of the world.

He wanted the people who had been gathered into the fold to remain supremely interested in the in-gathering of others. He had no wish that his Society should survive except as an organ of evangelism; hence, he placed his hymns of exhortation in the forefront, entitled as they are by the moving words, "Exhorting and Beseeching Sinners to return to God". It is also noteworthy that, though he did not print it in the Table of Contents, the sub-title of the section entitled "Outward and Inward Religion" is the single word "Convincing".

Thus, by his titles, he said to his followers the prime work of Methodists is to exhort and beseech people to turn to God, and then, when they have turned, to convince them of the reality, not only of sin and judgment, but of all inward religion.[1]

"England and then the world" – Lord, wherever I live, help me to establish my witness there first; within my family, along my street, in my village or town.

1 From *The Evangelical Doctrines of Charles Wesley's Hymns.*

August 27th

Therefore I say unto you, Take no thought for your life, what ye shall eat, or what ye shall drink; nor yet for your body, what ye shall put on. Is not the life more than meat, and the body than raiment? Behold the fowls of the air: for they sow not, neither do they reap, nor gather into barns; yet your Heavenly Father feedeth them. Are ye not much better than they? Which of you by taking thought can add one cubit unto his stature? And why take ye thought for raiment? Consider the lilies of the field, how they grow; they toil not, neither do they spin: And yet I say unto you, That even Solomon in all his glory was not arrayed like one of these. Wherefore, if God so clothe the grass of the field, which today is, and tomorrow is cast into the oven, shall he not much more clothe you, O ye of little faith?

(Matthew 6:25–30 *KJV*)

Verse 25. *Therefore take not thought* – That is, be not anxiously careful. Beware of worldly cares; for these are as inconsistent with the true service of God as worldly desires. Is not life more than meat? – And if God gives the greater gift, will he deny the smaller?

Verse 27. *And which of you* – If you are ever so careful, can even add a moment to your own life? This seems by far the most easy and natural sense of the words.

Verse 29. *Solomon in all his glory was not arrayed like one of these* – Not in garments of so pure a whiteness. The eastern monarchs were often clothed in white robes.

Verse 30. *The grass of the field* – Is a general expression, including both herbs and flowers. Into the still[1] – This is the natural sense of the passage. For it can hardly be supposed that grass or flowers should be thrown "into the oven" the day after they were cut down. Neither is it the custom, in the hottest countries, where thy dry fastest, to heat ovens with them.

If God so clothe – The word properly implies, putting on a complete outfit that surrounds the body on all sides; and beautifully expresses that external membrane which (like the skin in a human body) adorns the fabric of the vegetable, and guards it from the injuries of the weather. Every microscope in which a flower is viewed gives a lively comment on this text.[2]

Jehovah-jireh – God my provider.

1 Apparatus for distilling liquid by boiling and then cooling to condense vapours. Stills are sometimes used to produce perfume and herbal medicine.

2 From *Notes on the New Testament.*

AUGUST 28TH

JUST AS A BODY, THOUGH ONE, HAS MANY PARTS,
BUT ALL ITS MANY PARTS FORM ONE BODY

(1 Corinthians 12:12 *NIV*)

There is no doubt that the "cellular" organization of the Methodist movement was almost its greatest strength, and not only other religious movements, but also the Trades Unions, the Chartists,[1] the Labour Movement,[2] and to some extent the Communist Party, have paid it the compliment of imitating it.

What happened in the Class Meetings must have varied from place to place, time to time, and leader to leader; but the leader was normally a layman – that is, he was neither an ordained clergyman nor a Methodist itinerant preacher – and very often of humble origin and little or no education; the same applied to members of his Class for the most part, although it was by no means unknown for an employer to be in the Class led by one of his employees. Prayer at the meetings was certainly extemporaneous, and not limited to the leader; the conversation concerned personal matters, and included confession of sin as well as testimony to the power of God. Members absent through sickness or old age were regularly visited by the leader and others and, if necessary, financially supported, and those absent for other reasons were pleaded with to resume their attendance. Classes for women were separate from those for men, and for this reason women Class leaders played an important part from the start.[3]

Lord of the Church, a wonderful picture emerges here, of a structure that was inclusive and informative. Help your Church today to learn from the Church of yesteryear, and to value those traditions which have much to offer, even if they might need updating.

1 A movement that campaigned on behalf of the working classes for political reform.
2 Similar to, but distinct from, the British Labour Party, which didn't come into being until 1900.
3 From *Methodism*.

August 29th

The well is deep

(John 4:11 *NIV*)

It is hard to believe, but it is certainly the case, that even this type of fellowship was not sufficiently intimate for all of Wesley's purposes. Membership of Class, and therefore of the Methodist Society, required ... simply "the desire to flee from the wrath to come" (which might be thought to be an almost universal desire); but those who had experienced the New Birth and were advancing towards Christian Perfection (and in Wesley's mind, to be regenerate implied at once the obligation to go on to perfection) were gathered into "bands", smaller groups, also led by laymen, in which the higher reaches of the Christian life could be explored. What was said "in band" was held to be completely secret and unrepeatable; and even today when Methodists wish to say something highly confidential to each other they sometimes describe themselves as being "in band". How far this further elaboration of the Methodist system was actually carried out in Methodism as it spread far and wide is a matter of conjecture, but it was certainly part of Wesley's original intention.[1]

Lord, give me that faith which will enable me to swim in the deep(er) waters of my relationship with you. Spiritual paddling is tempting, Lord, and relatively easy, but not very productive. Grant me a desire to explore new depths with you, I pray.

1 From *Methodism.*

AUGUST 30TH

THE RIGHTEOUS PERSON MAY HAVE MANY TROUBLES,
BUT THE LORD DELIVERS HIM FROM THEM ALL

(Psalm 34:19 *NIV*)

Easter Day 1749. John Nelson[1] met me … On Easter Sunday, at eight. He preached … to a large number of serious hearers. Towards the end of his discourse, a mob came from York, hired and led by some (mis-called) gentlemen.

They stood still, until an eminent Papist cried out, "Why do you not knock the dog's brains out?" They immediately began throwing anything that was at hand, so that the congregation quickly dispersed.

John spoke a few words, and walked towards York. They followed with showers of bricks and stones; one of which struck him on the shoulder, part of a brick hit him on the back of the head, and he fell to the ground. When he came to, two men lifted him up, and led him forward between them. The gentlemen followed, throwing as before, until he came to the city-gate, near which lived an honest tradesman, who took him by the arm, and pulled him into his house. Some of the rioters swore they would break all his windows, if he did not turn him out. But he told them resolutely, "I will not, and let any of you touch my house at your peril. I shall make you remember it as long as you live." They thought it wise to leave.[2]

Thank you, Lord, for the "honest tradesman" who offered sanctuary. Lord, wherever your people need such help and protection, please rush to their aid. As the battle rages, surround them according to their need.

1 Methodist lay preacher, often referred to as the pioneer of Methodism in Yorkshire.
2 From *The Journal of the Rev. John Wesley, Volume 2.*

August 31st

A fool gives full vent to his spirit,
but a wise man quietly holds it back

(Proverbs 29:11 *ESV*)

After a surgeon had dressed the wound in his head, John went softly on to Acomb[1] … He went out in order to preach, and began singing a hymn. Before he had finished, the same gentleman came in a coach from York with a number of people. They threw clods and stones so fast on every side that the congregation soon dispersed.

John walked down into a little ground, not far from Thomas Slaton's[2] house. Two men quickly followed; one of whom swore desperately he would have his life … He struck [John Nelson] several times, with all his force, on the head and breast, threw him down and stamped upon him, leaving him for dead. By the mercy of God, being carried into a house, he soon came to himself, and after a night's rest was so recovered that he was able to ride to Osmotherly.[3, 4]

Today, Lord, I am impressed by John Nelson's spirit of quiet determination in the face of such dreadful intimidation. Thank you, Lord, for his example.

1 A suburb of York.
2 Leader of a Methodist Society in York.
3 North Yorkshire.
4 From *The Journal of the Rev. John Wesley, Volume 2.*

People look at the outward appearance, but the Lord looks at the heart

(1 Samuel 16:7 *NIV*)

If the one who is asleep is not outwardly vicious, his sleep is usually the deepest of all; whether he be of the Laodicean spirit, "neither cold nor hot,"[1] but a quiet, rational, inoffensive, good-natured professor of the religion of his fathers; or whether he be zealous and orthodox and after the straightest sect of our religion, like a Pharisee; that is, according to the Scriptural account, one that justifies himself; one who works to establish his own righteousness as the grounds of his acceptance with God.

Meanwhile, the wretched self-deceiver thanks God that he is "not as other men are";[2] adulterers, for example, or the unjust, or executioners: no, he does no wrong to anyone. He fasts twice a week, uses all the means of grace, is constant at church and sacrament, and gives tithes of all he has. With regard to the righteousness of the law, he is blameless, but he wants nothing of the spirit of godliness.[3]

Lord, external appearances are one thing; an inward change of heart is another. Grant me, Lord, the wisdom to know one from the other, and to give preference to the latter.

1 Revelation 3:16, *KJV*.
2 See Luke 18:9–14 .
3 From *Fifty Three Sermons.*

September 2ND

YE ARE NOT IN THE FLESH, BUT IN THE SPIRIT,
IF SO BE THAT THE SPIRIT OF GOD DWELL IN YOU

(Romans 8:9 *KJV*)

However highly esteemed among men such a Christian as this may be, he is an abomination in the sight of God, and an heir of every woe which the Song of God denounces against scribes and Pharisees, hypocrites.

He has "made clean the outside of the cup and the platter,"[1] but within is full of all filthiness. "An evil disease cleaveth still unto him, so that his inward parts are very wickedness."[2] Our Lord compares him to "a painted sepulchre," which appears beautiful on the outside but, nevertheless, is "full of dead men's bones, and of all uncleanness".[3] The bones indeed are no longer dry; sinews and flesh are upon them, and skin covers them; but there is no breath in them, no Spirit of the living God. And, "if any man have not the Spirit of Christ, he is none of his".[4]

What a lovely truth it is, Lord, that inward change influences outward behaviour. Come, Holy Spirit, and bless me with your abiding presence this day.

1 See Luke 11:39, *KJV*.
2 See Psalm 41:8, *KJV*.
3 See Matthew 23:27, *KJV*.
4 From *Fifty Three Sermons*.

Decide never to put a stumbling block or hindrance in the way of a brother

(Romans 14:13 *ESV*)

It deserves particular notice that no fits or convulsions had ... been produced under Whitefield's preaching, though he preached the same doctrine as the Wesleys, and addressed himself with equal or greater vehemence to the passions, and with more theatrical effect. But when Wesley ... was preaching to a society in Wapping,[1] the symptoms reappeared with their usual violence, and were more than usually contagious.

A difference of opinion concerning these outward signs, as thy are called, was one of the subjects which had distracted the London Methodists, and rendered Wesley's presence among them necessary.

The French Prophets also had obtained considerable influence over some of the Society; these prophets had now for about half a century acted as frantic and as knavish a part for the disgrace of a good cause, as the enemies of that cause could have desired.[2]

God of wisdom, help me to act in such a way that I only ever attract people to Jesus. By your gracious Spirit's infilling, steer me along today, I pray, in the ways of Christ.

1 East London.
2 From *John Wesley.*

September 4th

Test everything

(1 Thessalonians 5:21 *ESV*)

Those [of the French Prophets] who had taken up their abode in England formed a sect here, and as soon as the Methodists began to attract notice, naturally sought to make converts among a people whom they supposed to be prepared for them.

The first of these extravagants with whom Charles Wesley was acquainted, was an English proselyte, residing at Wickham,[1] to whom he was introduced on his way to Oxford, and with whom it seems he was not only to take up his lodging, but to sleep.

This gentleman insisted that the French Prophets were equal, if not superior, to the prophets of the Old Testament. Charles, however, was not aware that his host and chum was himself a gifted personage, till they retired to bed, when as they were undressing, he fell into violent agitations, and gobbled like a turkey-cock. "I was frightened," he says, "and began exorcizing him with 'Thou deaf and dumb devil!' He soon recovered from his fit of inspiration. I prayed, and went to bed, not half liking my bed-fellow, nor did I sleep very sound with Satan so near me."[2]

God of wisdom, keep your people safe.

1 Hampshire, England.
2 From *John Wesley*.

I was kidnapped from my homeland

(Genesis 40:15 *NLT*)

It was the practice in this rough and rowdy century of Merrie England[1] to kidnap young men in the street and impress them into His Majesty's Navy.[2]

John Wesley did not escape the menace of such a destiny at the hands of his enemies. But hardly had his captors led him three quarters of a mile toward the nearest headquarters of the press gang, when their leader looked into Wesley's eyes and then and there decided to offer his own life in order to bring the preacher back safely through the mob.

Wesley started again on his methodical mission to build a hateless world.[3]

What a story! International God, I pray today for those who are victims of human trafficking – innocent people kidnapped and sold into the misery of modern-day slavery. Lord, in your mercy, hear their cries, soften the hearts of their kidnappers, and bless the efforts of all those agencies seeking to intervene. For those who have been rescued, Father, yet still suffer trauma, I pray your gentle, gradual healing.

1 A nickname for England during the years between the Middle Ages and the cultural revolution, when the nation was deemed to be a place of happiness and contentment; some kind of pastoral utopia that never actually existed, but to which peasants aspired, nonetheless. The reality was somewhat different.

2 From "impressment"; taking men into naval service by brute force. Warships belonging to the British Navy were always short of basic crew members, and men between the ages of 18 and 55 were beaten into submission, kidnapped, or plied with free ale until they were helpless to resist and woke up on board, often miles out to sea.

3 From *Living Biographies of Religious Leaders*.

September 6th

Better is open rebuke than hidden love

(Proverbs 27:5 *NIV*)

[George Whitefield] wrote to Wesley –

Honoured Sir,

I cannot think it right in you to give so much encouragement to those convulsions which people have been thrown into under your ministry. Was I to do so, how many would cry out every night? I think it is tempting God to require such signs. That there is something of God in it, I doubt not. But the Devil I believe interposes. I think it will encourage the French Prophets, take people from the written word, and make them depend on visions, convulsions, etc., more than on the promises and precepts of the Gospel.[1]

Thank you, Lord, for the gift of friends who will be lovingly honest with me.

1 From *Rev. John Wesley.*

September 7th

Our God is in the heavens; he does all that he pleases

(Psalm 115:3 *ESV*)

Wesley wrote as follows:

I had an opportunity to talk with Mr Whitefield of those outward signs which had so often accompanied the work of God. I found his objections were chiefly grounded on gross misrepresentation of matters of fact. But next day he had an opportunity of informing himself better; for in the application of his sermon, four persons sunk down close to him almost in the same moment. One of them lay without either sense or motion; a second trembled exceedingly; the third had strong convulsions all over his body, but made no noise unless by groans; the fourth, equally convulsed, called upon God, with strong cries and tears. From this time, I trust, we shall all suffer God to carry on his own work in the way that pleaseth him.[1]

You are God.

1 From *Rev. John Wesley.*

September 8th

I myself will tend my sheep and have them lie down, declares the Sovereign Lord. I will search for the lost and bring back the strays. I will bind up the injured and strengthen the weak

(Ezekiel 34:15, 16 *NIV*)

Thur. Jan. 3 [1740] – I left London, and the next evening came to Oxford, where I spent the following two days in looking over the letters which I had received over the past sixteen or eighteen years. How few traces of inward religion are in those letters! I found one of my correspondents who declared that God had "shed abroad his love in his heart",[1] and given him the "peace that passeth all understanding".[2]

He was expelled out of his society, as a madman; and was disowned by his friends, despised and forsaken by all. He lived obscure and unknown for a few months, then went to him whom his soul loved.[3]

Father of all, I pray for those who for one reason or another don't quite fit in at church; those who hover around the fringes but aren't fully integrated or, to be honest, all that welcome.

1 See Romans 5:5.
2 See Philippians 4:7, *KJV*.
3 From *John Wesley's Journal (Abridged)*.

September 9th

Every place where you set your foot will be yours

(Deuteronomy 11:24 *NIV*)

Wesley had a meeting with the Bishop of Bristol…[1]

"I hear … many people fall into fits in your societies, and that you pray over them."

"I do so, my lord, when any show, by strong cries and tears, that their soul is in deep anguish; I frequently pray to God to deliver them from it, and our prayer is often heard in that hour."

"Very extraordinary indeed! Well, sir, since you ask my advice, I will give it freely. You have no business here; you are not commissioned to preach in this diocese. Therefore I advise you to go hence."

"My lord," replied Wesley, "my business on earth is to do what good I can. Wherever, therefore, I think I can do most good, there I must stay, so long as I think so. At present, I think I can do most good here; therefore, here I stay. Being ordained a priest, by the commission I then received, I am a priest of the Church universal; and being ordained as a Fellow of a college, I am not limited to any particular cure, but I have an indeterminate commission to preach the word of God in any part of the Church of England … If I should be convinced in the meantime that I could advance the glory of God, and the salvation of souls in any other place more than Bristol, in that hour by God's help I go hence; which until then I may not do."[2]

Lord of the Church, wherever your people are located, may it be their prime motivation to preach the word. Put us where you want us each to be, then use us as you want us each to be used. Just where you need us, Lord.

1 Joseph Butler (1692–1752).
2 From *Rev. John Wesley*.

SEPTEMBER 10TH

THOSE WHO LOOK TO HIM ARE RADIANT;
THEIR FACES ARE NEVER COVERED WITH SHAME

(Psalm 34:5 *NIV*)

An article appeared in the *Weekly Miscellany*:[1]

"The Methodist preacher stands on an eminence," said the writer, "with admiring and subscribing crowds about him. He is young, which is good; looks innocent, which is better; and has no human learning, which is best of all."

When we consider that the chief Methodist preacher, Wesley, was then thirty-six, had spent most of his life in striving after holiness, and was a distinguished Fellow of Oxford College, we are astonished that an editor could be found who would insert such a libel in his journal! The article goes on to say:

"The Methodists are mad enthusiasts who teach dictates of the Holy Spirit, seditions, heresies, and contempt of the ordinances of God and man. They are buffoons in religion, and mountebanks[2] in theology; creatures who disclaim sense, and are below argument," and so on.[3]

Blessed are the unoffended! Lord, give your people the wit, and the grace, to shrug off ridicule without a second thought. Teach us not to care.

1 1732–1741.
2 A deceiver, a swindler.
3 From *Rev. John Wesley.*

SEPTEMBER 11TH

THE ACCUSER OF OUR BROTHERS AND SISTERS

(Revelation 12:10 *NIV*)

A certain James Bates, M.A., Rector of St Paul's, Deptford,[1] and formerly Chaplain to His Excellency Horatio Walpole, Esq.,[2] distinguished himself by producing two pamphlets, the first against Mr Whitefield in particular, and the second entitled "Quakero-Methodism; or, a Confutation of the First Principles of the Quakers and Methodists."

In the first, Whitefield is charged with causing numbers of poor tradesmen to leave their families to starve while they ramble about after him; his is also accused of violently dividing text from context in expounding the word of God, so that he makes arrant nonsense of both; and finally, "he shuffles and prevaricates; treats the bishop with saucy sneers; is guilty of flat falsehoods, disingenuous quirks, and mean evasions; perfidiously tramples upon the canons of the Church; and flies in the face of his diocesan with unparalleled pride and impudence." And the second pamphlet is equally abusive and untrue.[3]

Oh Lord, this is just nonsense. Enable your Church not to rise to such accusations, but to laugh them off and carry on.

1 Bate, not Bates. English writer (1703–75).
2 1st Baron Walpole MP (1663–1717).
3 From *Rev. John Wesley.*

September 12th

"No weapon that is fashioned against you shall succeed, and you shall confute every tongue that rises against you in judgment. This is the heritage of the servants of the Lord and their vindication from me, declares the Lord"

(Isaiah 54:17 *ESV*)

At last, after much bitterness and many blows, Methodism became a respectable organization. They years had softened the novelty of Wesley's prophecy. The army of Methodists had grown big enough to command respect. Wesley had travelled everywhere. Yet, unlike the earlier nomad prophets who had pitched their tents at random and had then vanished in the wind, this methodical builder remained everywhere long enough to establish his ideas upon a solid basis…

Let us now observe him in action … From dawn to sunset he gallops over the unpaved and muddy roads of England, preaching in every town on the way, feeding the hungry, tending the sick, praying for the dead. In addition to all these duties, he personally supervises the huge organization of his Methodist classes all over England, instructing the resident preachers, writing letters to the itinerant preachers, presiding over the conferences of a hundred delegates who meet annually as the governing body. He knows intimately every last preacher and teacher in the organization. His travels average no less than four thousand miles a year. He has made fifty trips across the water to his congregations in Ireland, and he has left the hoofprints of his horses upon two hundred and twenty thousand miles of British soil. He does all his reading as he sits in the saddle. To quote his own quaint words, "History, philosophy, poetry I read on horseback, having other employments at other times." He opens his book while the horse is "at a trot", slackens the reins, and allows the "knowing animal" to lead him "surely and safely" into the next familiar town.[1]

Thank you, Lord!

1 From *Living Biographies of Religious Leaders.*

The Lord will fulfil his purpose for me

(Psalm 138:8 *ESV*)

Wesley had now proposed to himself a clear and determinate object…

He hoped to give a new impulse to the Church of England, to awaken its dormant zeal, infuse life into a body where nothing but life was wanting, and lead the way to the performance of duties which the State had blindly overlooked, and the Church had scandalously neglected: thus he would become the author of a second Reformation,[1] whereby all that had been left undone in the former would be completed.[2]

Father, today I pray for those who are searching for their destiny in life; anyone looking to you for guidance regarding their future. Show them your will, and help them to discover what you would have them do.

1 The Protestant Reformation, a dramatic schism from the Roman Catholic Church, led by Martin Luther then continued by the likes of John Calvin and Huldrych Zwingli. Generally speaking, the Reformation as a process lasted from 1517, when Luther posted his *Ninety-five Theses*, until approximately 1648, when matters were established.

2 From *John Wesley.*

September 14th

Living in the fear of the Lord and encouraged by the Holy Spirit

(Acts 9:31 *NIV*)

[Wesley] began life with ascetic habits and opinions; with a restless spirit, and a fiery heart. Ease and comfort were neither congenial to his disposition nor his principles; wealth was not necessary for his calling, and it was beneath his thoughts: he could command not merely respectability without it, but importance. Nor was it long before he discovered what St Francis and his followers and imitators had demonstrated long before, that they who profess poverty for conscience sake, and trust for their daily bread … will find it as surely as Elijah in the wilderness…

The effects which he produced, both upon body and mind, appeared equally to himself and to his followers miraculous. Diseases were arrested or subdued by the faith which he inspired, madness was appeased, and in the sound and sane, paroxysms were excited which were new to pathology, and which he believed to be supernatural interpositions, vouchsafed … by the Spirit of God, or worked in opposition to them by the exasperated Principal of Evil.[1]

The contrast here, Lord, is fascinating; an ascetic, orderly man with methodical ways, whose ministry was accompanied by miracles or provision, healing and salvation. What does this demonstrate, Lord? That you accept and use anyone who is consecrated to your service, and that the power at work is entirely yours.

1 From *John Wesley*.

YOU WERE DEAD IN YOUR TRANSGRESSIONS AND SINS

(Ephesians 2:1 *NIV*)

In the midst of our "natural" life, we are in spiritual "death". And we remain in such a state until the Second Adam[1] becomes a quickening Spirit to us; until He raises the dead, the dead in sin; dead in pleasure, riches, or honours.

But before any dead soul can live, he "hears" (hearkens to) "the voice of the Son of God": he is made aware of his lost state, and receives the sentence of death in himself. He realizes himself to be "dead while he liveth";[2] dead to God, and all the things of God having no more power to perform the actions of a living Christian, than a dead body has to perform the functions of a living man...

One who is dead in sin does not have "senses exercised to discern spiritual good and evil".[3] "Having eyes, he sees not; he hath ears, and hears not."[4] He does not "taste and see that the Lord is gracious".[5] He "hath not seen God at any time"[6] ... In vain is the name of Jesus "like ointment poured forth"[7] ... He understands none of these things.[8]

Oh Lord, how gracious you are to wake the dead, and how powerful. You make the deaf to hear and the blind to see. You bring life where life does not exist. You are God, and you have conquered death.

1 See 1 Corinthians 15:47.
2 See 1 Timothy 5:6.
3 See Hebrews 5:14.
4 See Mark 8:18.
5 See Psalm 34:8.
6 See John 1:18.
7 See Song of Songs 1:3.
8 From *Fifty Three Sermons*.

September 16th

It is required of stewards that they be found trustworthy

(1 Corinthians 4:2 *ESV*)

I gave the following instructions to Stewards:

1. You are to be men full of the Holy Ghost and wisdom, that you may do all things in a manner acceptable to God. 2. You are to be present every Tuesday and Thursday morning, in order to transact the affairs of the Society. 3. You are to begin and end every Meeting with earnest prayer unto God, for a blessing on all your undertakings. 4. You are to produce your accounts on the first Tuesday in every month, so that they may be transcribed into the ledger. 5. You are to take it in turn, month by month, to be chairman. The chairman is to see that all the rules are punctually observed, and immediately to check with whoever breaks any of them. 6. You are to do nothing without the consent of the minister, either actually given, or presumed. 7. You are to consider, whenever you meet, that "God is here." Therefore, be deeply serious. Utter no trifling word. Speak as in his presence, and to the glory of his great name. 8. When anything is debated, let anyone stand up and speak, while everyone else pays attention; let him speak just loud enough to be heard, in love and the spirit of meekness. 9. You are to pray continually, and make sure a spirit of holy harmony exists among you; keep your unity in the bonds of peace. 10. In all debates, you are to watch over your spirits, avoiding all contention as you would avoid fire. Be swift to hear, and slow to speak; in honour preferring others before yourself. 11. Even if you cannot relieve, do not grieve the poor. Give them soft words, if nothing else. Abstain from sour looks and harsh words. Put yourself in the place of the poor, and deal with them as you would like God to deal with you. N.B. If any Steward shall break any of the preceding rules, after having been admonished by the chairman and notice given to the minister, he is no longer a Steward.[1]

Ten reasonable rules, Lord!

1 From *The Journal of the Rev. John Wesley, Volume 2.*

JOB'S THREE FRIENDS ... SET OUT FROM THEIR HOMES AND MET TOGETHER BY AGREEMENT TO GO AND SYMPATHIZE WITH HIM AND COMFORT HIM

(Job 2:11 *NIV*)

There was a small group of ordained clergymen who valued Wesley's work and gave it as much support as possible. William Grimshaw was vicar of Haworth in Yorkshire (and therefor a predecessor of Patrick Brontë) from 1742 until his death in 1763. He ruled his parishioners with a rod of iron, but seems to have had a heart of gold. He preached the Methodist message with fire and fervour ... and he certainly met with astonishing success in the number of conversions and attendances at Holy Communion recorded...

Vincent Perronet was vicar of Shoreham in Kent, and ten years older than Wesley. He was a man of quiet and studious habit, who stayed in his parish, but was always available to give help and advice to John and Charles, and to defend them in writing against their detractors when needed. He was called the Archbishop or umpire of Methodism, and many disputes were settled in his peaceful parsonage; there also John was occasionally prevailed upon to rest and read for a few days.[1]

Thank you, Lord, for friends who are loyal. Thank you, Lord, for friends whose friendship does not waver during difficult times. May I be a loyal friend.

1 From *Methodism.*

SEPTEMBER 18TH

IT IS WRITTEN, "WHAT NO EYE HAS SEEN, NOR EAR HEARD, NOR THE HEART OF MAN IMAGINED, WHAT GOD HAS PREPARED FOR THOSE WHO LOVE HIM"

(1 Corinthians 2:9 *ESV*)

John Berridge, vicar of Everton (Bedfordshire) … was a good scholar in his Cambridge days, but few traces of this were in evidence when he began his own revival in the parish in 1756. He was not officially linked with the Wesleys, but was in close accord with them, and they thought it best to allow him to conduct his own mission in his own way. The Everton revival, which reached its height in 1759 … spread far over the neighbouring countryside…

His theology turned gradually towards Calvinism, and away from Wesley's; but on his deathbed, he was very willing to agree with a friend who said that Wesley and he would "unite in perfect harmony in Heaven". "Ay, ay," said the old man. "That we shall, to be sure; for the Lord washed our hearts here, and there He will wash our brains."[1]

What a lovely statement, Lord! And what a lovely truth!
When we all get to Heaven!

1 From *Methodism.*

September 19th

Brothers and sisters, stand firm and hold fast to the teachings we passed on to you, whether by word of mouth or by letter

(2 Thessalonians 2:15 *NIV*)

Manchester,

3 April 1790

Dear Tommy,

So you have reason to acknowledge that God has not forgotten to be gracious. If you can build preaching-houses without increasing the General Debt, it is well; but otherwise it will eat us up.

But I have no more to do with these matters. I have appointed a Building Committee and shall leave to them everything pertaining to building for the time to come.

In all these parts of the kingdom there is a fair measure of the work of God. There will be so everywhere if the preachers are holy and zealous men.

I am, dear Tommy, your affectionate friend and brother,

J. Wesley.[1, 2]

Thank you, Lord, for Wesley's pastoral interest in the preaching-house in Norwich, even when he was hundreds of miles away in Manchester. Lord, I pray for those places and people who remain close to my heart, even though they are far away geographically. I think of friends and churches, towns and countries that claim an interest in my prayers, and I lift them before you today.

1 Written to Mr Tommy (Thomas) Tattershall at the preaching-house in Norwich, Norfolk, England. John Wesley wrote often to men who supervised preaching-houses in his absence.

2 This letter hangs in a frame in The Square Methodist Church, Dunstable, Bedfordshire, England.

SEPTEMBER 20TH

THIS MAN IS MY CHOSEN INSTRUMENT

(Acts 9:15 *NIV*)

By far the most gifted, influential, and saintly of all Wesley's clerical friends – and perhaps of all his friends – was fletcher of Madeley. Jean Guillaume de la Flechère, born in Switzerland in 1729, the descendant of a noble Savoy family,[1] studied for a while in Geneva, and came to England to learn the language. Now calling himself John William Fletcher, he was appointed tutor to a Shropshire family, and a few months later met Wesley and became a Methodist. Wesley persuaded him in due course to be ordained, and in 1760 he was appointed to the living of Madeley, also in Shropshire. Here he ministered for the rest of his days, a model pastor of his flock, but by his gentleness and charity, his humility and courage, spreading the infection of holiness all through the ranks of the Methodists.[2]

Lord, this is an outstanding tribute to a devout minister. Thank you for those ministers who quietly and humbly go about their business without seeking recognition or reward. I pray for my minister today.

1 House of Savoy, historic European family.
2 From *Methodism.*

Rich and poor have this in common:
The Lord is the Maker of them all

(Proverbs 22:2 *NIV*)

Wesley became convinced that if any man on earth could claim to have been granted the gift of "Perfect Love", it was Fletcher, and urgently wished to designate him as his successor in the acknowledged leadership of the Methodists; but Fletcher, consistently with the whole tenor of his life, refused the honour. He was an acute and lucid theologian, and his *Checks to Antinomianism*[1] takes rank as a classic of courteous theological controversy.

[Wesley's friends] could not spend their whole time, or even most of their time, itinerating with the Gospel in the manner of Wesley himself. He came to rely more and more, reluctantly at first, but afterwards cheerfully, on preachers who came from every walk of life and often started from very humble origins … Thomas Maxfield,[2] a mere layman, was called of God [to preach], and took it upon himself to preacher at the Foundery … Once the principle was established, Wesley, with the inspired opportunism which enabled him to make use of any method – whether he had thought of it himself or not … for furthering his work … set about training and preparing his lay preachers for the work which he now saw that they would be able to do. He chose them for their personal knowledge of salvation, and at first set a period of one year for their "probation" (the word is still current in Methodism); later he extended it to four years.[3]

Lord, you accept and use learned theologians from noble families.
Lord, you accept and use those from humble origins. In the service of Jesus, there's a place for all.

1 1770.
2 Possibly the first officially recognized lay preacher in Methodism.
3 From *Methodism.*

September 22ND

Judge not, that ye be not judged. For with what judgment ye judge, ye shall be judged; and with what measure ye mete, it shall be measured to you again. And why beholdest thou the mote that is in thy brother's eye, but considerest not the beam that is in thine own eye? Or how wilt thou say to thy brother, Let me pull out the mote out of thine eye; and, behold, a beam is in thine own eye?

(Matthew 7:1–4 *KJV*)

Verse 1. *Judge not* – anyone without full, clear, certain knowledge, without absolute necessity, without tender love.

Verse 2. *With what measure ye mete, it shall be measured to you* – Awful words![1] So we may, as it were, choose for ourselves, whether God shall be severe or merciful to us. God … will favour the candid and benevolent: but those who exercise judgment without mercy cannot expect to be shown mercy.

Verse 3. In particular, who do you search for the fault in someone else, while you yourself are guilty of a greater sin?

Verse 4. *The mote* – The word properly signifies a splinter, or a sliver of wood. This and a beam, its opposite, were proverbially used by the Jews to denote on the one hand, small infirmities, and on the other, gross faults.[2]

Lord of mercy, keep my eyes focused on the mercy I have received, and receive daily, so that I may show mercy to others.

1 Literally "full of awe", not bad.
2 From *Notes of the New Testament.*

SEPTEMBER 23RD

LEARN TO DO RIGHT; SEEK JUSTICE. DEFEND THE OPPRESSED. TAKE UP THE CAUSE OF THE FATHERLESS; PLEAD THE CASE OF THE WIDOW

(Isaiah 1:17 *NIV*)

Christianity, John Wesley said, is a social religion; hence Methodism needed social hymns. Full salvation, in Wesley's view, was perfect love; the Methodists, therefore, not merely as individuals, but as bands of loving companions – as Societies – sang their way to Zion … The hymns that the Methodists sang, like all effective hymns must be, were emotional, but their content throughout was Scriptural and doctrinal. They did not merely stir emotion, but caused their singers to contemplate religious truth and meditate upon it.

So John Wesley took his brother's hymns, which expressed his own evangelical doctrine in vivid verse, as his declaration of what theology, speculative and practical, the Methodists believed.[1]

A "social religion" expressed in song! Compassion with crescendos!
Keep your people singing, Lord.

1 From *The Evangelical Doctrines of Charles Wesley's Hymns.*

September 24th

Seek the Lord while he may be found;
call on him while he is near

(Isaiah 55:6 *NIV*)

Thee will I love, my Strength, my Tower,
Thee will I love, my Joy, my Crown,
Thee will I love with all my power,
In all thy works, and thee alone;
Thee will I love, till the pure fire
Fill my whole soul with chaste desire.

Ah, why did I so late thee know,
Thee, lovelier than the sons of men!
Ah, why did I no sooner go
To thee, the only ease in pain!
Ashamed, I sigh, and inly mourn,
That I so late to thee did turn.[1, 2]

Last-minute God, I pray for those known to me personally who have resisted your mercy for years, even decades. Reach them, I pray.

1 Johann Scheffler, translated from the German by Wesley for *Hymns and Sacred Poems, 1739.*

2 A lovely story accompanies this hymn, as follows: The Rev. William Arthur gives a description of Gideon Ouseley, the great Irish evangelist, which, he says, presents him exactly as he had often heard him spoken of by those in whose house Ouseley stayed. It is from the pen of the Rev. John Hughes. When he was a boy at home, he says, "On a raw November evening Ouseley preached at the corner of the street in which we resided at Portarlington. After preaching, he came into our house for some refreshment, and to wait until his time came again to preach in the chapel. When he took a seat in the little back apartment it was dusk. A turf fire played fitfully, and there was no other light. I crouched in an obscure corner, and Ouseley thought himself alone. He took off his cloak and hat, ejaculated 'My blessed Master!' and wiped the perspiration from his head and face. He then poked the fire, and spread himself out before it. After musing a minute, he wept. Tear after tear rolled down his rugged cheeks. He repeated, in a low but distinct voice, the first two verses of the hymn, 'Thee will I love, my strength, my tower.' After repeating the line, 'Ah, why did I so late thee know,' he smote his forehead with his big hand, and finished the verse." (From cyberhymnal.org)

September 25th

Moses was a very humble man, more humble than anyone else on the face of the earth

(Numbers 12:3 *NIV*)

John Wesley regarded Christian Perfection as an ideal to be realized in the present life … The perfection John preached, which was so full pf qualifications and was capable of being improved upon, so he taught, seemed worthless to Charles. The tragedy of his spiritual life was that he never ceased to cry out for the unattainable, but perhaps the noblest thing about him was that his ideal never grew dim – he always struggled "to hitch his wagon to a star" – whereas John, practical organizer as he was, tried to pack the stars in his wagon.

Charles set perfection too high, John told him; he challenged him to find living examples of the perfection he and Whitefield taught. He, on the other hand, could call five hundred witnesses who would testify to the truth of his own doctrine. Well, perhaps he could, but when he did Charles did not like them; they seemed to lack one grace of perfection, humility. They reminded him much more of dingy lamps than of clear, shining stars. He made strong protests against glib claims to perfection.[1]

Lord, the moral of this story is clear. If I am to shine as a bright star for you, then please don't allow any lack of humility to dim that witness.

1 From *The Evangelical Doctrines of Charles Wesley's Hymns.*

SEPTEMBER 26TH

FAITH IS CONFIDENCE IN WHAT WE HOPE FOR AND ASSURANCE ABOUT WHAT WE DO NOT SEE. THIS IS WHAT THE ANCIENTS WERE COMMENDED FOR

(Hebrews 11:1 *NIV*)

John, of course, was right in his assertion that his brother was striving after an ideal unattainable by a man while living in the flesh. Charles really was not striving for practicable Christian Perfection, but for heavenly beatitude, which, as he once sang, "he must die to know". Like the heroes of Hebrews 11 his faith in the ideal persisted, though he died without realizing it on earth.

But was John's doctrine satisfactory? Did this very practical person formulate a successful dogma of the perfection he taught? Is not the word "perfection" a misnomer for so qualified an ideal as his? Did he ever present a clear and full statement of what he meant which his followers can teach? Writers like Drs Flew,[1] Sugden,[2] and Curtis[3] have to acknowledge contradictions and inconsistencies in his doctrine. These authorities point out … that it was based on an inadequate conception of sin. Perfection, even relative perfection, as a theory of salvation from all sin, must take into account the sins which Jesus stressed so emphatically – sins of omission as well as those of commission. John Wesley does not tell us how they are to be avoided.[4]

Father, whatever theories exist, help me today to be like Jesus. Let me start there.

1 Robert Newton Flew (1886–1962), English Methodist minister and theologian.
2 Edward Holdsworth Sugden (1854–1935) Master of Queen's College (University of Melbourne). He was in partnership with the Methodist Church.
3 Not sure who this is.
4 From *The Evangelical Doctrines of Charles Wesley's Hymns.*

SEPTEMBER 27TH

ENTER YE IN AT THE STRAIT GATE: FOR WIDE IS THE GATE, AND BROAD IS THE WAY, THAT LEADETH TO DESTRUCTION, AND MANY THERE BE WHICH GO IN THEREAT: BECAUSE STRAIT IS THE GATE, AND NARROW IS THE WAY, WHICH LEADETH UNTO LIFE, AND FEW THERE BE THAT FIND IT. BEWARE OF FALSE PROPHETS, WHICH COME TO YOU IN SHEEP'S CLOTHING, BUT INWARDLY THEY ARE RAVENING WOLVES

(Matthew 7:13–15 *KJV*)

Verse 13. *The strait gate* – Holiness. And this is the narrow way. *Wide is the gate, and many there are that go in through it* – They need not seek for this; they come to it of course. *Many go in through it, because strait is the* other *gate* – Therefore they do not care for it; they like a wider gate.

Verse 15. *Beware of false prophets* – Who, in their preaching, describe a broad way to heaven: it is their *prophesying*, their *teaching* the broad way, rather than their walking in it themselves, that is here chiefly spoken of. All those who teach any other way than that taught by our Lord are false prophets. *In sheep's clothing* – With external religion only, and only professing love. *Wolves* – those who do not feed souls, but destroy them.[1]

Lord, guide me by your Spirit in your ways, and protect me as I seek to follow. I pray too for those who are just embarking on their Christian experience, and who are vulnerable. Surround them with your protection.

1 From *Notes on the New Testament.*

YE SHALL KNOW THEM BY THEIR FRUITS. DO MEN GATHER GRAPES OF THORNS, OR FIGS OF THISTLES? EVEN SO EVERY GOOD TREE BRINGETH FORTH GOOD FRUIT; BUT A CORRUPT TREE BRINGETH FORTH EVIL FRUIT. A GOOD TREE CANNOT BRING FORTH EVIL FRUIT, NEITHER CAN A CORRUPT TREE BRING FORTH GOOD FRUIT. EVERY TREE THAT BRINGETH NOT FORTH GOOD FRUIT IS HEWN DOWN, AND CAST INTO THE FIRE

(Matthew 7:16–20 *KJV*)

Verse 16. *By their fruits ye shall know them* – A short, plain, easy rule, whereby to know true from false prophets; and one that may be applied even by people unaccustomed to deep reasoning. True prophets convert sinners to God; or, at least, confirm and strengthen those that are converted. False prophets do not. False prophets are not sent from the Spirit of God, but come in their own name.

Verse 18. *A good tree cannot bring forth evil fruit, neither a corrupt tree good fruit* – It is certain, though, that the goodness and badness referred to here is in respect of the doctrine, not necessarily personal character, for even a bad man, preaching this doctrine, can be an instrument of converting sinners to God.

Verse 19 – *Every tree that bringeth not forth good fruit is hewn down and cast into the fire* – How dreadful, then is the condition of the teacher who has brought no sinners to God![1]

Gracious God, how may I serve you this day?

1 From *Notes on the New Testament.*

September 29th

Male and female he created them

(Genesis 1:17 *NIV*)

Wesley had many women helpers; in fact, women participated freely in all the activities of the eighteenth-century Methodists in a manner which would have shocked their nineteenth-century successors, and which surprised their non-Methodist contemporaries.

Foremost among them was undoubtedly Mary Bosanquet (1739–1815). She was brought up in comfortable circumstances, but the influence of the Methodists caused her to devote her life to the care of the underprivileged. For a number of years she ran an orphanage in her own home, and later became a preacher. In fact, in 1787 she was authorized as an itinerant preacher in the Methodist Connexion[1] "so long as she preaches our doctrine and attends to our discipline".[2]

Lord of the Church, thank you for all that women bring to ministry, fellowship and social care. I think of women in my own church and denomination, and all that they do – and are – and ask you to bless them.

1 A formal association of Methodist churches.
2 From *Methodism.*

September 30th

Like a fluttering sparrow or a darting swallow,
an undeserved curse does not come to rest

(Proverbs 26:2 *NIV*)

Wesley and his lieutenants encountered [fierce opposition] as soon as their work got into full swing and became widely known. Some of it sprang from reasonable doubts as to the wisdom of his unconventional methods and the effectiveness of his apparently untrained assistants, as well as from questions about the orthodoxy of his theology.

Much of it came from sheer jealousy and malice. Among the sober and reasonable attacks must be counted that of Joshua Tucker,[1] the humane and progressive Dean of Gloucester, who blamed the errors and extravagances of Wesley on the teaching of William Law[2] – in a sense, with good reason.

Personal attacks on Wesley labelled him as hypocrite, libertine, Papist, Jacobite – and most insistently of all, "enthusiast" ... Wesley's custom was to pass over the great majority of such diatribes in silence, and only to answer those which might do harm to the Methodists at large.[3]

Lord Jesus, you knew what it was like to be ridiculed and insulted; grant me your grace to put today's text into action, should I be called to endure ridicule for the sake of the gospel.

1 Or Josias (1713–99).
2 Anglican priest and writer (1686–1761). Law refused to swear an oath of allegiance to King George I, and was regarded with suspicion.
3 From *Methodism.*

October 1st

He breathed on them and said, "Receive the Holy Spirit"

(John 20:22 *NIV*)

On the authority of God's word, and our own Church, I must repeat the question, 'Hast thou received the Holy Ghost?'

If you have not, you are not yet a Christian.

A Christian is someone "anointed with the Holy Ghost and with power".

You are not yet made a partaker of pure religion, undefiled. Do you know what religion is – it is a participation of the divine nature; the life of God in the soul of an individual; Christ formed in the heart; "Christ in thee, the hope of glory"; happiness and holiness; Heaven begun on earth; a Kingdom of God within; an everlasting Kingdom brought into your soul.[1]

Gracious Spirit, dwell with me, for I would be gracious. Holy Spirit, dwell with me, for I would be holy. Spirit of Jesus, dwell with me, for I would be like Jesus.

1 From *Fifty Three Sermons.*

October 2nd

He has saved us and called us to a holy life – not because of anything we have done but because of his own purpose and grace

(2 Timothy 1:9 *NIV*)

Are you thoroughly convinced that without inward change and spiritual birth, no one shall see the Lord? Are you labouring after such things? Are you working out your salvation with fear and trembling? Can you tell the searcher of hearts, 'Thou, O God, art the thing that I long for!'?[1]

You hope to be saved; but what reason do you have for the hope within you? Is it because you have done no harm? Is it because you have done much good? Is it because you are not like other men?[2] Or wise, or learned, or honest, or morally good, esteemed, with a fair reputation?

Alas! None of this will bring you to God. In his account, such things are lighter than vanity. Do you know Jesus Christ, whom He sent? Has he taught you that "by grace we are saved through faith; and that not of ourselves: it is the gift of God: not of works, lest any man should boast"?[3]

Jesus Christ came into the world to save sinners.[4] Have you learned what that means?

O that in all these questions you may hear the voice that wakes the dead; and feel that hammer of the word, which breaks the rock in pieces![5] "If ye will hear His voice today … harden not your hearts."[6, 7]

Lord, in your mercy, hear my prayers once again for friends, family and loved ones who are not saved. Impress our love upon their lives, I pray.

1 Psalm 71:4, *KJV*.
2 See Luke 18:11.
3 See Ephesians 2:8, 9, *KJV*.
4 1 Timothy 1:15.
5 Jeremiah 23:29.
6 See Hebrews 3:15, *KJV*.
7 From *Fifty Three Sermons*.

October 3rd

The multitude was divided

(Acts 23:7 *KJV*)

Schism, according to Wesley, has almost always been wrongly defined a separation *from* a church, instead of a separation *in* a church. Upon his own definition, he himself was … guilty of the offence; and however much he contended against those of his followers who were for separating from the Establishment, it is scarcely possible that he should not have foreseen the separation to which all his good measures tended.

Those measures were taken in good faith, and with good intent; most of them indeed arising, unavoidably, from the circumstances in which he found himself; but this was their direct, obvious, inevitable tendency. One step drew on another. Because he preached an enthusiastic and dangerous doctrine, which threw his hearers into convulsions, he was … by most clergymen, refused the use of their pulpits. [1, 2]

The law of unintended consequences! Even with our best efforts at church unity, Lord, divisions are inevitable. Help us, therefore, to disagree with grace and goodwill, even if we can't imagine ever seeing eye-to-eye.

1 From *John Wesley.*

2 Methodism was slowly but surely emerging as a denomination in its own right, separating from the Church of England.

October 4th

"Has not my hand made all these things,
and so they came into being?" declares the Lord

(Isaiah 66:2 *NIV*)

He was … refused the use of their pulpits…

This drove him to field-preaching; but field-preaching is not for all weathers, in a climate like [England's]. Prayer-meetings also were a part of his plan: and thus it became expedient to build meeting-houses. Meeting-houses required funds: they required ministers too, while [Wesley] was itinerating.

Few clergymen could be found to co-operate with him; and though at first he abhorred the thought of admitting uneducated laymen to the ministry, lay preachers were soon forced upon him, by their own zeal, which was too strong to be restrained, and by the plain necessity of the case.[1]

Lord God, how often do we see your work only in hindsight! You steer our ways, and when we look back, we understand what you were developing. To that end, help me to trust your steering, even when the fuller picture is not yet evident. Grant me faith to trust you one step at a time.

1 From *John Wesley.*

October 5th

We were gentle among you, like a nursing mother taking care of her own children

(1 Thessalonians 2:7 *ESV*)

The business of the leaders was to see every person in their classes at least once a week, in order to inquire how their souls prospered; to advise, reprove, comfort, or exhort, as occasion might require; and to receive what they were willing to give towards the expenses of the Society and the relief of the poor … At first they visited each person at his own house; but this was soon found, on many accounts, to be inexpedient, and even impracticable. It required more time than the leaders could spare; many persons lived with masters, mistresses, or relations, who would not suffer them to be thus visited; and when this frequent and natural objection did not exist, it often happened that no opportunity could be had of speaking to them, except in the presence of persons who did not belong to the Society, so that the purpose of the visit was rendered useless. Differences also, and misunderstandings, between members of the same class could not be cleared up, unless the parties were brought face to face. For these reasons it was soon determined that every class should assemble weekly.[1]

Thank you, Lord, for ministers and pastoral visitors who visit faithfully. Theirs is an important ministry, yet not always an easy one. Bless them as they give of their time and energy in such ways, that they in turn may be a blessing.

1 From *John Wesley.*

October 6th

The Lord will watch over your coming and going
both now and for evermore
(Psalm 121:8 *NIV*)

Nothing could shake [John Wesley] from his purpose – not even the frequent conspiracy of the elements. If the ferry was not at hand when he came to a river, he swam across. "The winds and Wesley," laughed his intimates, "go hand in hand." If a boat to Ireland floundered in a tempest, "John Wesley was certain to be aboard". Time and again he came near to drowning, or galloping over a precipice in the fog. No one knew the pitfalls of nature and the foibles of man better than he. But he never yielded either to the one or to the other. "One morning," he records in his journal, "our servant came up and said, 'Sir, there is no travelling today. Such a quantity of snow has fallen in the night that the roads are quite filled up.' I told him, 'At least we can *walk* twenty miles a day, with our horses in our hands.' So in the name of God we set out. The north-east wind was piercing as a sword, and had driven the snow into such uneven heaps that the main road was unpassable." But they made the next town.[1]

Look after those who travel, trudge and traverse for your sake, Lord. Bless those whose ministry sees them criss-crossing countries and continents.

1 From *Living Biographies of Religious Leaders.*

October 7th

Surely goodness and mercy shall follow me all the days of my life

(Psalm 23:6 *KJV*)

Magazines and newspapers ... were filled with ... abuse of the poor Methodists. One paper complains that, "in Yorkshire, by the preaching of the Methodists, the spirit of enthusiasm had so prevailed that almost every man who could hammer out a chapter in the Bible had turned an expounder of the Scripture, to the great decay of industry, and the almost ruin of the woollen manufacture, which seemed threatened with destruction for want of hands to work it."[1]

Such ... were the premonitory mutterings of the storm in which the Methodist movement was cradled. Mobs threatened; newspapers, magazines, and other periodicals fulminated their malicious squibs; prelates, priests, and doctors of divinity became militant pamphleteers; but, in the midst of all, Wesley and his friends calmly proceeded in their glorious calling.[2]

What a wonderful turn of phrase: "Calmly proceeded in their glorious calling"! Help me, I pray, to proceed calmly in my calling today, safe in the knowledge of your unfailing goodness and mercy. Thank you, Lord.

1 Until the advent of the Industrial Revolution in England, the wool industry kept thousands in employment, especially in Yorkshire and Cumberland. It was not uncommon for almost the entire male population of a small Yorkshire town to be engaged in this industry in one way or another.

2 From *Rev. John Wesley.*

October 8th

Whoever heeds reproof is honoured

(Proverbs 13:18 *ESV*)

Dr Doddridge[1] writes in a letter, dated 24 May 1739:

"I think the Methodists sincere; I hope some may be reformed, instructed, and made serious by their means. I saw Mr Whitefield preaching on Kennington Common last week to an attentive multitude, and heard much of him at Bath; but, supposing him sincere and in good earnest, I still fancy that he is but a *weak* man – much too positive, says rash things, and is bold and enthusiastic. I am most heartily glad to hear that any *real* good is done anywhere to the souls of men; but whether these Methodists are in a right way – whether they are warrantable in all their conduct – whether poor people should be urged through different persons successively to pray from four in the morning till eleven at night, is not clear to me; and I am less satisfied with the high pretences they make to the divine influence. I think what Mr Whitefield says and does comes but little short of an assumption of inspiration or infallibility."[2]

Lord, grant me that grace whereby I may receive criticism with humility, appreciating the fact that there may be a kernel of useful truth within what is said. By the same token, help me not to be discouraged.

1 (1702–51), Doctor of Divinity, English Nonconformist leader.
2 From *Rev. John Wesley.*

October 9th

WE ARE CHRIST'S AMBASSADORS; GOD IS MAKING HIS APPEAL THROUGH US. WE SPEAK FOR CHRIST WHEN WE PLEAD, "COME BACK TO GOD!"

(2 Corinthians 5:20 *NLT*)

Sometimes the Methodists met with a friend. For instance, "godly Joseph Williams", of Kidderminster, [1, 2] sympathized with their indefatigable endeavours to save the souls of their fellow-men, and on 17 September 1739, he writes…

"The common people flock to hear them, and in most places hear them gladly. They commonly preach once or twice every day; and expound the Scriptures in the evening to religious societies, who have their society rooms on purpose." He then gives an account of his hearing Charles Wesley preach at Bristol. The preacher stood on a table in a field, and, with eyes and hands lifted up to Heaven, prayed with uncommon fervour and fluency. "He then preached about an hour," said Williams, "in such a manner as I have scarce heard any man preach. Thou I have heard many a finer sermon, yet I think I never heard any man discover such evident signs of vehement desire (to benefit his hearers). With unusual fervour he acquitted himself as an ambassador for Christ."[3]

am·bas·sa·dor

n.

1. A diplomatic official of the highest rank appointed and accredited as representative in residence by one government or sovereign to another, usually for a specific length of time.

2. A diplomatic official heading his or her country's permanent mission[4]

1 Author, prolific letter writer, ardent Methodist.
2 Worcestershire, England.
3 From *Rev. John Wesley.*
4 Thefreedictionary.com.

October 10th

Watch and pray

(Matthew 26:42 *NIV*)

Fri. 20 [March 1741] – A gentleman came to me full of goodwill, to exhort me not to leave the Church;[1] or (which was the same thing in his account) to use extemporary prayer; which, said he, "I will prove to a demonstration to be no prayer at all. For you cannot do two things at once. But thinking how to pray, and praying, are two things. *Ergo*, you cannot both think and pray at once."

Now, may it not be proved by the self-same demonstration, that praying by a form is no prayer at all? For example, "You cannot do two things at once. But reading and praying are two things. *Ergo*, you cannot both read and pray at once."[2]

Lord, how I pray and when I pray is no one else's business. What matters is that I pray, and make the most of the gift of fellowship and dialogue with you. Thank you so much for the gracious privilege of prayer.

1 The Church of England (to establish a separate denomination).
2 From *John Wesley's Journal (Abridged).*

Do not take advantage of a hired worker who is poor and needy … Pay them their wages each day before sunset, because they are poor and are counting on it

(Deuteronomy 24:14, 15 *NIV*)

Thur. May 7 [1741] – I reminded the United Society that many of our brethren and sisters didn't have food, or suitable clothing; many were out of work, through no fault of their own; many were sick and dying. I had done what I could to feed the hungry, to clothe the naked, to employ the poor, and to visit the sick, but this was not enough and I therefore desired the help of all those whose hearts were as my heart to bring what clothes each could spare to be distributed and to give a penny a week, or what they could afford, for the relief of the poor and sick.

My design, I told them, is to employ all the women who are out of business, and would like to work, in knitting, paying them the common price for the work they would do; and then add, according to their need. Twelve people will be invited to inspect these women, and to visit and provide things needful for the sick. Each of these is to visit the sick within their district every other day.[1]

God of justice, I pray for those who campaign on behalf of the poor, for fair wages. Bless their efforts as they work hard to secure decent pay for a day's work. Guide those responsible for official legislation in such matters.

1 From *John Wesley's Journal (Abridged).*

October 12th

TRUST YE IN THE LORD FOR EVER: FOR IN THE LORD JEHOVAH *IS* EVERLASTING STRENGTH

(Isaiah 26:4 *KJV*)

Mon. Dec. 7 [1741] – I preached on, "Trust ye in the Lord Jehovah; for in the Lord is everlasting strength."

I was showing what reason we had to trust in the Captain of our salvation, when someone came into the middle of the room and cried out,

"Who was your captain the other day, when you hanged yourself? I know the man who saw you when you was cut down."

This story, it seems, had been spread around, and was believed by many in Bristol. I asked those present to make room for the man to approach me, but the moment he saw the way open, he ran away with all possible speed, not even stopping to look behind him.

Sat. 12 – In the evening someone asked to speak to me. He was utterly confused, and was unable to speak for a while. Eventually, he said, "I am he that interrupted you at the new room, on Monday. I have had no rest since, day or night, nor will I have until I speak with you. I hope you will forgive me, and that this will be a warning to me all the days of my life."[1]

Gracious God, draw close to those who are in the grip of mental health troubles. Look kindly upon them, however bizarre their behaviour and however illogical their reasoning. Bring peace and healing to the disturbed. Help them, please.

1 From *John Wesley's Journal (Abridged).*

October 13th

TRUE WORSHIPERS WILL WORSHIP THE FATHER IN THE SPIRIT AND IN TRUTH

(John 4:23 *NIV*)

The meetings of … bands, or societies as they were often called, were looked upon by many with suspicion and even abhorrence. We find only one … clergyman giving the excellent advice to his people, "Not to censure any professed members of the Church *who live good lives*, for resorting to religious assemblies in private houses, to perform in society acts of *divine worship*, when the same seems to have been practised by the primitive Christians; and when, alas, there are so many parishes where a person *piously* disposed has no opportunity of joining in the public service of our Church more than one hour and a half in a week."

The same clergyman advises, "Not to condemn those who are constant attendants on the *communion* and *service* of our Church if they sometimes use other prayers in private assemblies, since the best divines of our Church have composed and published many *prayers* that have not the sanction of public authority, which implies a general consent that our Church has not made provision for every private occasion."[1]

Father, when I consider today's text, I am convinced that my worship of you is acceptable if it is sincere, and from the heart. The format or style is secondary. Thank you, Lord, that you graciously accept my humble expressions of worship; may they always please you as I acknowledge your greatness.

1 From *Rev. John Wesley.*

October 14th

I AM NOT ASHAMED: FOR I KNOW WHOM I HAVE BELIEVED, AND AM PERSUADED THAT HE IS ABLE TO KEEP THAT WHICH I HAVE COMMITTED UNTO HIM AGAINST THAT DAY

(2 Timothy 1:12 *KJV*)

Wesley's eldest sister, Emilia,[1] who had always been accustomed to correspond with him, and for whose opinions he had much respect, wrote to him very angrily … abusing the Methodists as bad people, and telling him she understood he could work miracles, cast out devils, etc.

Dr Whitehead's[2] comment upon this is as simple as it is beautiful:

"Mr Wesley knew in whom he had believed, and in the midst of abuse poured out upon him by friends and enemies, went on his way as if he heard not."[3]

Thank you, Lord, for John Wesley's remarkable ability to keep his focus in place, come what may. Help me to learn from his example of steadfast resolution.

1 1692–1771.

2 1740?–1804, English physician and preacher, biographer of John Wesley (*Life of Wesley*, published in 1793).

3 From *Rev. John Wesley.*

He who finds a wife finds what is good

(Proverbs 18:22 *NIV*)

Twice on his travels following his youthful adventure in Georgia, [John Wesley] turned aside to canter in lover's lane.

At the halfway milestone of his life he fell in love with the attractive young widow of a Scotch seaman. This woman was one of his most ardent disciples. When he was sick, she nursed him back to health. "She … understands my physical constitution better than most doctors."

Unfortunately, however, she ran afoul of the social standards of the day. For she was a woman of "low station" and therefore "unfit to be wedded to a prophet". The rumour of the impending marriage created a scandal in the ranks of his followers. A conspiracy was formed to marry off the young lady secretly to one of his subordinates, a man "whose position could do no harm to the cause." And before Wesley could discover what was afoot, he was denied the fruits of his love.[1, 2]

God of love, today I bring before you in prayer, those who are seeking relationships, and those who are seeking your will regarding their choice of a husband or wife. Help them, Lord, especially if they are uncertain. Guide their minds and hearts.

1 Wesley endured the catastrophe of his relationship with Sophia Hopkey (Williamson), and this account refers to an aborted relationship with Grace Murray, whom he loved dearly and hoped to marry. His brother Charles, however, interfered in the relationship as he saw it distracting John from his mission, and enlisted the help of Methodist friends to arrange her marriage to someone else, resulting in a furious spat between the brothers and terrible heartache for John.

2 From *Living Biographies of Religious Leaders.*

October 16th

With such nagging she prodded him day after day

(Judges 16:16 *NIV*)

Finally [Wesley] did succeed in finding himself a wife, the daughter of a London merchant – a giddy young woman who understood neither his character nor his mission.

For thirty years she niggled and nagged and scolded and threatened. She intercepted his private correspondence, destroyed his letters, ridiculed him to his enemies and struck him blows.

And then, when she had worn herself and her husband to the point of prostration, she took sick and died. And Wesley's friends breathed a sigh of relief…

He had gambled with his heart and lost.[1] But he never lost his courage. His friends needn't have pitied him. "The one lasting and absorbing passion of John Wesley was God."[2, 3]

Oh Lord, please help those whose marriages are something of a disaster, with all the heartache and stress that entails. Help your Church to be kind, gracious and understanding towards those whose marriages have collapsed.

1 Out of respect for John Wesley the prophet and man of God, I have chosen not to dwell on his relationships with women within these pages; likewise, his disastrous marriage. The details I have included demonstrate his imperfect humanity, some of his vanity, and his occasional lapses in wisdom, and will suffice for that reasonable purpose.

2 In 1750, Wesley began a correspondence with Molly Vazeille, who had been widowed for three years. After a friendship of just a few months, Wesley announced to his brother Charles that he planned to marry Molly. Charles was filled with dread as he certainly didn't approve of Molly. When John announced the news of the engagement to his church congregation, it was said they hid their faces from him. John and Molly were married in February 1751.

3 From *Living Biographies of Religious Leaders.*

These are the names of the tribes

(Ezekiel 48:1 *ESV*)

Methodism had ... taken root in the land. Meeting-houses had been erected in various parts of the kingdom and ... Wesley [was] the acknowledged head and sole director of the Society which he had raised and organized. Funds were provided by a financial regulation, so well devised, that the revenues would increase in exact proportion to the increase of its numbers. Assistant preachers were ready, in any number that might be required, whose zeal and activity compensated ... for their want of learning; and whose inferiority of rank and education disposed them to look up to Mr Wesley with deference as well as respect ... A system of minute inspection had been established ... to give the preacher the most perfect knowledge of those who were under his charge. No confession of faith was required from any person who desired to become a member: in this Wesley displayed that consummate prudence which distinguished him whenever he was not led away by some darling opinion. The door was thus left open to the orthodox of all descriptions, Churchmen or Dissenters, Baptists or Paeodbaptists,[1] Presbyterians, Presbyterians or Independents, Calvinists or Arminians; no profession, no sacrifice of any kind, was exacted. The person who joined the new Society was not expected to separate himself from the community to which he previously belonged. He was only called upon to renounce his vices, and follies which are near akin to them.[2]

Lord, I pray your blessing upon those looking for a church in which to settle – a "tribe" that can become their spiritual home. As they search, I pray you will guide them to a Christian fellowship that will best suit them, whichever denomination that might be. May my own church be ever-welcoming.

1 People who were baptized as children, but not as adults.
2 From *John Wesley.*

OCTOBER 18TH

PRECIOUS IN THE SIGHT OF THE LORD IS THE DEATH OF HIS SAINTS

(Psalm 116:15 *ESV*)

Methodism had advanced when Wesley lost his mother, in a good age,[1] ready and willing to depart. Arriving in London from one of his circuits, he found her "on the borders of eternity; but she had no doubt or fear, nor any desire but, as soon as God should call, to depart and to be with Christ."

On the third day after his arrival, he perceived that her change was near. "I sat down," he says, "on the bedside. She was in her last conflict, unable to speak, but I believe quite sensible. Her look was calm and serene, and her eyes fixed upward while we commended her soul to God. From three to four the silver cord was loosing … and then, without any struggle, or sigh, or groan, the soul was set at liberty. We stood round the bed, and fulfilled her last request, uttered a little before she lost her speech: 'Children, as soon as I am released sing a psalm of praise to God.'"

[Wesley] performed the funeral service himself.[2]

God of compassion, draw close to those who mourn this day; whose loved ones have departed. Embrace them with comfort as they tread the path of bereavement. In the darkness of loss, may they sense your tender care.

1 Susanna Wesley died on 23 July 1742, aged 73. She is sometimes referred to as the "Mother of Methodism".

2 From *John Wesley.*

October 19th

This, in essence, is the message we heard from Christ and are passing on to you: God is light, pure light; there's not a trace of darkness in him

(1 John 1:5 *MSG*)

If you even now "awakest, and arise from the dead",[1] [God] has bound himself to "give thee light". "The Lord shall give thee grace and glory"[2] : the light of his grace here, and the light of his glory when you receive the crown that does not fade away.[3] "Thy light shall break forth as the morning, and thy darkness be as the noon-day."[4] "God, who commanded the light to shine out of darkness, shall shine in thy heart; to give the knowledge of the glory of God in the face of Jesus Christ."[5] "On them that fear the Lord shall the Sun of Righteousness arise with healing in his wings."[6] And in that day it shall be said unto you, "Arise, shine; for thy light is come, and the glory of the Lord is risen upon thee."[7] For Christ shall reveal himself in you: and he is the true Light. God is light,[8] and will give himself to every awakened sinner who waits for him; you shall be a temple of the living God, and Christ shall "dwell in thy heart by faith".[9]

Lord God, you are light. You are brilliant. There is nothing shadowy or shady about you. You give of yourself, in shining your light into the hearts of sinners. Thank you, God; light-bearer and light-sharer.

1 See Ephesians 5:14.
2 See Psalm 84:11, *KJV*.
3 See 1 Peter 5:4.
4 See Psalm 36:7, *KJV*.
5 See 2 Corinthians 4:6, *KJV*.
6 Malachi 4:2, *KJV*.
7 See Isaiah 60:1, *KJV*.
8 1 John 1:5.
9 From *Fifty Three Sermons*.

October 20th

Do you give the horse his might?
Do you clothe his neck with a mane?
(Job 39:19 *ESV*)

Wesley continue, with his constitutional fervour, to preach the doctrines of instantaneous regeneration, assurance, and sinless perfection. These doctrines gave … offence, and became still more offensive when they were promulgated by unlettered men, with all the vehemence and self-sufficiency of … inspiration.

Wesley himself added to the offence by the loftiness of his pretensions. In the preface to his third journal, he says, "It is not the work of man which hath lately appeared; all who calmly observe it must say, 'This is the Lord's doing, and it is marvellous in our eyes.' The manner in which God has wrought this is as strange as the work itself. These extraordinary circumstances seem to have been designed by God for the further manifestation of his work, to cause his power to be known, and to awaken the attention of a drowsy world."

Wesley related accounts of cures brought about by faith and prayer, which he considered positively miraculous. When his own teeth ached, he prayed, and the pain left him. His faith was so strong that is sometimes sufficed for his horse too. "My horse," he says, "was so exceedingly lame, that I was afraid I would have to retire him. We could not discern what was wrong, yet he would not set his foot to the ground. After riding for seven miles I was thoroughly tired, and my head ached more than it had done for some months. What I hear state is the naked fact: let everyone account for it as they see fit. I thought, 'Cannot God heal either man or beast, by any means?' Immediately my weariness and my headache ceased, and my horse's lameness in the same instant. Nor did he halt any more, either that day or the next."[1]

What a story! Well, why not, Lord! You are the God of human and horses! Remind me to pray about everything, knowing that if it matters to me, then it matters to you.

1 From *John Wesley.*

October 21st

PRAY … FOR KINGS AND ALL WHO ARE IN AUTHORITY SO THAT WE CAN LIVE PEACEFUL AND QUIET LIVES MARKED BY GODLINESS AND DIGNITY

(1 Timothy 2:2 *NLT*)

It was commonly reported that [John Wesley] was a Papist, if not a Jesuit; that he kept Popish priests in his house … that he received large remittances from Spain…[1]

Sometimes it was reported that he was in prison on a charge of high treason … Reports to this effect we so prevalent, that when, in the beginning of the year 1744, a proclamation was issued requiring all Papists to leave London, he thought it prudent to remain a week there … This did not prevent the Surrey magistrates from summoning him, and making him take the oath of allegiance, and sign the declaration against Popery.[2]

Wesley was indifferent to all other accusations; but the charge of disaffection, in such times, might have serious consequences, and he drew up a loyal address to the king, in the name of "The Societies in derision called Methodists".[3]

I pray for kings and queens today, Lord – monarchs and rulers who to some extent hold the lives of their subjects in their hands. Grant them wisdom and courage to reign with kindness and righteousness, for the benefit of their nations.

1 At a time in English history when the very throne of monarchy was at stake, in the tussle between Protestants and Catholics, this was a serious allegation, with important implications of treason.

2 Roman Catholics were required to sign an oath of allegiance to the king. They were obliged to register their names and details of their estates. In times of such political turmoil, Roman Catholics were regarded with hostility and suspicion, hence their expulsion from London.

3 From *John Wesley*.

October 22nd

DO YOUR BEST TO PRESENT YOURSELF TO GOD AS ONE APPROVED,
A WORKER WHO HAS NO NEED TO BE ASHAMED,
RIGHTLY HANDLING THE WORD OF TRUTH

(2 Timothy 2:15 *ESV*)

In the early stages of his career Wesley was content to leave the good done by his ministry to the clergymen of the parish in which the persons who received it dwelt.

Afterwards, we have seen that he formed bands and societies for the mutual assistance of his converts, and these were usually left in the charge of persons who would instruct them in religious matters.

In these days the Church provides for the careful instruction and religious fellowship of her members; in those [days] the clergy in general made no provision for the religiously disposed people of their parishes; and hence, asks Mr Wesley, "what was to be done in a case of … extreme necessity?' No clergyman would assist at all. The question that remained was to find someone among themselves who was upright in heart, and of sound judgment in the things of God, and to ask him to meet the rest as often as he could, in order to confirm them as he was able in the ways of God.[1]

Thank you, Lord, for clergy. Thank you too for those who step in and help when no clergy are available. Their work is invaluable, and I ask you bless them; lay workers, readers, church helpers, volunteers, and those whose absence would quickly be noticed.

1 From *Rev. John Wesley*.

David spake to the chief of the Levites

(1 Chronicles 15:16 *KJV*)

In these measures there was no *intention* of a separation from the Church [of England]...

[John Wesley] took care, and all his principles and feelings favoured the caution, that no obstacles should be placed in the way of the closest connection of the societies with the Establishment. None of their services were held in the hours of her public service; the Methodists formed in many parishes formed the great body of her communicants; thousands of them died in her communion; and the preachers, though separated to the work by solemn prayer and a mode of ordination, though without the imposition of hands,[1] were not permitted to administer either of the sacraments to the people among whom they laboured.[2]

These are tremendous steps in careful diplomacy, Lord, and today my prayers are with those who negotiate delicate and sensitive issues within church life, often confidentially. Make them holy diplomats, Lord, as they seek to balance every opinion and work towards positive solutions.

1 1 Timothy 4:14.
2 From *Rev. John Wesley.*

October 24th

Test your servants for ten days; let us be given vegetables to eat and water to drink

(Daniel 1:12 *ESV*)

Sun. July 6 [1746] (London) – After talking largely with both the men and women leaders, we agreed it would prevent great expense, as well of health as of time and money, if the poorer people of our society could be persuaded to leave off drinking tea.

We resolved ourselves to begin and set the example. I expected some difficulty in breaking off a custom of six-and-twenty years' standing. And, accordingly, the three first days, my head ached, more or less, all day long, and I was half asleep from morning till night. The third day, on Wednesday, in the afternoon, my memory failed, almost entirely. In the evening I sought my remedy in prayer. On Thursday morning my headache was gone. My memory was as strong as ever. And I have found no inconvenience, but a sensible benefit in several respects, from that very day to this.[1]

Is there anything, Lord, that I should give up?

1 From *John Wesley's Journal (Abridged).*

October 25th

In a desert land he found him, in a barren and howling waste. He shielded him and cared for him; he guarded him as the apple of his eye

(Deuteronomy 32:10 *NIV*)

Tues. March 24 [1747] – I rode to Blanchland,[1] about twenty miles from Newcastle. The rough mountains round about were still white with snow. In the midst of them is a small winding valley, through which the [River] Derwent runs. On the edge of this the little town stands, which indeed is little more than a heap of ruins. There seems to have been a large cathedral church, the vast walls of which remain. I stood in the churchyard, under one side of the building, upon a large tombstone, around which, while I was praying, all the congregation knelt down on the grass. They were gathered out of the lead mines from all parts; many from Allandale, six miles off. A row of little children sat under the opposite wall, all quiet and still. The whole congregation drank in every word with such earnestness in their looks, I could not but hope that God will make this wilderness sing for joy.[2]

Oh Lord, bring revival where there is wilderness! Gather your people together where there is no church witness, to become a witness! Look at the barren areas and bring new life, new hope.

1 Northumberland, England.
2 From *John Wesley's Journal (Abridged).*

October 26th

The horse is prepared ... but safety is of the Lord

(Proverbs 21:31 *KJV*)

Thur. Jan. 28 [1748] – I set out for Deverel Longbridge.[1] About ten o'clock we were met by a loaded wagon, in a deep, hollow way. There was a narrow path between the road and the bank: I stepped into this…

When the wagon came near, my horse began to rear, and to attempt climbing up the bank. This frightened the horse which was close behind, and made him prance and throw his head to and fro, till the bit of the bridle caught hold of the cape of my greatcoat, and pulled me backward off my horse.

I fell onto the path, between the wagon and the bank, as if someone had taken me in his arms and laid me down there.

Both our horses stood stock still, one just behind me, the other before; so, by the blessing of God, I rose unhurt, mounted again, and rode on.[2]

Lord, when life knocks me down – when circumstances conspire – help me, I pray, to take stock and "ride on" as soon as I possibly can. Be with those today, Lord Jesus, who have suffered blows or sudden setbacks. Bless us with that special gift of perseverance.

1 Almost certainly Longbridge Deverill, Wiltshire, England.

2 From *John Wesley's Journal (Abridged).*

October 27th

They were harassed and helpless, like sheep without a shepherd

(Matthew 9:36 *NIV*)

[Wesley found] the success of the work of the societies depended in great measure upon the leaders who were chosen to look after them during his absence. The affairs of the first organized society in Fetter Lane fell into confusion, again and again, during his absence in Bristol, and when he came to town much of his time was taken up in trying to restore order...[1]

Wesley ... did not find one woman of the Society who had not been on the point of casting away her confidence in God. However ... he found one who, although others had laboured hard to persuade her she had no faith, replied, "with a spirit they could not resist, 'I know that the life which I now live, I live by faith in the Son of God, who loved me, and gave himself for me; and he has never left me one moment since the hour he was made known to me in the breaking of bread.'"[2]

Oh Lord, how quickly the devil moves in whenever he spots an opportunity. Protect your flock, I pray, from any such disarray. Bless those who lead. Give them strength! Lord, we don't want to continually be a problem-solving Church – we want to be a soul-saving Church. Stay with us.

1 Power struggles were rife, as various people assumed positions of authority in Wesley's absences. Various strands of teaching were implemented and numerous members of the congregation were advised that their faith was sub-standard because of one reason or another.

2 From *Rev. John Wesley*.

October 28th

The glory of the Lord filled the temple

(Ezekiel 43:5 *ESV*)

In general [Wesley] was heard with deep attention [when he preached], for his believers listened with deep reverence; and those who were not persuaded listened … from curiosity, and behaved respectfully…

"I wonder at those," says he, who talk of the *indecency* of field-preaching. The highest *indecency* is in St Paul's Church, where a considerable part of the congregation are asleep, or talking, or looking about, not paying attention a word the preacher says. On the other hand, there is the highest *decency* in a churchyard, or field, where the whole congregation behave and look as if they saw the Judge of all, and heard Him speaking from Heaven."

Sometimes when he had finished speaking, and pronounced the blessing, not a person offered to move: the charm was upon them still; and every man, woman and child remained where they were, till he set the example of leaving.[1]

Thank you, Almighty God, for those times when your Spirit seems especially close; when worship is touched with splendour, and no one wants to go home. More of the same, please!

1 From *John Wesley*.

October 29th

You shall go out in joy and be led forth in peace; the mountains and the hills before you shall break forth into singing, and all the trees of the field shall clap their hands

(Isaiah 55:12 *ESV*)

The situations in which [Wesley] preached sometimes contributed to the impression [he made upon his hearers]; and he himself perceived that natural influences operated upon the multitude. Sometimes, in a hot and cloudless summer day, he and his congregation were under the cover of the sycamores … In such a scene, he observed that bird, perched on one of the trees, sung without intermission from the beginning of the service to the end. No instrumental concert would have fitted so well with the place and the feeling of the hour. Sometimes, when he had not finished preaching until twilight, he saw that the calmness of the evening agreed with the seriousness of the people…

One of his preaching places in Cornwall was in what had once been the courtyard of a rich and honourable man. But he and all his family were in the dust, and his memory had almost perished. "At Gwenap, in the same county," he says, "I stood on the wall, in the calm still evening, with the setting sun behind me, and almost an innumerable multitude before, behind, and on the other hand. May likewise sat on the little hills, at some distance from the bulk of the congregation. But they could all hear distinctly while I read." This amphitheatre was one of his favourite stations.[1]

What a lovely picture this creates, Creator God.

1 From *John Wesley*.

October 30th

God so loved the world that he gave his one and only Son, that whoever believes in him shall not perish but have eternal life

(John 3:16 *NIV*)

The development of the [Methodist] Revival was not hampered by either verbal or physical violence. Wesley went on serenely with his work while the rabble raged. Much more serious was the internal strife which from time to time broke out among his supporters. As often happens at a time of spiritual awakening, some people joined the movement because of the sensations that they might expect to receive. If they are disappointed in this, such people go off to start religious movements on their own. This happened once or twice in the growth of Methodism, and there were some also who quarrelled with Wesley … But by and large, his strong personality prevented outbursts of personal feeling. What he could not prevent was theological controversy.

Whitefield was convinced that God had from eternity predestined the majority of mankind to damnation, and a few to salvation through Jesus Christ. The purpose of his evangelistic activity was to gather to Christ those who were predestined to salvation … Both the Wesleys rejected predestination root and branch. They were quite sure that Christ had really and truly died for all men. "For all, for all, my Saviour died" was the burden of one of Charles's most frequently sung hymns. The restriction of God's grace to the elect few was utterly repugnant to their understanding of the New Testament … They agreed that the initiative in salvation was wholly God's, and that faith itself was the gift of God; but they refused to draw from this the conclusion that man was denied the free choice between damnation and salvation.[1]

"Whosoever will may come,
And who comes to him shall never
Disappointed turn away;
Praise the Lord! 'tis whosoever."[2]

1 From *Methodism.*
2 William John McAlonan (1863–1925), *The Song Book of The Salvation Army, 2015.*

Do not let the sun go down while you are still angry

(Ephesians 4:26 *NIV*)

The argument between the two parties broke out soon after the beginning of the Revival, but it was kept within bounds by the agreement between Whitefield and John Wesley that the two principals should not engage in public controversy, and that each should work in his own sphere without interruption from the other. But the expulsion of six Methodists of the Calvinistic persuasion from St Edmund Hall, Oxford, in 1768 set the controversy alight,[1] and many of the Calvinistic pamphlets were directed personally against John Wesley...

[The words of Augustus Montague Toplady][2] about Wesley were so vitriolic that his opponent lost his habitual calm and answered back by publishing a highly tendentious summary of Toplady's argument ... This precipitated a further flood of abuse from Toplady and his associate, Roland Hill;[3] the Minutes of Wesley's Conference in 1770 took an uncompromising line; and Whitefield's death in the same year removed the last restraints.[4]

Lord, forgive us when we argue and anger gets the upper hand.

1 The vice-principal of the college, John Hingson, was alarmed by the presence of students "who talked of regeneration, inspiration and drawing nigh unto God". An enquiry was convened, resulting in the expulsion of six Methodists with Calvinistic sympathies on the grounds that they refused to desist from publicly praying and exhorting.
2 1740–78. Anglican cleric, hymn-writer, and a major proponent of Calvinism.
3 Or Rowland (1744–1833), evangelical Calvinist.
4 From *Methodism*.

November 1st

And, behold, there came a leper and worshipped him, saying, Lord, if thou wilt, thou canst make me clean. And Jesus put forth his hand, and touched him, saying, I will; be thou clean. And immediately his leprosy was cleansed. And Jesus saith unto him, See thou tell no man; but go thy way, shew thyself to the priest, and offer the gift that Moses commanded, for a testimony unto them

(Matthew 8:2–4 *KJV*)

Verse 2. *A leper came* – Leprosies in those countries were seldom curable by natural means, any more than palsies or lunacy were. Probably this leper, though he might not mix with people, had heard our Lord at a distance.

Verse 4. *See thou tell no man* – Perhaps our Lord only meant here, not until you have spoken to a priest, who was appointed to inquire into the cause of the leprosy. [1]But many other Jesus commanded absolutely to tell no one of the miracles he had wrought. This he seems to have done for one or more of these reasons: 1. To prevent the multitude from thronging him, in the manner related in Mark 1:45. To fulfil the prophecy of Isaiah 42:2, that he would not be vain or ostentatious. Matthew offers this reason on chapter 12:17. To avoid being taken by force and made a king; John 6:15. That he might not enrage the chief priests, scribes, and Pharisees, who were the most bitter against him, any more than was unavoidable and inevitable; Matthew 16:20, 21.[2]

What a lovely picture of Jesus: the One who is worshipped, the One who heals and cleanses, and the One who counsels in great wisdom. Jesus is Lord.

1 Leviticus 4:1–9.
2 From *Notes on the New Testament.*

November 2nd

In the beginning was the word,
and the word was with God,
and the word was God

(John 1:1 *KJV*)

Verse 1. *In the beginning* – Referring to Genesis 1:1 and Proverbs 8:23, when all things began to be made by the word. In the beginning of Heaven and earth, and the whole frame of created beings, the word existed without any beginning. He was when all things began; whatsoever had a beginning. *The word* – so termed in Psalm 33:6 … so that St John did not borrow this expression from … any heathen writer. He was not yet named Jesus, or Christ. He is the word whom the Father begat or spoke from eternity; by whom the Father made all things, through whom the Father speaks to us … *And the Word was with God* – Therefore distinct from God the Father. The word with denotes a perpetual tendency, as it were, of the Son to the Father, in unity of essence. He was with God alone; because nothing beside God had any being at that time. *And the word was God* – Supreme, eternal, independent.[1]

Another stunning picture of Christ: eternal God, begotten, not created.

1 From *Notes on the New Testament.*

November 3rd

What does it profit, my brethren, if someone says he has faith but does not have works? Can faith save him? If a brother or sister is naked and destitute of daily food, and one of you says to them, "Depart in peace, be warmed and filled," but you do not give them the things which are needed for the body, what does it profit? Thus also faith by itself, if it does not have works, is dead

(James 2:14–17 NKJV)

Wesley's emphasis of holiness as perfect love was entirely admirable. It was a complete statement of what holiness means. Even sins of omission rise from selfishness and are driven out by love. The soul possessed with the divine love could find no room for any sort of sin.

This emphasis was most important in the Calvinist circles of the eighteenth century, in which salvation was taught as the final privilege of the elect rather than a present deliverance from sin. Wesley's emphasis was always on present salvation – a salvation, not only from the guilt, but from the power of sin, which could only be complete when love absolutely dominated the soul.

His doctrine gained much from his practical character. He did teach love as a mystical and emotional relation of the soul to Christ, as a bride to her husband; all such doctrines he disliked; he thought that they were smudged with sentimentality, and led to exotic extravagances. The love which he taught was practical and social.[1]

Hearts to God and hands to mankind; Christianity with its sleeves rolled up.
Faith with its boots on.

1 From *The Evangelical Doctrines of Charles Wesley's Hymns.*

November 4th

These three remain: faith, hope and love.
But the greatest of these is love

(1 Corinthians 13:13 *NIV*)

Probably [Wesley's] favourite chapter in the Bible was 1 Corinthians 13, which described love in social and practical actions.

The love which he taught was the divine love which saved others and ministered to every sort of necessity, and expressed itself in social service and mutual unselfishness. Few men, either by their precepts or their examples, have illustrated so forcibly the practical character of the Christian ideal.

Whatever may be said against his notional doctrines, he found the path of perfection and directed his people to walk on that most excellent way. The practical benefits his teaching rendered to them were immense. They were protected from mystical extravagances on the one hand, and from the antinomian perils of an unbalanced stress on "faith only", on the other.[1]

"Love divine, all loves excelling,
Joy of Heaven to earth come down;
Fix in us thy humble dwelling;
All thy faithful mercies crown!
Jesus, Thou art all compassion,
Pure unbounded love Thou art;
Visit us with Thy salvation;
Enter every trembling heart."[2]

1 From *The Evangelical Doctrines of Charles Wesley's Hymns.*
2 Charles Wesley.

November 5th

Now Jacob's well was there. Jesus therefore, being wearied with his journey, sat thus on the well: and it was about the sixth hour. There cometh a woman of Samaria to draw water: Jesus saith unto her, Give me to drink. (For his disciples were gone away unto the city to buy meat.) Then saith the woman of Samaria unto him, How is it that thou, being a Jew, askest drink of me, which am a woman of Samaria? for the Jews have no dealings with the Samaritans

(John 4:6–9 *KJV*)

Verse 6. *Jesus sat thus* – Weary as he was. It was the sixth hour – Noon; the heat of the day.

Verse 7. *Give me to drink* – In this one conversation he brought her to the knowledge that knowledge which the Apostles were so long in attaining.

Verse 8. *For his disciples were gone* – Else he need not have asked her.

Verse 9. *How dost thou* – Her open simplicity appears from her very first words. *The Jews have no dealings* – Not by way of friendship. They would receive no kind of favours from them.[1]

In these four verses, we see a stunning picture of God made man: weary, thirsty, alone, breaking down barriers. A vulnerable God who reaches out across social norms and cultural expectations. This is God. This is the Incarnation.

1 From *Notes on the New Testament.*

November 6th

Built on the foundation of the apostles and prophets, with Christ Jesus himself as the chief cornerstone

(Ephesians 2:20 *NIV*)

Through all the years of persecution and strife Wesley was protecting the organization of his Societies. They were grouped early on into "Circuits", very large at first, and gradually decreasing in size as the movement advanced. After 1748 the representatives of each Society in the Circuit met once a quarter, and soon came to issue each quarter a "Plan" of the preachers appointed from week to week in each Society.

Wesley retained the general control of all the Circuits as the "Superintendent", but appointed an "Assistant" to each of them; these Assistants came to be called Superintendents.

It gradually became customary for a preacher to stay in a Circuit for three years, though Wesley at first thought that even this was too long … he calculated that a preacher would have preached to the same congregation all that he useful could in about three years. In 1745 he began the practice of calling together his clerical supporters and his preachers to a conference. In due course this gathering became annual, and settled the main affairs of the "Connexion" (as it came to be called) for the ensuing year.[1]

Slowly but surely, Lord, you have, over the centuries, built, developed and moulded your Church. You are a patient, painstaking God who works graciously and slowly.

1 From *Methodism.*

November 7th

GOD PLACED ALL THINGS UNDER HIS FEET AND APPOINTED HIM TO BE HEAD OVER EVERYTHING FOR THE CHURCH

(Ephesians 1:22 *NIV*)

At the same time the Societies developed their devotional and liturgical practices. The "preaching service", held at a different time from the services of the Parish Church,[1] became exceedingly popular.

Love-feasts, the revival of the New Testament "Agape",[2] were borrowed from the Moravians and widely practised ... Each person present received a piece of plain cake and a cup of water, and these were taken together in token of fellowship. Afterwards, each one present, if possible, gave a testimony to God's power and love, and many hymns were sung.

Most characteristically Methodist of all was the "Covenant Service". It originated in one of the London Societies when Wesley read the words of the Covenant which Richard Alleine, the Puritan,[3] had suggested that every Christian should make with his Lord.[4]

Thank you, Lord, for John Wesley, who persevered under hostile opposition in order to create something beautiful for God. He never gave up, and you rewarded his efforts. May that example encourage me, albeit in smaller, more personal ways.

1 An interesting point, demonstrating, perhaps, that John Wesley was still anxious to avoid a collision with the Church of England, and keen to observe such protocol.
2 Something less formal than the Anglican rite of Holy Communion.
3 Richard Alleine (1610 or 1611–1681), English Puritan divine.
4 From *Methodism.*

November 8th

Have respect unto the covenant

(Psalm 74:20 *KJV*)

The practice [of reading the words of Richard Alleine's Covenant] still holds, and every Methodist is expected to assent to the demanding words:

Christ has many services to be done: some are easy, others are difficult; some bring honour, others bring reproach; some are suitable to our natural inclinations and temporal interests, others are contrary to both. In some way we may please Christ and please ourselves, in others we cannot please Christ except by denying ourselves. Yet the power to do all these things is assuredly given us in Christ, who strengtheneth us. Therefore let us make the Covenant of God our own. Let us engage our heart to the Lord, and resolve in His strength never to go back…

and to take upon his lips this prayer:

> **I am no longer my own, but thine. Put me to what thou wilt, rank me with whom thou wilt; put me to doing, put me to suffering; let me be employed for thee or laid aside for thee, exalted for thee or brought low for thee; let me be full, let me be empty; let me have all things, let me have nothing; I freely and heartily yield all things to thy pleasure and disposal. And now, O glorious and blessed God, Father, Son and Holy Spirit, thou art mine, and I am thine. So be it. And the Covenant which I have made on earth, let it be ratified in Heaven[1] Amen.**

1 From *Methodism.*

November 9th

Blessed are they whose iniquities are forgiven, and whose sins are covered

(Romans 4:7 *KJV*)

The plain Scriptural notion of justification is pardon the forgiveness of sins.

It is that act of God the Father, whereby, for the sake of his son and his shed blood, he "showeth forth his righteousness" (or mercy) "by the remission of the sins that are past".

This is the easy, natural account of it given by St Paul … "Blessed are they," says he, "whose iniquities are forgiven, and whose sins are covered: blessed is the man to whom the Lord will not impute sin."

To him that is justified or forgiven, God "will not impute sin" to his condemnation. He will not condemn him … either in this world or in that which is to come. His sins, all his past sins, in thought, word, and deed, are covered, are blotted out, shall not be remembered or mentioned against him, any more than as if they had not existed.

God will not inflict on that sinner what he deserves to suffer, because his son has suffered for him … He loves, and blesses, and watches over us for good, as if we had never sinned.[1]

What an astonishing gospel. So simple. So profound. So complete.

1 From *Notes on the New Testament.*

NOVEMBER 10TH

WHOEVER CONCEALS THEIR SINS DOES NOT PROSPER, BUT THE ONE WHO CONFESSES AND RENOUNCES THEM FINDS MERCY

(Proverbs 28:13 *NIV*)

Is there ... sin in him that is in Christ? Does sin *remain* in one that believes in him? Is there any sin in them that are born of God, or are they wholly delivered from it? Let no one imagine this to be a question of mere curiosity; or that it is of little importance whether it is determined one way or another. It is a point of the utmost importance to every serious Christian; the resolving of which concerns both his present and eternal happiness ...

The whole body of ancient Christians, those who have left us anything in writing, declare with one voice that even believers in Christ, till they are "strong in the Lord and in the power of his might,"[1] have need to "wrestle with flesh and blood,"[2] with an evil nature, as well as with "principalities and powers"[3] ... The same testimony is given by all other Churches; not only by the Greek and Romish Church, but by every Reformed Church in Europe, of whatever denomination . . .

For the sake of those who really fear God, and desire to know "the truth as it is in Jesus," it is not inappropriate to consider the point with calmness and impartiality.[4]

Great Guardian of my soul, help me to be honest with you regarding such matters, and to "keep short accounts" whereby any lingering sins quickly wither and die. Holy Spirit, dwell with me and convict me of anything that concerns you.

1 Ephesians 6:10, *KJV*.
2 See Ephesians 6:12.
3 See Ephesians 6:12.
4 From *Fifty Three Sermons*.

November 11th

The flesh lusteth against the Spirit, and the Spirit against the flesh: these are contrary the one to the other

(Galatians 5:17 *KJV*)

By sin, I mean inward sin; any sinful temper, passion, or affection; such as pride, self-will, love of the world, in any kind or degree; such as lust, anger, peevishness; any disposition contrary to the mind that was in Christ. The question is not concerning outward sin; whether a child of God can commit sin or not. We all agree and maintain, "He that commiteth sin is of the Devil."[1] We agree, "Whosoever is born of God doth not commit sin."[2] We now enquire, Is a justified or regenerate person freed from all soon? Is there no sin in their heart – nor ever after, unless they fall from grace?

The state of a justified person is inexpressibly great and glorious ... Born again ... A child of God ... A member of Christ ... A temple of the Holy Ghost ... Created anew in Christ Jesus ... And so long as that person "walketh in love" he worships God in spirit and in truth.[3]

But was he not freed from all sin, so that there is no sin in his heart? I cannot say this; I cannot believe it; because St Paul says the contrary, describing the state of believers in general: "The flesh lusteth against the Spirit, and the Spirit against the flesh: these are contrary the one to the other." He expresses this clearly. The Apostle directly affirms that the flesh, evil nature, opposes the Spirit, even in believers; that even in the regenerate there are two principles, "contrary the one to the other".[4]

This may be true, Lord Jesus – St Paul and John Wesley in agreement on this point – but it is by no means the whole story. Because of Calvary, all my sins – all of them – are forgiven, "covered by the blood". Thank you, Lord, for Calvary.

1 1 John 3:8, *KJV*.
2 1 John 3:9, *KJV*.
3 John 4:24.
4 *From Fifty Three Sermons*.

November 12th

A farmer went out to sow his seed. As he was scattering the seed, some fell along the path, and the birds came and ate it up. Some fell on rocky places, where it did not have much soil. It sprang up quickly, because the soil was shallow. But when the sun came up, the plants were scorched, and they withered because they had no root

(Matthew 13:3–6 *NIV*)

[The itinerant] life led [Wesley] into a lower sphere of society than that wherein he would otherwise have moved; and he thought himself a gainer by the change. Writing to some earl, who took a lively interest in the revival of religion which, through the impulse given, directly or indirectly, by Methodism, was taking place, he says, "To speak rough truth, I do not desire any intercourse with any persons of quality in England. I mean, for my own sake. They do me no good, and, I fear, I can do none to them."

But though Wesley preferred the middling and lower classes of society to the rich, the class which he liked least were the farmers.

Wesley was likely to judge thus unfavourably of the agricultural part of the people, because they were the least susceptible of Methodism. For Methodism could be kept alive only by associations and frequent meetings; and it is difficult, or impossible, to arrange these among a scattered [rural] population. Where converts could not be made, and the discipline could not be introduced among them, and the effect kept up by constant preaching and inspection, they soon fell off.[1]

Lord of the harvest, my prayers today are with those who have heard your word, but don't do much about developing its impact, for one reason or another. Stay with them, I pray, and graciously warm whatever influence has taken place.

1 From *John Wesley.*

November 13th

TAKE THEREFORE NO THOUGHT FOR THE MORROW:
FOR THE MORROW SHALL TAKE THOUGHT FOR THE THINGS OF ITSELF

(Matthew 6:34 *KJV*)

At first there was no provision made for the lay preachers. The enthusiasts who offered themselves to the work literally took no thought for the morrow, what they should eat, nor what they should drink, nor yet for the body what they should put on. They trusted in him who feedeth the fowls of the air, and who sent his ravens to Elijah in the wilderness[1] ... They were lodged and fed by some of the Society wherever they went; and when they wanted clothes, if they were not supplied by individual friends, they presented their need to the stewards. St Francis and his followers did not commit themselves with more confidence to the care of Providence, nor with a more entire disregard of all human means...

In England [however], rags were no recommendation, and it was inconvenient that the more popular itinerants should be clothed in the best apparel, while the usefulness of some of their colleagues, who were equally devoted to the cause, was lessened by the shabbiness of their appearance. To remedy this evil, it was agreed that every circuit should allow its preacher three pounds per quarter, to provide himself with clothing and books. But further relief was still necessary for those married preachers who gave themselves up wholly to the service of Methodism.[2]

Lord, bless those groups, charities, churches and societies who care for the poor and underprivileged. Bless and guide too, I pray, government legislation regarding those in need. Keep an eye on my personal giving too, please.

1 1 Kings 17.
2 From *John Wesley*.

NOVEMBER 14TH

EXCEPT YE BE CONVERTED, AND BECOME AS LITTLE CHILDREN,
YE SHALL NOT ENTER INTO THE KINGDOM OF HEAVEN

(Matthew 18:3 *KJV*)

[Wesley] went back to Bristol, but … was again summoned to London by appeal to him on account of the wranglings and divisions of the Fetter Lane Society…

He writes, "I accordingly came to London, though with a heavy heart. Here I found every day the dreadful effects of our brethren's reasonings and disputings with each other. Scarce one in ten retained his first love; and most of the rest were in the utmost confusion, biting and devouring one another. I pray God ye be not consumed one of another."

"One came to me," says Wesley, the following Sunday," by whom I used to profit much. But her conversation was now too high for me. It was far above, out of my sight. My soul is sick of this sublime divinity! Let me think and speak as a little child! Let my religion be plain, artless, simple! Meekness, temperance, faith, and love, be these my highest gifts; and let the highest words wherein I teach them, be those I learn from the book of God!"[1]

Lord, my heart goes out to John Wesley here! After all his work, after all his struggle, it has come to squabbles and in-fighting. Preserve your Church from such wastes of energy, I pray, that we might not grieve your heart. Hold our tongues, please.

1 From *Rev. John Wesley.*

November 15th

The Lord preserveth the simple: I was brought low, and he helped me

(Psalm 116:6 *KJV*)

[Wesley] ... returned home, and after praying for divine aid, in his usual clear and logical way ... He sought [faith] by doing all these things:

"To go to church;

"To communicate;

"To fast;

"To use as much private prayer as he could; and,

"To read the Scriptures;

"Because I believe these are 'means of grace.'"[1]

Oh Lord, forgive us when we overcomplicate matters of faith and belief! Help us to take a leaf out of Wesley's books and, every so often, come "back to basics" in our dealings with you, for there is much profit in doing so. Make us simple saints.

1 From *Rev. John Wesley.*

November 16th

Look beneath the surface so you can judge correctly

(John 7:24 *NLT*)

Reflecting … on the case of a poor woman who had continual pain in her stomach, I could not but notice the inexcusable negligence of most physicians in cases of this nature. They prescribe drug upon drug, without knowing a jot of the matter concerning the root of the disorder. And without knowing this they cannot cure, though they can murder, the patient. Whence came this woman's pain? (which she would never have explained, had she never been questioned about it) – it came from fretting for the death of her son. And what use medicines, while she fretted like that? Why do physicians not consider how far our bodily disorders are caused or influenced by the mind; and in those cases, which are utterly out of their sphere of expertise, call in a minister; as indeed ministers, when they find the mind disordered by the body, call in the assistance of a physician? But why are these cases out of their sphere? Because they know not God. It follows, no man can be a thorough physician without being an experienced Christian.[1]

Reading this, Lord, I can but thank you for the tremendous advances made in holistic medicine, whereby such matters are nowadays better understood and appreciated. Grants us each, Lord – ministers, doctors and all your people – wisdom to look beyond the obvious for what might be distressing someone, and to listen carefully before jumping to a conclusion.

1 From *John Wesley's Journal (Abridged).*

November 17th

The Lord bless thee, and keep thee: The Lord make his face shine upon thee, and be gracious unto thee: The Lord lift up his countenance upon thee, and give thee peace

(Numbers 6:24–26 *KJV*)

Thurs. 17 [May 1759] – When a coal-pit runs far underground it is customary to build a partition wall from the shaft to within three or four years of the end, in order to make air circulate; it moves down one side of the wall, turns at the end, and then moves briskly up the other side. In a pit … which ran four hundred yards under the ground, and had long been neglected, several parts of the wall were fallen down. Four men were sent down to repair it. They were about three hundred yards from the shaft, when the foul air caught fire. In a moment it tore down the wall from end to end; and, burning on until it came to the shaft, it then burst and went off like a large cannon. The men instantly fell on their faces, or they would have been burned to death in a few moments. One of them, who once knew the love of God (Andrew English), began crying aloud for mercy. But in a very short time his breath was stopped. The other three crept on their hand and knees, till two got to the shaft and were pulled up; but one of them died in a few minutes. John McCombe was drawn up next, burned from head to foot, but rejoicing and praising God. They then went down for Andrew, whom they found senseless; the very circumstance which saved his life. Losing his senses, he lay flat on the ground, and the greatest part of the fire went over him; whereas, had he gone forward on his hands and knees, he would undoubtedly have been burned to death. But life or death was welcome; for God had restored the light of his countenance.[1], [2]

"My times are in your hand,
My God, I wish them there!
My life, my friends, my soul I leave
Entirely to your care."[3]

1 From *John Wesley's Journal (Abridged).*

2 Wesley was in the habit of riding his horse to the entrances of pits and waiting for miners to appear at the end of their shift, when he would preach to them.

3 William Freeman Lloyd (1791–1853), *The Song Book of The Salvation Army, 2015.*

NOVEMBER 18TH

MY DOCTRINE SHALL DROP AS THE RAIN

(Deuteronomy 32:2 *KJV*)

Wesley never departed willingly or knowingly from the doctrines of the Church of England, in which he had been trained up, and with which he was conscientiously satisfied, after full and free enquiry. Upon certain points which were not clearly stated in the doctrine, he formed opinions for himself, which were generally clear, and consistent with the Christian system, and credible. He laid no stress upon these opinions, though, and never proposed them to be anything more than they were.[1]

I love today's text, Lord, because it teaches me that your doctrines are light, and refreshing, not heavy or burdensome. You do not seek to overload your people, but to instruct and guide. Help me to receive your doctrines as grass receives rain. By the same token, help me to hold my own opinions lightly, and to remember that I might be mistaken!

1 From *John Wesley.*

November 19th

Where were you when I laid the earth's foundation? Tell me, if you understand. Who marked off its dimensions? Surely you know! Who stretched a measuring line across it? On what were its footings set, or who laid its cornerstone – while the morning stars sang together and all the angels[1] shouted for joy?

(Job 38:4–7 *NIV*)

Wesley traced what he called the Adamic law to beyond the foundation of the world, to that period unknown to mankind … when the morning stars first sang together, having been newly called into existence.

It pleased the Creator to make his first-born sons intelligent beings,[2] so that they might know him who had created them. He endued them with understanding, to discern truth from falsehood and good from evil; and, as a necessary result of this, with the gift of liberty – a capacity to choose. They were therefore able to offer their Creator a free and willing service; a service acceptable to their gracious Master.

It was God's intention to offer them an opportunity for the continued increase of their happiness whereby every instance of obedience would add to the perfection of their nature.[3]

Here we begin to trace, Lord, glimpses of your character; that you were willing to give angels – and then human beings – the marvellous gift of freewill, even though you always knew it would lead to rebellion and the crucifixion of Jesus. This is love. This is grace.

1 Hebrew: "Sons of God".
2 This is referring to angelic beings, the celestial host, not humankind.
3 From *John Wesley*.

November 20th

God created mankind in his own image, in the image of God he created them; male and female he created them

(Genesis 1:27 *NIV*)

In like manner. When God, in his appointed time, had created a new order of beings – when he had raised man from the dust of the earth, breathed into him the breath of life, and caused him to become a living soul,[1] he gave to this free intelligent creature the same law as to his first-born children; not written upon tablets of stone, but engraved on his heart[2] by the finger of God, written in the inmost spirit, both of men and angels, so that it would never be far off, never hard to understand, but always at hand, and always shining with clear light, even as the sun shines in the midst of the heavens.

Such was the original law of God. It shone in its full splendour and mankind was created holy, just as he that created him is holy; perfect as his Father in Heaven is perfect.[3] God made mankind to be an image of his own eternity. God gave a perfect law. He required full obedience on every point.[4]

Eternally engraved as evidence of eternal love and concern – thank you, God.

1 Genesis 2:7.
2 See Hebrews 8:10.
3 Matthew 5:48.
4 From *John Wesley*.

November 21st

The serpent was more crafty than any of the wild animals the Lord God had made. He said to the woman, "Did God really say, 'You must not eat from any tree in the garden'?" The woman said to the serpent, "We may eat fruit from the trees in the garden, but God did say, 'You must not eat fruit from the tree that is in the middle of the garden, and you must not touch it, or you will die.'" "You will not certainly die," the serpent said to the woman. "For God knows that when you eat from it your eyes will be opened, and you will be like God, knowing good and evil." When the woman saw that the fruit of the tree was good for food and pleasing to the eye, and also desirable for gaining wisdom, she took some and ate it. She also gave some to her husband, who was with her, and he ate it. Then the eyes of both of them were opened

(Genesis 3:1–7 *NIV*)

Man disobeyed this law, and from that moment he died. God had told him, "In the day that thou eatest of that fruit [the forbidden fruit] thou shalt surely die." Accordingly, on that day, he did die: he died to God, the most dreadful of all deaths: he was separated from him in union with whom his spiritual life consisted. His soul died. The body dies when it is separated from the soul; correspondingly, the soul dies when it is separated from God. This separation occurred when Adam ate of the forbidden fruit … We understand this to be spiritual death, but his body too became corruptible and mortal; dead to God, dead to sin, and hurrying on to death everlasting, to the destruction of both body and soul, in the fire that is never quenched.[1, 2]

Paradise lost. Lord, have mercy.

1 Mark 9:48.
2 From *John Wesley.*

November 22nd

My dear children … I am again in the pains of childbirth until Christ is formed in you

(**Galatians 4:19** *NIV*)

Can Christ be in the same heart where sin is? Undoubtedly He can; otherwise it could never be saved therefrom, for where the sickness is, there is the Physician;

Carrying on His work within,
Striving till he cast out sin.[1]

Christ cannot *reign* where sin *reigns*, and neither will He *dwell* where any sin is allowed. But He is in – and dwells in – the heart of every believer who is *fighting* against all sin, even though it may not yet be purified.

The opposite doctrine – that there is no sin in believers – is quite new in the Church of Christ … but whatever doctrine is *new* must be wrong; for the *old* religion is the only *true* one; and no doctrine can be right unless it is the very same "which was from the beginning".[2]

Lord, I pray for anyone fighting sin today; anyone who is struggling. Stay with them, Lord Jesus, and assist them, so that you may reign in their hearts.

1 This ditty appears to be Wesley's own work. I am unable to find a reference to it elsewhere.
2 From *Fifty Three Sermons.*

November 23rd

Looking unto Jesus the author and finisher of *our* faith

(Hebrews 12:2 *KJV*)

Some will argue using the text "If any man be a believer in Christ, he is a new creature. Old things are passed away; behold all things become new".[1] The argument will run that a person cannot be an old creature and a new creature at the same time.

I respond, yes, he may. He may be partly renewed, but he does not yet have the whole mind of Christ. Whereas his old judgement concerning such matters as justification, holiness, happiness and indeed the things of God in general is now passed away, and his old desires, plans, loves, tempers and conversations, they are not yet wholly new. Still he feels, to his sorrow and shame, remains of the old man – taints. The difference is, these can no longer gain any advantage over him, so long as he watches over them in prayer.

Every babe in Christ is holy, and yet not altogether so. He is saved from sin; yet not entirely: it remains, thought it does not reign … Believers, though, "walk after the Spirit" (Romans 8:1), and the Spirit of God dwells in them; consequently, they are being delivered from the guilt, the power, or, in one word, the being of sin.[2]

Lord, a double cure is needed; a merciful deliverance from guilt, backed home by a powerful protection against temptation. God of mercy and power, pour out these blessings on any who needs them this very hour.

1 1 Corinthians 5:17.
2 From *Fifty Three Sermons.*

NOVEMBER 24TH

CAST ALL YOUR ANXIETY ON HIM BECAUSE HE CARES FOR YOU

(1 Peter 5:7 *NIV*)

Fri. 20 [November 1747] I was informed of a remarkable providence: Someone going home last night met a woman in Blackfriars,[1] who enquired about the way to the waterside.[2] She said, "It is so late, you will not be able to get a boat now." The woman answered, "I don't want one." At this point, she stopped and began to question her more closely; "what was she going to do?" After a while, she confessed she was going to drown herself, being under a heavy affliction. But she was soon brought to a better frame of mind, and soon resolved to cast her care on him who had cared for her.[3]

Lord, in your great mercy, rush to help those who are afflicted today; who are carrying secret burdens and can see no way out of their problems. Send someone along just at the right time.

1 South London.
2 The River Thames.
3 From *The Journal of the Rev. John Wesley, Volume 2.*

November 25th

Create in me a pure heart, O God

(Psalm 51:10 *NIV*)

Sun. 22 [November 1747] I spent an hour with Mary Cheesebrook, who is a strange monument to the mercy of God. About six years ago, she was without God in the world, being a kept mistress.[1] An acquaintance brought her one evening to the chapel in West Street, where God gave her a new heart. She shed an abundance of tears, she "plucked out the right eye and cast it from her";[2] and from that time applied herself by hard labour to all that was needed for life and godliness.[3] She missed no opportunity of coming to the preaching, often after a hard day's work; she came to the Foundery in the evening, often running all the way. Every Saturday, after paying her little debts, she gave away all the money that remained.

Two years ago she caught a violent cold, which she neglected, until it settled on her lungs. I knew nothing about this until her illness was beyond a cure and she herself was worn to a skeleton. I mentioned her plight to Mrs —, and she sent her half a guinea.[4] Mary immediately sent for a poor man, a baker, from whom she had lately taken bread. She owed him about ten shillings, but a dispute arose between them, for the man would not take the money, saying, "She wanted it more than he." But she prevailed, saying, "She could not die in peace, if she owed any man anything."[5]

Lord, you are in the soul-saving business. Thank you for the transformation that you alone can impart. Your touch is unique.

1 A sexual partner who is not a wife; sometimes, a maid or servant too.
2 See Matthew 5:29, 30.
3 See 2 Peter 1:3.
4 A full guinea was worth about 21 shillings in 1747.
5 From *The Journal of the Rev. John Wesley, Volume 2.*

NOVEMBER 26TH

RELIGION THAT GOD OUR FATHER ACCEPTS AS PURE AND FAULTLESS IS THIS: TO LOOK AFTER ORPHANS AND WIDOWS IN THEIR DISTRESS

(James 1:27 *NIV*)

I found something still troubled Mary Cheesebrook; something was still on her mind. She told me it was her concern for her little child, a girl about eight years old, who, after she had died, would have no friend to take care of her. I replied, "Be at rest in this thing; I will take care of the child." From that time she lay (two or three weeks) quietly waiting for the salvation of God.[1]

This leads me to think today, Lord, of parents around the world who are concerned for the welfare of their children; refugees who are separated from their families by warfare and/or economic necessity. May your Church, Lord, respond as John Wesley did, with compassion and practical support.

Can I help, Lord?

1 From *The Journal of the Rev. John Wesley, Volume 2.*

NOVEMBER 27TH

OPEN YOUR MOUTH FOR THE MUTE, FOR THE RIGHTS OF ALL WHO ARE DESTITUTE. OPEN YOUR MOUTH, JUDGE RIGHTEOUSLY, DEFEND THE RIGHTS OF THE POOR AND NEEDY

(Proverbs 31:8–9 *ESV*)

John Wesley did not confine his interest and his activities to the welfare of the Methodists. He took "the whole world as his parish" in more than one sense. He was greatly concerned by the terrible conditions, for instance, in which French prisoners of war were kept in Bristol,[1] and took steps to help them; he campaigned for the improvement of prisons in general; he opened dispensaries for the sick poor, and published his own treatise on *Primitive Physic* (an up-to-date document by the standard of the times); he took steps to counteract the activities of smugglers in Cornwall, where his influence was especially great; and, above all, his last years were marked by his determined support of those who were trying to abolish that execrable villainy, the scandal of religion, of England, and of human nature, slavery.[2]

John Wesley – preacher and political activist. What can I do, Lord, at local level? Can I exercise an influence somewhere? Letter-writing? Campaigning?

1 Stapleton Prison, adapted for use when France declared war on Britain in 1739. French prisoners were incarcerated there until 1814, when the Treaty of Paris was signed. Conditions were horrendously cramped and disease was rife.

2 Wesley published *Thoughts Upon Slavery* in 1774, and is sometimes regarded as the first attack upon slavery by a man of status and influence. Bristol Docks routinely hosted slave ships importing slaves from Africa, which meant that Wesley would have had personal, first-hand experience of seeing slaves disembarking from ships chained and bullied into place.

November 28th

We are surrounded by such a great cloud of witnesses

(Hebrews 12:1 *NIV*)

The popular image of an evangelist, and still more of a revivalist, is of a man with a crude, ill-thought-out, hell-fire theology, who alternately weedles and terrifies his hearers into accepting his message; the theology he is thought to have taken over ready-made from some literalist interpreter of the Bible; his emotionalism is believed to spring from a defect in his own personality. There have indeed been revivalists and evangelists of whom these criticisms have been perfectly just, and some of them have added to their ill-fame and an undue financial astuteness. These men have brought discredit on the honourable enterprise of evangelism, without which there could have been no Christian Church and can be no expansion of its influence. But, so far at least as Great Britain is concerned, they all came after the time of the Wesleys, and it would be unhistorical in the extreme to have the modern evangelist image in one's mind when studying the Methodist Revival.[1]

Father, Great Britain owes a debt to those who established Christianity within its shores. Thank you for pioneers whose influence has been positive and lasting – not least John Wesley. Granted, mistakes have been made and your gospel has not always been well represented, but that does not negate the tremendous heritage you have graciously bestowed upon the British Isles. Thank you for your grace.

1 From *Methodism.*

November 29th

Devote yourself to the public reading of Scripture, to exhortation, to teaching

(1 Timothy 4:13 *ESV*)

John Wesley was a theologian before he became an evangelist, and he remained a theologian all through the years of his evangelistic mission. In fact, it would be true to say that his primary interest never ceased to be theological, since it was by the exposition of Scriptural truth that he brought men and women to the point of repentance and faith, and after they had been converted he continued to see that they were interested in Scriptural truth to the end of their days. Christian doctrine was for him no mere means to the end of emotional conversion; it was the truth which made men free,[1] and he devoted his best powers of mind and spirit all through his life to its understanding and proclamation. Emotionalism he despised as much as any modern sceptic, though of course the modern sceptic would always see emotionalism where Wesley saw the operation of the Holy Spirit. A casual glance at any one of his published sermons – and these were the sermons, perhaps embellished by some illustrations, by which people were converted in their hundreds – will show how little Wesley valued an emotional appeal, and how much he valued theological exposition.[2]

Lord of the word, you have gifted some as theologians and teachers. Theirs is a high calling of great responsibility. Bless them as they study. Keep them on the right lines. Fill their studies with your Spirit. Bless their students too, at theological colleges and the like. Fill your Church with intelligent witnesses.

1 John 8:32.
2 From *Methodism*.

November 30th

As he went along, he saw a man blind from birth. His disciples asked him, "Rabbi, who sinned, this man or his parents, that he was born blind?" "Neither this man nor his parents sinned," said Jesus, "but this happened so that the works of God might be displayed in him"

(John 9:1–3 *NIV*)

Verse 2. *Who sinned, this man, or his parents, that he was born blind* – This is, was it for his own sins, or for the sins of his parents? They suppose (as many of the Jews did, though without any ground from Scripture) that he might have sinned in a pre-existent state, before he came into the world.

Verse 3. *Jesus answered, Neither hath this man sinned, nor his parents* – It was not the manner of our Lord to answer any questions that were of no use, but to gratify an idle curiosity … It was neither for any sins of his own, nor of his parents; but that the power of God might be displayed.[1]

Healing God, you cut to the heart of the matter. You deal with us honestly. Thank you that you speak truth into this world, without fear or favour. Please speak truth into my life, as a token of your great love.

1 From *Notes on the New Testament.*

December 1st

As long as it is day, we must do the works of him who sent me. Night is coming, when no one can work. While I am in the world, I am the light of the world

(John 9:4, 5 *NIV*)

Verse 4. *The night is coming* – Christ is the light. When the light is withdrawn, night comes. *When no man can work* – No man can do anything towards working out his salvation after this life is ended. Yet Christ can work always. But he was to work upon earth only during the day, or season which was appointed to him.

Verse 5. *I am the light of the world* – I teach men inwardly by my Spirit, and outwardly by my preaching, regarding the will of God; and I show them, by my example, how they must do it.[1]

Lord of my days, help me to work for you while the light lingers; before this brief day of my life closes. Light of the world, show me the way.

1 From *Notes on the New Testament.*

December 2nd

The pot he was shaping from the clay was marred in his hands; so the potter formed it into another pot, shaping it as seemed best to him

(Jeremiah 18:4 *NIV*)

John Wesley saw, and nothing he said was of greater practical value, that salvation was not only the work of Christ done for us and accepted by faith by the man who was justified, but that it was also done in us by the regenerative and sanctifying power of the Holy Spirit…

Entire sanctification, then – Christian perfection – is not a higher form of justification, but a completion, so Wesley himself teaches, of regenerative work wrought as Charles wrote by "degrees insensible", though realized, according to John, instantaneously in some supreme moment of divine visitation. It does not depend primarily on an acceptance by faith of Christ's finished work, but is the result of his unfinished work in the heart and on the character.[1]

Both instant and constant! The mystery of salvation and sanctification! The work is done, yet is still being done! Thank you, Lord, that you save and sanctify; you bless, and then continue to bless. Keep me in your sanctifying will, I pray.

1 From *The Evangelical Doctrines of Charles Wesley's Hymns.*

December 3rd

Remain in me, as I also remain in you.
No branch can bear fruit by itself; it must remain in the vine.
Neither can you bear fruit unless you remain in me

(John 15:4 *NIV*)

The following questions and answers at an early Conference (1744) should not be overlooked. Conference preachers were asked:

"Why are not *we* more holy?" "Chiefly because we are enthusiasts, looking for the end without using the means."

To touch upon two or three examples:

"Who of you rises at four in the summer? Never at five when he does not preach?"

"Do you recommend to all our Societies that five o'clock hour for private prayer? Do you observe it? Or any other time? Do you find by experience that any time is no time?"

"Do you know the obligation and benefit of fasting? How often do you practise it?"

Entire sanctification, Wesley teaches, is by faith, but also by rising at four o'clock in the morning and by fasting.[1]

"Take time to be holy, speak oft with thy Lord;
Abide in him always, and feed on his Word;
Make friends of God's children; help those who are weak;
Forgetting in nothing his blessing to seek."[2]

1 From *The Evangelical Doctrines of Charles Wesley's Hymns.*
2 William Dunn Longstaff (1822–94), *The Song Book of The Salvation Army, 2015.*

Be conformed to the image of his Son

(Romans 8:29 *ESV*)

[John Wesley's] outward life was undoubtedly healthier than that of Charles. He was a happy man, so much engaged in missionary work that as he grew older he was decreasingly introspective. His whole career was an example of holiness and zeal; he was possessed with a spirit of love, entirely unselfish, giving every hour of his long, disciplined day to the service of God and man. He was vigorous and healthy, and, for all his zeal, became remarkably tolerant. No doubt he had the mental limitations of his time and age, but no man has ever packed into eighty-eight years of life more of holy love and devoted service than John Wesley. One of his critics, even, wrote "his countenance shone with goodness, truth, purity, benevolence; a sanctity belonged to him which those near him felt as if it were a power with which the atmosphere was fraught".[1]

To be like Jesus!

1 From *The Evangelical Doctrines of Charles Wesley's Hymns.*

December 5th

Now a certain man was sick, named Lazarus, of Bethany, the town of Mary and her sister Martha.

(It was that Mary which anointed the Lord with ointment, and wiped his feet with her hair, whose brother Lazarus was sick.) Therefore his sisters sent unto him, saying, Lord, behold, he whom thou lovest is sick. When Jesus heard that, he said, This sickness is not unto death, but for the glory of God, that the Son of God might be glorified thereby

(John 11:1–4 *KJV*)

Verse 1. *One Lazarus* – It is probable that Lazarus was younger than his sisters.... Ecclesiastical history informs us that Lazarus was now thirty years old, and that he lived thirty years after Christ's ascension.

Verse 2. *It was that Mary who afterwards anointed* – She was more known than her elder sister Martha, and as such is named before her.

Verse 4. *This sickness is not to death, but for the glory of God* – The final event of this sickness will not be death, in the usual sense of the word; a final separation of his soul and body, but a manifestation of the power of God.[1]

Lord, in the midst of our lives, and all that we experience – life, sickness, death, bereavement – you call us by name. We are not merely abstract subjects to you, but dearly loved individuals whose lives you care about.

1 From *Notes on the New Testament.*

December 6th

Wisdom will enter your heart, and knowledge will be pleasant to your soul

(Proverbs 2:10 *NIV*)

[Wesley] based his theology on the Bible and "experience", but far more based on the Bible than experience. The Bible was for him the "book of God", and he placed implicit trust in all its statements. When any passage was obscure to him, he compared it with more other lucid passages, and so arrived at what he took to be its true meaning. He quotes Scripture in much the same way as a modern fundamentalist does, but this does not mean that he was a fundamentalist in the modern sense. He lived before the days of modern Biblical criticism, and so can hardly be expected to have taken its findings into account. He was not aware of the sources which lie behind the Pentateuch, or of the theory that there is more than one author of the prophecy of Isaiah, or of the Synoptic problem ... he eagerly accepted a theory of the meaning of the Book of Revelation which turned into a kind of Old Moore's Almanack[1] of the last year of human existence. But in all these matters he was in complete accord with the other theologians of his time.[2]

Lord, even without so many of the modern aids to study, Wesley excelled as an outstanding theologian. Thank you, Lord, for books, for the internet, and for the modern evolution of critical study whereby I have countless opportunities to learn more about you and your word. Help me to take advantage of them.

1 An astrological publication published annually in Great Britain since 1697.
2 From *Methodism.*

December 7th

A time to weep and a time to laugh,
a time to mourn and a time to dance

(Ecclesiastes 3:4 *NIV*)

The Methodist emphasis on "religious experience" is well-known in religious circles, and is of course very vulnerable to psychological attack.

But it is only in small part derived from Wesley. He never based a single doctrine on it, but always appealed to Scripture. If, however, a doctrine was propounded by Scripture and therefore trustworthy, he was very willing to show that it was confirmed by experience – which is, of course, a respectably traditional method of establishing a proposition.

Still less did he found any doctrine on "feelings". Charles Wesley says a great deal about feelings in his hymns … and seems to lay great emphasis on them. But he did not mean … mere emotions; he refers, rather, to that consciousness of personal relationship or of truth which comes to the whole personality, and not to the mind and senses alone…

Feelings in the fuller sense were part of what [John Wesley] meant by experience, and of what caused him constantly to refer to real Christianity as "experimental (we should say *experiential*) religion".[1]

Thank you, Creator God, for the precious gift of feelings and emotions, all the better to appreciate life in all its shades. Thank you for the emotions of spirituality – most of all that I can bring every feeling to you, in any situation, knowing you understand.

1 From *Methodism.*

December 8th

Repent and believe the good news!

(Mark 1:15 *NIV*)

It is generally supposed that repentance and faith are only the gate of religion; that they are necessary only at the beginning of our Christian course, when we are setting out on the way to the Kingdom...

This is undoubtedly true, that there is a repentance and a faith which are, more especially, necessary at the beginning: a repentance which is a conviction of our utter sinfulness, and guilt, and helplessness...

But, there is also a repentance and a faith ... which are requisite after we have "believed the gospel"; and in every subsequent stage of our Christian course, or we cannot "run the race which is set before us".[1]

This repentance and faith are necessary to our continuance and growth in grace ... so that we may say, not only,

Every moment, Lord, I want
The merit of thy death;
but, likewise, in the full assurance of faith,
Every moment, Lord, I have
The merit of thy death![2, 3]

Gracious Lord, I want – need – to drink fresh spiritual water every day. If repentance is helpful to that end, then keep me repenting! Keep me fresh in Christ!

1 See Hebrews 12:1.
2 From Charles Wesley's hymn *To the haven of thy breast, O Son of man, I fly!*
3 From *Fifty Three Sermons.*

December 9th

You are all one in Christ Jesus

(Galatians 3:28 *ESV*)

For many years the leader of Methodism was unaware that he had founded a new church. It didn't occur to him that his clubs and congregations and preachers would ever find it necessary to separate themselves from the Church of England into which he had been born, and which he loved in spite of her faults. Wesley abhorred the idea of separation in any sphere – political as well as spiritual. The latter years of his life were deeply saddened by the struggle of England with her colonial children in America. In 1776 he published an address to the people of "New Britain" in which he prayed for an end to "this business of men of the same blood and language murdering each other with all possible speed".[1]

He had more than a casual interest in his friends of the New World. Throughout the thirteen colonies his preachers had organized large flocks of Methodists. When the Americans, much to his sorrow, broke definitively away from the Church of England, he ordained a priest in his own name to head the "Wesleyan" Methodists in the New World.[2] And thus John Wesley lived to see not only a separate government in America, but a separate church as well.[3]

Lord Jesus, whether we be labelled Wesleyan Methodists, Methodists, or something else, you are Head of the Church. Whether we worship in England or America or somewhere else.

1 A violent clash of cultures and religious opinions.
2 Methodists in America had already parted from its British parentage in terms of policy and leadership. It had formulated its own policies and styles of worship.
3 From *Living Biographies of Religious Leaders*.

December 10th

Cast thy burden upon the Lord, and he shall sustain thee

(Psalm 55:22 *KJV*)

[John Wesley] lived to face still another and far more bitter separation.

For the time came when his life-long companion and fellow worker, his younger brother Charles, passed away.

John Wesley, now in his eighty-sixth year, felt very lonely. He climbed into the pulpit and led the singing of his brother's greatest hymn, one of the several thousand that Charles Wesley had given to the English language:

"Come, O thou traveller unknown
Whom still I feel but cannot see,
My company before has gone
And I am left alone with thee."

For a moment he bowed down beneath his burden. He broke off his singing and sat down wearily at the foot of God's altar. Then he gathered himself and journeyed on.[1]

Father God, I pray today for those who are bowed down beneath their burdens. Draw alongside them, I ask, and gently enable them to gather themselves up again and journey on.

1 From *Living Biographies of Religious Leaders.*

DECEMBER 11TH

BEING JUSTIFIED BY FAITH, WE HAVE PEACE WITH GOD THROUGH OUR LORD JESUS CHRIST: BY WHOM ALSO WE HAVE ACCESS BY FAITH INTO THIS GRACE WHEREIN WE STAND, AND REJOICE IN HOPE OF THE GLORY OF GOD

(Romans 5:2 *KJV*)

God in justifying us, does something *for* us; in reclaiming us again, He does the work *in* us. The former changes our outward relation to God, so that we are transformed from enemies to children. By the latter, our *inmost* souls are changed; sinners become saints. The former restores us to favour. The latter to the image of God.

Justification is another word for pardon. It is the forgiveness of all our sins ... our acceptance with God. The immediate effects are the peace of God ... and a "rejoicing in hope of the glory of God, with joy unspeakable and full of glory".

At the same time that we are justified – in that very moment – sanctification begins. In that instant we are born again; and when we are born again, our sanctification begins, and we gradually "grow up in him who is our head".[1] This expression, says Wesley, points out the exact analogy between natural and spiritual things: a child is born of a woman. Afterwards, he gradually and slowly grows until he attains the stature of a man. In like manner a person is born of God in a short time, but it is by slow degrees that he afterwards grows up to the measure of the full stature of Christ. The same relationship exists between our new birth and our sanctification.[2]

Paradise restored. Thank you, Lord.

1 Ephesians 4:15.
2 From *John Wesley*.

December 12th

The Lord is my rock and my fortress and my deliverer

(2 Samuel 22:2 *ESV*)

Deliverance [from sin, Wesley acknowledged] might be gradually wrought in some. He says, in this sense, they do not claim a single particular moment wherein sin ceases to be. It is, however, desirable (if it is the will of God), that it should be done instantaneously; that the Lord should destroy sin in a moment, in the twinkling of an eye – and he generally does. This, Wesley insisted, was a plain fact, with evidence enough to satisfy any unprejudiced person. And why might it not be instantaneous? he argued. A moment to him is the same as a thousand years[1]...

Wesley's confidence is that God is both able and willing to sanctify us now ... [deliverance] will come, it will not tarry. Therefore, look for it every day, every hour, every moment. Why not this hour? Why not this moment? Certainly you may look for it now, if you believe it is by faith.[2]

Gracious Deliverer, you work in wisdom, and everything you do is predicated upon love. You minister to us in proportion to our ability to receive your presence in our lives. Sometimes you deliver gradually, sometimes instantly. Either way, Lord, you seek to remove sin from our lives, so that we become more like you.

1 See 2 Peter 3:8.
2 From *John Wesley.*

December 13th

I tell you, her sins, which are many, are forgiven – for she loved much. But he who is forgiven little, loves little

(Luke 7:47 *ESV*)

Christ is ready, and he is all you want. He is waiting for you! He is at the door.[1] Whoever you are, if you desire forgiveness, first believe. Believe in the Lord Jesus Christ.

Do not say, "I cannot be accepted yet, because I am not yet good enough." Who is good enough – who ever was – to merit acceptance at God's hands?

Do not say, "I am not contrite enough; I am not aware enough of all my sins." I would to God that you were more aware of your sins, and a thousand times more contrite than you are!

But do not stay where you are for this reason. It may be that God will make you more contrite. It may be that you will not weep much over your sins until you love much because you have had much forgiven.[2]

No one so good that they don't need to be forgiven. No one so bad that they can't be forgiven. This is grace. Lord, in your mercy, speak to those who feel unable to approach you for forgiveness; cover them with mercy and dissolve their reluctance.

1 See Revelation 3:20.
2 From *John Wesley*.

December 14th

I REJOICE BECAUSE OF YOU; BUT I WANT YOU TO BE WISE ABOUT WHAT IS GOOD, AND INNOCENT ABOUT WHAT IS EVIL

(Romans 16:19 *NIV*)

Sun. Jun 1 [1783] – About nine in the morning we sailed, and at nine on Friday, 13, landed at Helvoetsluys. Here we hired a coach for Briel, but were forced to hire a waggon also, to carry a box which one of us could have carried on his shoulders. At Briel we took a boat to Rotterdam.[1]

We had not been there long when Mr Bennett, a bookseller, who had invited me to his house, called upon me. But as Mr Loyal, the minister of the Scotch congregation,[2] had invited me, he ... went with us to Mr Loyal's. I found a friendly, sensible, hospitable and pious man.

We took a walk together round the town, all as clean as a gentleman's parlour. Many of the houses are as high as those in the main street at Edinburgh; and the canals, running through the chief streets, make them convenient, as well as pleasant; bringing the merchants' goods up to their doors. Stately trees grow on all their banks. The whole town is encompassed with a double row of elms; so that one may walk all round it in the shade.[3]

Lord, it is hard to escape Wesley's sense of awe and wonder here; his fascination with the work of God in another country, and his great interest in a culture and an environment different to his own. Place such a childlike heart within me, I pray, that I may always enjoy the world you have created; grant me the gift of wonderment.

1 Wesley was fascinated by reports of a "blessed work" taking place in Holland, whereby people were converted to a better way of life. He was interested in comparing this with his Methodist work and taking notes.

2 An English-speaking congregation in the heart of Rotterdam.

3 From *John Wesley's Journal (Abridged).*

December 15th

Cry aloud, spare not, lift up thy voice like a trumpet, and shew my people their transgression, and the house of Jacob their sins

(Isaiah 58:1 *KJV*)

Mon. April 5 [1784] – As soon as I set foot in Georgia, I began preaching at five in the morning; and every communicant, that is, every serious person in the town, continually attended throughout the year: I mean, every morning, winter and summer, unless in the case of sickness. They did so till I left the province. In the year 1738, when God began his great work in England, I began preaching at the same hour, winter and summer, and was never without a congregation. If they will not attend now, they have lost their zeal; and then, it cannot be denied, they are a fallen people. And then, at the same time, we are labouring to secure the preaching-houses to the next generation! In the name of God, let us, if possible, secure the present generation from drawing back to perdition! Let all the preachers that are still alive to God join together as one … fast and pray, lift up their voice as a trumpet … in season, out of season, to convince them they are fallen; and exhort them instantly to repent.[1]

How wonderful it is, Lord, to see Wesley reflecting on the decades, still with the same fire in his heart, still with the same undimmed passion. As I too glance back over the years, I thank you, Lord, for sustaining grace that lasts a lifetime. Thank you for your inexhaustible love.

1 From *John Wesley's Journal (Abridged)*.

Stand up in the presence of the aged, show respect for the elderly and revere your God

(Leviticus 19:32 *NIV*)

At Lowestoft,[1] one evening, all adjourned to a … chapel to hear the venerable John Wesley.… He was exceedingly old and infirm, and was attended and almost supported in the pulpit by a young minister on each side. The chapel was crowded to suffocation.

In the course of his sermon Mr Wesley repeated … the lines from Anacreon:[2]

"Oft am I by woman told,
Poor Anacreon! thou grow'st old.
See, thine hairs are falling all;
Poor Anacreaon, how they fall!
Whether I grow old or no,
By these signs I do not know;
But this I need not to be told,
'Tis time to live if I grow old."

Once, as the old man was going to mount into his pulpit, he found a little child had perched herself upon the pulpit steps, and as he lifted her out of his way he kissed her; and we are told that simple loving action melted the heart of a papist who had come to hear him preach, and led to his conversion. The children loved Wesley, and crowded round him in the streets, longing to have a touch of his kind hand, or a smile from his benevolent face.[3]

Physically old, yet spiritually young.
Lord, grant me that blessing as the years go by.

1 Coastal town in Suffolk, England.
2 c.570–478 BC, Greek poet.
3 From *Rev. John Wesley.*

Samuel took a flask of olive oil and poured it on Saul's head

(1 Samuel 10:1 *NIV*)

The Head-Ach. (sic.)

Rub the head for a quarter of an hour: tried.

Or, be electrified: tried.[1]

Or, apply to each temple the thin yellow rind of a lemon, newly peeled.

Or, pour upon the palm of the hand a little brandy, and some zest of lemon, and hold it to the forehead; or a little ether.

Or, if you have caught cold, boil a handful of rosemary in a quart of water. Put this in a mug, and hold your head (covered with a napkin) over the steam, as hot as you can bear. Repeat this until the pain ceases: tried.

Or, snuff up the nose camphorated spirits of lavender.

Or, a little juice of horseradish.[2]

Lord, you graciously preserved John Wesley's life for the best part of nine decades. Whether or not that was down to any of these remedies, I don't know – I am just grateful to you for his lasting influence, and for your hand upon his long ministry. Raise up more John Wesleys, Lord!

1 In 1756, Wesley acquired some electrical apparatus and began testing it on himself, whenever he felt ill. He would either "electrify" himself or ask one of his assistants to electrify him. He was quite convinced that electric shocks could cure at least twenty known diseases, and was one of the first people in the world to advocate this theory. He used his "static electricity machine" over and over again, though he was never actually licenced to practise medicine.

2 From *Primitive Physic.*

December 18th

An angel of the Lord appeared and a light shone in the cell. He struck Peter on the side and woke him up. "Quick, get up!" he said, and the chains fell off Peter's wrists. Then the angel said to him, "Put on your clothes and sandals." And Peter did so. "Wrap your cloak around you and follow me," the angel told him. Peter followed him out of the prison, but he had no idea that what the angel was doing was really happening; he thought he was seeing a vision. They passed the first and second guards and came to the iron gate leading to the city. It opened for them by itself, and they went through it. When they had walked the length of one street, suddenly the angel left him

(Acts 12:7–10 *NIV*)

Mon. 19 [May 1784] – As I was sitting down to supper, I was informed that publicity had been given to my preaching, and that the congregation was waiting. I would not disappoint them; but preached immediately on salvation by faith. Among them were a gentleman and his wife, who shared a remarkable story … She said she had often heard her mother repeat a story told to her by an intimate acquaintance; that her husband had been involved in the rebellion of 1745.[1] He was tried at Carlisle,[2] and found guilty. The evening before he was to [be hanged], sitting and musing in her chair, she fell asleep. She dreamed that someone came to her and said, "Go to such a part of the wall, and among the loose stones you will find a key, which you must carry to your husband." She woke up, but thinking it a common dream, thought nothing of it. Presently she fell asleep again, and dreamed the very same dream. She started up, put on her cloak and hat, and went to that part of the wall, and found a loose key among the stones. Having, with some difficulty, procured admission to the jail, she gave this to her husband. It opened the door of his cell, as well as the lock of the prison door. So at midnight he escaped with his life.[3]

You are the God of dreams and miracles. Don't ever let me put you in a box. You cannot be confined by prison bars or narrow minds. Almighty God.

1 The Jacobite uprising, an attempt by Chares Edward Stuart ("Bonnie Prince Charlie") to regain the British throne for the House of Stuart.

2 Cumbria, England.

3 *John Wesley's Journal (Abridged).*

DECEMBER 19TH

THE LORD REIGNETH

(Psalm 97:1 *KJV*)

Mon. June 28 [1784] (Epworth) –

Today I entered on my eighty-second year, and found myself just as strong to labour, and as fit for any exercise of body or mind, as I was forty years ago. I do not impute this to second causes, but to the Sovereign Lord of all. It is he who bids the sun of life stand still, so long as it pleaseth him.

I am as strong at eight-one as I was at twenty-one; but abundantly more healthy, being a stranger to the headache, toothache, and other bodily disorders of my youth.

We can only say, "The Lord reigneth!" While we live, let us live to him!"[1]

I think the moral of the story here, Sovereign Lord, is to give you all the glory.

1 From *John Wesley's Journal (Abridged).*

December 20th

When you pray, do not keep on babbling like pagans, for they think they will be heard because of their many words

(Matthew 6:7 *NIV*)

Wesley continually inculcated the duty of early rising, as equally good for body and soul.

"It helps the nerves," he said, "better than a thousand medicines; and especially preserves the sight, and prevents lowness of spirits. Early preaching," he said, "is the glory of the Methodists. Whenever this is dropped, they will dwindle away into nothing."

He advised his preachers to begin and end always precisely at the time appointed, and always to conclude the service in about an hour; to suit their subject to their audience, to choose the plainest texts, and keep close to the text; neither rambling from it, nor allegorizing, nor spiritualizing too much.

More than once, in his journal, he has recorded the death of men who were martyrs to long and loud preaching, and he frequently cautioned his followers against it. They were instructed also not to pray above eight or ten minutes at most, without intermission, unless for some pressing reason.[1]

Lord, deliver your Church from long-windedness!

1 From *John Wesley.*

DECEMBER 21ST

ONE OF THOSE DAYS JESUS WENT OUT TO A MOUNTAINSIDE TO PRAY, AND SPENT THE NIGHT PRAYING TO GOD

(Luke 6:12 *NIV*)

The watch-night [service] was [one of] Wesley's objectionable institutions. It originated with some reclaimed colliers of Kingswood, who, having been accustomed to sit late on Saturday nights at the ale-house, transferred their weekly meeting, after their conversion, to the school-house, and continued there praying and singing hymns far into the morning.

Wesley was advised to put an end to this: but, upon "weighing the thing thoroughly, and comparing it with the practice of the ancient Christians," he could see no cause to forbid it; because he ... shut his eyes to the obvious impropriety of midnight meetings. So he appointed them to be held once a month ... He also appointed three love-feasts in a quarter: one for the men, a second for the women, and the third for both together; "that we might eat bread," he says, "as the ancient Christians did, with gladness and singleness of heart ... we seldom return from them without being fed not only with the meat which perisheth, but with that which endureth to everlasting life."[1] A travelling preacher presides at these meetings: anyone who chooses may speak; and the time is chiefly employed in relating what they call their Christian experience. In this point, also, Mr Wesley disregarded the offence which he gave.[2]

Lord of the hours, I think today of those who can't sleep at night; people who are worried, or in pain. I pray that you would meet with them in their lonely, dark hours. May they find great blessing in finding you there.

1 See John 6:27, *KJV*.
2 From *John Wesley*.

December 22ND

MOSES WAS A HUNDRED AND TWENTY YEARS OLD ... YET HIS EYES WERE NOT WEAK NOR HIS STRENGTH GONE

(Deuteronomy 34:7 *NIV*)

"Leisure and I," said Wesley, "have taken leave of one another. I propose to be busy as long as I live, if my health is so long indulged to me."

This resolution was made in the prime of life, and never was resolution more carefully observed. "Lord, let me not live to be useless!" was the prayer he uttered after seeing one, whom he had long known as an active and useful magistrate, reduced by age to be "a picture of human nature in disgrace, feeble in body and mind, slow of speech and understanding".

He was blessed with a vigorous constitution beyond that of ordinary men, and with an activity of spirit even rarer than his health and strength. Ten thousand cares of various kinds, he said, were no more weight or burden to his mind than ten thousand hairs were to his head. But, in truth, his only cares were those of superintending the work of his ambition, which continually prospered under his hands. He had no real cares: no anxieties, no sorrows, no griefs which touched him. His manner of life was the most favourable that could have been devised for longevity. He rose early, and lay down at night with nothing to keep him awake, or trouble him in sleep. His mind was always in a pleasurable and wholesome state of activity; he was temperate in his diet, and lived in perpetual motion: and frequent change of air is perhaps of all things that which is most conducive to joyous health and long living.[1]

Have I been useful, Lord? I hope so!

1 From *John Wesley.*

December 23rd

Who can count the dust of Jacob, and the number of the fourth part of Israel? Let me die the death of the righteous, and let my last end be like his!

(Numbers 23:10 *KJV*)

"Let my last end be like his!"

How many of you join me in this wish? Perhaps there are a few of you who do not, even in this numerous congregation! And O that this may rest upon your minds! – that it may not die away till your souls are safely lodged "where the wicked cease from troubling, and where the weary are at rest"![1]

O God, with thee nothing is impossible![2] O that you would cause the mantle of your prophet, whom you have taken up, now to fall upon us that remain![3, 4, 5]

"Teach me to live that I may dread
The grave as little as my bed.
Teach me to die that so I may
Rise glorious at the awe-ful Day."[6]

Lord of eternity, my prayers today are for those who are facing the reality of death. As they come to terms with the closure of life, draw near to them and reassure them of the great gift of salvation in Christ.

1 See Job 3:17–19, *KJV*.
2 See Luke 1:37.
3 See 2 Kings 2:14.
4 A very brief excerpt from a lengthy sermon Wesley preached following the death of his friend and colleague Reverend George Whitefield; London, Sunday 18 November 1770. Whitefield died aged just 55 in Massachusetts, on 30 September 1770.
5 From *Fifty Three Sermons.*
6 Thomas Ken (1637–1711), from his hymn *All praise to Thee, my God, this night.*

December 24th

THANKS BE TO GOD FOR HIS INDESCRIBABLE GIFT!

(2 Corinthians 9:15 *NIV*)

Wesley had no delight in speaking of the Fall and doom of man, or of the small remnant of God's gifts still left with him. He referred to these matters only because otherwise the announcement of God's grace would be made *in vacuo*; he had to remind his hearers of the situation which elicited the divine mercy.

But it is with the divine mercy and grace that he is really concerned. Nothing that man has ever done, or can possibly do, bestows any merit of any kind on man – Wesley will not agree that all good works done before a man is justified are "splendid sins", as the Calvinists were inclined to call them; they come in some way from the divine grace, and have some virtue, though they are not done as God wills good works to be done. But they confer no merit at all, and it is the very depth and height of blasphemy to suggest that man in any sense *deserves* the grace of God. Grace is wholly unmerited ... It is free for all and to all. The grace of God is the centrepiece of the whole Wesleyan theology.[1]

Lord, at this time of year, when thoughts turn to gifts and presents, I pause to thank you for your gift of grace in Christ. I bow low and give thanks.

1 From *Methodism.*

December 25th

There were shepherds living out in the fields nearby, keeping watch over their flocks at night. An angel of the Lord appeared to them, and the glory of the Lord shone around them, and they were terrified. But the angel said to them, "Do not be afraid. I bring you good news that will cause great joy for all the people. Today in the town of David a Saviour has been born to you; he is the Messiah, the Lord. This will be a sign to you: You will find a baby wrapped in cloths and lying in a manger." Suddenly a great company of the heavenly host appeared with the angel, praising God and saying, "Glory to God in the highest heaven, and on earth peace to those on whom his favour rests"

(Luke 2:8–14 *NIV***)**

Hark! The herald angels sing,
"Glory to the newborn King;
Peace on earth, and mercy mild,
God and sinners reconciled!"
Joyful, all ye nations rise,
Join the triumph of the skies;
With th'angelic host proclaim,
"Christ is born in Bethlehem!"

Christ, by highest Heav'n adored;
Christ the everlasting Lord;
Late in time, behold him come,
Offspring of a virgin's womb.
Veiled in flesh the Godhead see;
Hail th'incarnate Deity,
Pleased with us in flesh to dwell,
Jesus our Emmanuel.

Hail the heav'nly Prince of Peace!
Hail the Sun of Righteousness!
Light and life to all he brings,
Ris'n with healing in his wings.
Mild he lays his glory by,
Born that man no more may die;
Born to raise the sons of earth,
Born to give them second birth.

Come, Desire of nations, come,
Fix in us thy humble home;
Rise, the woman's conqu'ring Seed,
Bruise in us the serpent's head.
Now display thy saving pow'r,
Ruined nature now restore;
Now in mystic union join
Thine to ours, and ours to thine.

Adam's likeness, Lord, efface,
Stamp thine image in its place:
Second Adam from above,
Reinstate us in thy love.
Let us thee, though lost, regain,
thee, the Life, the inner man:
Oh, to all thyself impart,
Formed in each believing heart.[1]

Thank you, God, for Christ. Thank you, God, for Christ-mas.

1 Charles Wesley, *library.timelesstruths.org*

DECEMBER 26TH

THE CHURCH OF GOD, WHICH HE BOUGHT WITH HIS OWN BLOOD

(Acts 20:28 *NIV*)

Nothing that Wesley taught was at variance with the formularies of the Church of England, nor did he ever wish to question any of its doctrines. In a contest of orthodoxy with the prevailing school of thought among the bishops at any stage of his ministry, there is little doubt that he would have come off best … It was the methods used by Wesley and his friends to expand the Societies that were offensive. In spite of his own natural predilection for established order, Wesley felt himself obliged by the necessity of the Gospel not only to preach in the open air, but also to do so in other men's parishes without invitation or permission. He was careful never to do so at the time of statutory services in the Parish Church, and he persistently urged all his followers to attend all such services, including Holy Communion above all. But to gather round him a vast crowd of people who had for the most part never been seen in Church, to have them singing noisy hymns, to produce outbursts of religious fervour such as the neighbourhood had never seen before, to organize those affected in this way into Societies which met in large numbers every week, to preach things which sounded dangerously near the suggestion that Jack is as good as his master (for did he not teach that God loved master and man alike?) – and to do all this without permission under the very nose of the man who was responsible for the souls of all who lived in the parish – was this not rank "*enthusiasm*"? It is easy to see how devout parish priests who faithfully carried out their cure of souls and the others who spent their time drinking and gaming with the squire were equally incensed.[1]

Lord of the Church, today I pray specifically for the Church of England. I pray your blessing on the Anglican communion worldwide in all the issues it faces today. I lift that unique worshipping community before you.

1 From *Methodism.*

December 27th

Moses the servant of the Lord died

(Deuteronomy 34:5 *NIV*)

There was no hope at all that the authorities of the Church of England would take up and further the work of Methodism (many of them were surely hoping that it would peter out when the old man died)...

After John Wesley's death in 1791, the separation [of Methodism and Anglicanism] was soon consummated. Many of the Methodist Societies were painfully divided within themselves until 1795 on the question whether the Methodist preachers, not ordained episcopally, should give them the sacrament of Holy Communion. Those members who had been appointed as trustees of the property (mostly by Wesley himself) sturdily maintained that they should not, and went so far as to ban from their pulpits (as they were legally entitled to do) any preachers who had given the Sacrament. The rest of the members tended to take the other view. They could not see why the men who ministered to them in all other spiritual matters should not minister to them in this one too. The Conference therefore had to deal each year with disputes liable to lead to a split in the whole body of Methodists. In 1793 it was agreed that when a Society unanimously wished for the Sacrament from a Methodist preacher it should receive it.

Lord, when leaders die – even great ones – or when ministers move on, help us to keep our eyes on Jesus. When we face change in our churches – times of upheaval, maybe – help us to remember that you never change.

December 28th

These stones shall become a memorial to the sons of Israel forever

(Joshua 4:7 *NASB*)

[Wesley had] lived to preach under the shade of trees which he had planted; and he outlived the lease of the Foundry, the place which had been the cradle of Methodism.

In 1777, the headquarters of the Society were removed to the City Road, where a new chapel was built upon ground leased by the City [of London]. Great multitudes assembled to see the ceremony of laying the foundation, so that Wesley could not, without much difficulty, get through … to lay the first stone, in which his name and the date were inserted upon a plate of brass:

"This was laid by John Wesley, on April 1. 1777."[1]

How wonderful, Lord! After the dreadful struggles in Georgia, after so much dedicated work against opposition that would overwhelm many, John Wesley's ministry is formally recognized and Methodism is established.
Thank you, Lord.

1 From *John Wesley.*

December 29th

He knoweth the way that I take: when he hath tried me,
I shall come forth as gold. My foot hath held his steps,
his way have I kept, and not declined

(Job 23:10–11 *KJV*)

The days of his childhood returned upon him when [late in life Wesley] visited Epworth; and, taking a solitary walk in the churchyard of that place, he says, "I felt the truth of '*one generation goeth, and another cometh*'.[1] See how the earth drops its inhabitants, as the tree drops its leaves!"

Wherever he went, his old disciples had passed away, and other generations had succeeded in their stead; and at the houses to which he looked on with pleasure in the course of his yearly rounds, he found more and more frequently, in every succeeding year, that death had been before him.

Whole families dropped off, one by one, while he continued still in his green old age, full of life, and activity, and strength, and hope, and ardour. Such griefs were felt by him less keenly than by other men; because every day brought with it to him change of scene and change of persons; and because, busy as he was on earth, his desires were in Heaven.

"I had hopes," says he, in his journal, "of seeing a friend at Lewisham[2] in my way: and so I did: but it was in her coffin. It is well, since she finished her course with joy. In due time I shall see her in glory."[3]

The life to come! The promise of Paradise! Heaven as home!
Thank you, Lord Jesus!

1 See Ecclesiastes 1:4.
2 South-east London.
3 From *John Wesley.*

December 30th

The angels carried him to Abraham's side

(Luke 16:22 *NIV*)

On 2 March [1791] he died in peace; being in the eighty-eighth year of his age, and the sixty-fifth of his ministry. During his illness (Wesley had caught a cold on 17 February, while preaching in London, and this became a fever) he said, "Let me be buried in nothing but what is woollen; and let my corpse be carried in my coffin into the chapel." Some years before, he had prepared a vault for himself, and for those itinerant preachers who might die in London. In his will he directed that six poor men should have twenty shillings each for carrying his body to the grace; "for I particularly desire," said he, "that there may be no hearse, no coach, no escutcheon,[1] no pomp, except the tears of them that loved me, and are following me to Abraham's bosom. I solemnly adjure my executors, in the name of God, punctually to observe this." At the desire of many of his friends, his body was carried into the chapel of the day preceding the internment, and there lay in a kind of state becoming the person, dressed in his clerical habit, with gown, cassock, and band; the old clerical cap on his head; a Bible in one hand, and a white handkerchief in the other. The face was placid, and the expression which death had fixed upon his venerable features, was that of a serene and heavenly smile.[2, 3, 4]

The battle won! A good fight fought! Lord, keep me faithful unto death, I pray.

1 A shield, or coat of arms.

2 From *John Wesley*.

3 The crowds who flocked to see John Wesley "lying in state" were so great that it was decided to hold his funeral service between 5 a.m. and 6 a.m. the next day, for fear of accidents. News of this arrangement quickly spread, though, and hundreds attended, even at that hour.

4 As a mark of respect, the usual words of commendation during the funeral service – "Forasmuch as it hath pleased Almighty God to take unto himself the soul of our dear *brother*" – were changed to "our dear *father*".

SEE WHAT GOD HAS DONE!

(Numbers 23:23 *NIV*)

Mr Wesley left no other property behind him than the copyright and current editions of his works, and this he bequeathed to the use of the [Methodist] Connection after his debts should have been paid. There was a debt of one thousand six hundred pounds to the family of his brother Charles; and he had drawn also for some years upon the fund for superannuated preachers, to support those who were in full employment. When he was told that some persons murmured at this, he used to answer, "What can I do? Must the work stand still? The men and their families cannot starve. I have no money. Here it is: we must use it; it is for the Lord's work." The money thus appropriated, and the interest due upon it, amounted to a considerable sum. In building chapels, also, the expenses of the Connection outran its means, so that its finances were left in an embarrassed state. The number of his preachers at the time of his death amounted in the British dominions to 313, in the United States to 198; the number of members in the British dominions was 76,968, in the United States 57,621.[1]

To God be the glory!

1 From *John Wesley.*

Notes

Notes

NOTES